FROM EVIDENCE TO OUTCOMES IN CHILD WELFARE

From Evidence to Outcomes in Child Welfare

Welfare

AN INTERNATIONAL READER

Edited by Aron Shlonsky

Rami Benbenishty

OXFORD
UNIVERSITY PRESS

Oxford University Press is a department of the University of Oxford.
It furthers the University's objective of excellence in research, scholarship,
and education by publishing worldwide.

Oxford   New York
Auckland   Cape Town   Dar es Salaam   Hong Kong   Karachi
Kuala Lumpur   Madrid   Melbourne   Mexico City   Nairobi
New Delhi   Shanghai   Taipei   Toronto

With offices in
Argentina   Austria   Brazil   Chile   Czech Republic   France   Greece
Guatemala   Hungary   Italy   Japan   Poland   Portugal   Singapore
South Korea   Switzerland   Thailand   Turkey   Ukraine   Vietnam

Oxford is a registered trademark of Oxford University Press
in the UK and certain other countries.

Published in the United States of America by
Oxford University Press
198 Madison Avenue, New York, NY 10016

Library of Congress Cataloging-in-Publication Data
From evidence to outcomes in child welfare : an international reader / edited by Aron Shlonsky,
Rami Benbenishty.
   pages cm
ISBN 978-0-19-997372-9 (hardcover : alk. paper)   1. Child welfare.   2. Children—Services for.
I. Shlonsky, Aron, editor of compilation.   II. Benbenishty, Rami, editor of compilation.
HV713.F76 2013
362.7—dc23
2013023789

9 8 7 6 5 4 3 2 1
Printed in the United States of America
on acid-free paper

Contents

Acknowledgments

DESPITE NOTIONS TO the contrary, modern-day academics rarely have the opportunity to discuss big ideas with our colleagues. Mostly, we work from project to project, often in specialist roles with other specialists, chasing after the next grant, publishing the next paper, and interacting with the larger field of scholars only through reading publications or attending short presentations at conferences. This volume grew out of two extraordinary meetings in which a small group of scholars from around the world had the opportunity to debate, at length, what evidence can tell us and how we might use this knowledge to improve the welfare of vulnerable children and youth. We thank our gracious hosts in the Haruv Institute in Jerusalem, Israel, and the Chapin Hall Center for Children at the University of Chicago for providing such inspiring conditions for our work.

This book could not have been written without the generous support of Mrs. Lynn Schusterman. Her dedication and devotion to the welfare of children across the globe has been an inspiration. Also instrumental was the leadership of Hillel Schmid, the first director of the Haruv Institute in Israel, who brought us all together and made us all feel welcome, but also kept us on task and reminded us of the importance of our work.

The editors also wish to thank all of the volume's contributing authors. Our pace may have been slower than we wished but, at the end of the day, we think the book is better for it. To our readers who work in child welfare practice and policy, we thank you for your dedication and tenacity in trying to help those less fortunate than you, often doing so in extreme circumstances and without much support or guidance. Finally, and most importantly, we would like to acknowledge the many children and families who have received services from child welfare providers throughout the world. We hope that this book will make a small but important contribution to the safety and well-being of children everywhere.

Aron: I would like to thank Rami Benbenishty for being a patient colleague and friend, gently but firmly pushing us to finish this important project. I would also like to thank my sister, Liana, for stepping up and caring for our mother in this very difficult time. Thanks also to my universities, the University of Toronto and the University of Melbourne, for creating environments where these types of ideas can flourish.

Rami: I would like to acknowledge that many of the ideas shared in this volume came out of my long and fruitful collaboration with Ron Avi Astor, a colleague and dear friend. Our shared ideas, debates, and disagreements have enriched my thinking in so many ways. I would like to thank my wife Ruthy, the one and only, my children and grandchildren, Inbar, Rami, Rowee, Tamar, Amit, Adi, Yaara, Ariel, Aniam, and Imri. Everything I do comes from my love to you all.

We both would like to thank all the many scholars, professionals, and clients who have made our lives so rich. We hope that in our work we are sharing your wisdom with readers across the globe.

List of Contributors

Richard P. Barth, PhD, MSW, is dean and professor at the University of Maryland School of Social Work.

Donald J. Baumann, PhD, teaches at Saint Edwards University, Austin, Texas.

Rami Benbenishty, PhD, is a professor at the Louis and Gabi Weisfeld School of Social Work at Bar Ilan University, Israel.

Katherine L. Casillas, PhD, is an assistant professor in the Department of Pediatrics at the University of Colorado School of Medicine, Kempe Center for the Prevention and Treatment of Child Abuse & Neglect.

Mark E. Courtney, PhD, is a professor of social service administration at the University of Chicago.

Len Dalgleish, PhD, was a professor at the Department of Nursing and Midwifery, University of Stirling, UK.

Nancy S. Dickinson, MSSW, PhD, is clinical professor and director of the National Child Welfare Workforce Institute at the University of Maryland School of Social Work.

Tonino Esposito, PhD, is a senior research associate at McGill University School of Social Work.

Laura Ferrer-Wreder, PhD, is an associate professor of psychology, at Stockholm University's Department of Psychology.

John Fluke, PhD, is the associate director for systems research and evaluation and associate professor in the Department of Pediatrics at the University of Colorado School of Medicine, Kempe Center for the Prevention and Treatment of Child Abuse & Neglect.

Mathieu-Joel Gervais, BA, is a PhD student and research assistant at University of Quebec at Montreal.

Homer D. Kern, PhD, is a child welfare consultant at the American Humane Association, Child Protection Research Center, Englewood, Colorado.

Claude Laurendeau, MSW, is the former director of professional services at Batshaw Youth & Family Centres in Montreal, Quebec.

Bethany R. Lee, PhD, MSW, is associate professor and associate dean for research at the University of Maryland School of Social Work.

Bridgette Lery, PhD, is a senior analyst at Chapin Hall Center for Children at the University of Chicago.

Marla McDaniel, PhD, is a senior research associate at the Center on Labor, Human Services and Population at The Urban Institute, Washington DC.

Robyn Mildon, PhD, is the director of knowledge exchange and implementation at the Parenting Research Centre in Melbourne Australia.

Lise Milne, MSW, is a doctoral student and research associate at McGill University School of Social Work.

Michael Pergamit, PhD, is a senior fellow at the Center on Labor, Human Services and Population at The Urban Institute, Washington DC.

Hillel Schmid, PhD, is a professor emeritus at Paul Baerwald School of Social Work and Social Welfare, The Hebrew University of Jerusalem.

Aron Shlonsky, PhD, is professor of evidence informed practice at the University of Melbourne Faculty of Health Sciences, Department of Social Work and associate professor at the University of Toronto Factor-Inwentash Faculty of Social Work.

Lonnie Snowden, Professor Of Health Policy and Management at the University of California at Berkeley School of Public Health.

Knut Sundell, PhD, is an associate professor of psychology, and senior advisor for social affairs at the National Board of Health and Welfare, Sweden.

Nico Trocmé, PhD, is a professor of social work at McGill University, where he holds the Philip Fisher Chair in Social Work and directs the Centre for Research on Children and Families.

Maria Woolverton, PhD, is child welfare research team leader/senior social science research analyst at the Office of Planning, Research and Evaluation, Administration for Children and Families, US Department of Health and Human Services.

Fred Wulczyn, PhD, is a senior research fellow at the Chapin Hall Center for Children at the University of Chicago.

Anat Zeira, PhD, is an associate professor at the Paul Baerwald School of Social Work and Social Welfare, The Hebrew University of Jerusalem.

INTRODUCTION

Aron Shlonsky and Rami Benbenishty

WHAT IS EVIDENCE? Where can it be found? How can it best be used to improve outcomes? Is all evidence equally useful? What do we do if there is precious little evidence? What can be done if there is contradictory evidence? What can we do if research evidence is from another location? Will it apply here? These are questions that scholars in many fields have attempted to answer, but precious few have done so in the field of child welfare.

Comparative studies of child welfare systems demonstrate that context shapes the way systems are conceptualized and structured, and how services are chosen and delivered. There are several comparative studies of welfare systems in general and child welfare systems in particular (see, for example, N. Gilbert, Parton, & Skivenes, 2011; R. Gilbert et al., 2012; Kamerman, Phipps, & Ben-Aryeh, 2010). They will not be reviewed here except to bring to the forefront the importance of considering the transportability of evidence created in one policy and practice context that is brought to another. These comparative studies should sensitize us to the multiple ways in which historical, social, and cultural contexts influence the ways in which policymakers and social workers function, creating major differences in terminology, conceptual frameworks, and service structures. These authors and many other scholars (e.g., Weightman & Weightman, 1995) have observed that social workers in general, and child welfare workers in particular, are acting within institutional contexts that are informed by child care policy, local policy interpretation, professional concerns, and legislative requirements. Their forms of thought, routines, and practices are influenced by larger, more collective representations of appropriate interventions and competent practice.

As such, our definition of child welfare in this book is broad, encompassing services (public and voluntary) and policies designed to promote the well-being, positive development, and safety of children. This includes the prevention, amelioration, or remediation of social problems related to the functioning of the parent-child relationship network (Kadushin & Martin, 1988), as well as to the negative impact of social institutions and policies on children, their families, and caregivers (e.g., discrimination, social inequality, poverty, and marginalization). Hence, we include in our discussions direct services to support children and families, child protection services, services in the community and out of home, and policies that affect (intentionally or unintentionally) the welfare of children as individuals and as part of their families and communities.

The book brings together insights from several child welfare systems around the world. While not representative of all child welfare systems, these perspectives nonetheless reveal substantial differences that are of major importance to efforts aimed at creating, understanding, and using evidence to support the welfare of children. In particular, these perspectives make a strong case for understanding the role of context in generating, interpreting, and employing evidence.

Shlonsky and Benbenishty (Chapter 1) provide an introduction to evidence-informed practice and a broad overview of the different types of evidence that can be useful in guiding difficult decisions under uncertain conditions. This chapter describes the evolution of evidence-informed practice, as originally described in Sackett, Richardson, Rosenberg, and Haynes (1997) and later translated from medicine into the helping professions (Gambrill, 1999; Gibbs, 2003). An expansive interpretation of evidence-informed practice is depicted, including the historical, political, professional, and economic contexts in which child welfare services are provided. Noteworthy is the chapter's attention to how evidence can be identified, collected, and used by individual practitioners, service providers, and policymakers.

Policymakers, practitioners, and child welfare clients need to base their decisions on the best evidence available. Bauman, Fluke, Dalgleish, and Kern (Chapter 2) present the decision-making ecology/general assessment and decision-making model (DME/GADM) and vividly show the interplay between individual or group decision processes and the contexts in which these decisions are contemplated. Based on a comprehensive historical review of the development of theoretical and empirical decision-making frameworks, the authors' model outlines a decision-making continuum and a host of factors (such as decision-maker characteristics, case characteristics, and organizational context) that impact on assessments and decisions. In line with this book's overall approach to evidence, the model illustrates the iterative and cyclical process in which evidence influences decision-making. The chapter nicely demonstrates how choices can be related to specific outcomes (e.g., whether a decision to close a case ended in a child fatality) and the outcomes themselves become both evidence and context for future decisions.

Our assertion that context is essential for understanding the applicability of empirically supported treatments is underscored by Sundell and Ferrer-Wreder (Chapter 3), who describe what happens when such interventions are implemented in different countries and cultures. The authors note that, whereas some interventions did well in international replications, many others failed when transported from the place they were developed. They analyze possible explanations as to why results across contexts might vary. Some of these are related to methodological issues, whereas others stem from deeper contextual factors. The authors emphasize how the social service systems, sociodemographic, and cultural contexts impact the ways interventions should be adapted and implemented in new contexts. They address the complexity inherent in balancing fidelity and necessary adaptations, and the difficulties in distinguishing between the "surface" level and "deep" structures of empirically supported programs. One of the important implications of this chapter is the need to develop our theoretical and empirical understanding of both the intervention itself and the context in which it is being implemented.

Manualized, empirically supported treatment programs are often touted as the beginning and end of evidence-based practice. Barth and Lee (Chapter 4) challenge this convention by introducing the use of common factors and common elements to address some of the more pressing difficulties faced by children and families receiving child welfare services. The authors begin by reviewing the limitations associated with manualized programs, including the fact that practitioners are embedded in agencies that may lack the supports required for their use. They then argue that common factors (general approaches by practitioners that are associated with better outcomes) and common elements (individual practices that cut across effective treatment programs for specific problems) offer ways to implement evidence in practice that can be effective and are potentially more accessible to child welfare practitioners and agencies than manualized programs. The authors review specialized software designed to support the common elements approach in everyday practice, and examine in detail the "client-directed, outcome-informed" (Duncan, Miller, Wampold, and Hubble, 2010) approach. The chapter ends with a description of an integrative framework that brings together both common elements and common factors that can be used to generate services in child welfare that have a high likelihood of being effective.

Mildon, Dickinson, and Shlonsky (Chapter 5) argue that the adoption of a program by a child welfare agency is only one step in the process of effectively implementing an evidence-supported program to achieve better outcomes for children and families. The authors review the literature demonstrating the complexities involved in implementing programs in child welfare agencies and the strong relationships between the quality of implementation and service outcomes. The chapter presents "frameworks of implementation" (key attributes, facilitators, and challenges related to implementation), describes key actionable elements to be used to facilitate successful implementation of empirically supported interventions and practices, and discusses the implementation of common elements in agency settings. In line with our emphasis on agency context, the authors describe a framework developed by Aarons, Hurlburt, and Horwitz (2011) that connects the specifics of child welfare agency context with the most appropriate and effective implementation processes. Of the many strategies identified as key for successful implementation, the authors focus on critical components that have the strongest evidence in child welfare settings: staff recruitment and selection, training and ongoing technical assistance, and use of ongoing fidelity monitoring with staff evaluation. This chapter clearly supports the idea that the creation and evaluation of evidence is an ongoing process that underlies all agency practices, and does not end after an evidence-supported program has been adopted. Child welfare agencies are urged to use evidence in the implementation process and to create evidence on the degree to which the interventions or practices are successfully implemented and are achieving better outcomes for their clients.

Our approach in this volume rests on the idea that the definition and use of evidence should not be restricted to a simplistic focus on empirically supported treatments and their attendant outcomes. Wulczyn Lery and Snowden (Chapter 6) use an applied example to illustrate how other forms of evidence, specifically epidemiological data, can shed light on complex phenomena and can drastically alter future practice and policy responses. In their chapter, they show how a complex empirical investigation of the overrepresentation of black children in the foster care system can result in findings that are counterintuitive and lead to very different decisions with respect to social service response. Using a multilevel analysis of existing state data, the authors show how differences in child placement rates are a function of poverty, but that the effect of poverty differs among racial groups. Specifically, placement rates of children from high White poverty areas were more influenced by poverty than were placement rates for children in high Black poverty areas. The findings clearly demonstrate that placement rates are highly context sensitive and that, rather than relying on an intuitive approach that just considers high placement rates across jurisdictions, a more nuanced approach would consider how poverty and race work together to influence child placement.

Courtney, Pergamit, Woolverton, and McDaniel (Chapter 7) present the Multi-Site Evaluation of Foster Youth Programs, designed to determine the effects of independent living programs in achieving improvement in key outcomes in the lives of foster youth transitioning from care. This is the first experimental study in this area. As such, it presents an impressive example of a large-scale, multisite evaluation study that addresses questions about the "impact" of an important and widely used program, the quality of its implementation, and the external validity of findings generated in experimental designs. Based on their experience, the authors state that "objections from the field that experimental evaluation of child welfare programs is not feasible should be put to rest" (p. 125). They support this argument by showing that random assignment in field experiments is feasible and that high response rates can be achieved even among hard-to-reach participants such as youth in foster care. Nevertheless, they also offer analyses and examples that describe when such experiments are not possible and, even when they are, some of the lingering limitations they hold with respect to knowledge generation. In particular, they address issues such as constraints on external validity due to the unique characteristics of the service delivery systems they chose to evaluate, distinguishing between the impact of "programs" and treatment as usual ("practice"), and the possibility of confounding due to changes in policy context that occurred during the study. The authors provide valuable advice on how to plan experimental and nonexperimental studies that generate useful evidence for policy.

This volume presents a wide perspective on the use of evidence in a wide range of tasks in child welfare. Casillas and Fluke (Chapter 8) focus on evidence related to needs of clients culminating in a model that integrates both needs and outcomes in child welfare. The chapter uses reports of the National Survey of Child and Adolescent Well-Being (NSCAW) to develop an overall picture of the needs of children involved in various aspects of the US child welfare system. The authors identify a wide range of serious and overlapping needs of both children and their caregivers, show that many of these needs are not being met, and conclude that the child welfare field must better understand the multiple and complex issues faced by their clients. Integration across different service systems is required if these needs are to be addressed. The authors offer an integrative, person-oriented approach, to guide integrated assessment, treatment planning, and service delivery. Such an approach is based on a thorough examination of available evidence and the identification of empirically driven patterns of needs that may be co-occurring. Such a classification can serve child welfare services, policymakers, and researchers in their efforts to match certain classes of clients with interventions with evidence of effectiveness, and to identify other groups of clients for whom such programs have not yet been developed or validated.

Another of the contributions of this volume is an exploration of the importance attached to the child welfare agency as a primary site for the generation and use of evidence. Hillel Schmid (Chapter 9) analyzes the use of evidence in the context of nonprofit human service organizations. The author presents what he describes as an evidence-based approach for management (EBMgt), and discusses both the barriers and restraining forces that prevent implementation of the approach in organizations and the conditions that may facilitate the assimilation of this approach in child welfare agencies. The chapter presents the implementation of this approach as a demanding second-order change in organizations, requiring major shifts in existing organizational strategies, structures, and administrative processes. In line with the overall approach of this volume, the organizational culture change advocated in this chapter is not simply limited to making the use of empirically supported treatments more palatable to agencies, but also pertains to a major shift in organizational learning culture that promotes context-sensitive identification, generation, and utilization of evidence. Interestingly, the author emphasizes the role played by clients in contributing to an organizational culture that is informed by evidence. Finally, the chapter addresses several dilemmas related to the relative weights of facts and values, rational and irrational considerations, systematic work versus innovation and improvisation, and evidence as a support for tactical as opposed to long-term decisions.

Discussion of the agency context and management brings to the forefront not only managers but the practitioners who are expected to generate and use evidence in child welfare agencies. The importance of the workforce in implementation has already been touched on in Mildon et al. (Chapter 5). Zeira (Chapter 10) addresses this issue from a different angle—preparing child welfare practitioners to understand and use evidence. The chapter explores some of the difficulties associated with bridging the gap between research evidence and practice, and suggests strategies for training social workers to understand and systematically use research-generated knowledge in their everyday practice. The author argues that training social workers to routinely evaluate their own practice will promote a greater respect for, and use of, research evidence in practice. The chapter analyzes factors (both personal and environmental-organizational) that promote or hinder the implementation of systematic evaluation as part of practice. The author suggests that university-agency partnerships can be used to promote this evaluation process, discusses challenges that such partnerships might face, and identifies factors that might influence their success. Finally, the chapter presents the systematic planned practice model as one guide for systematic evaluation that can be incorporated in the routine work of social workers.

Trocme and associates (Chapter 11) also focus on the importance of an organizational culture in which evidence is a central component of clinical orientations, program development and activities, and overall decision-making. The authors describe a university-agency collaboration similar to what Zeira advocates (Chapter 10). Student-faculty knowledge mobilization (KMB) teams were deployed at several levels in the agency to assist managers in multiple ways to create and use evidence. These activities included service statistics integration groups, clinical integration groups, clinical surveys, and a shared newsletter. The authors describe the challenges (e.g., investment of resources and cultural differences between the teams) and the many strengths of this university–child welfare agency collaboration and conclude that this was a successful endeavor that generated interest beyond the target agency. This chapter is a rich example of the many ways in which evidence can become part of the organizational culture of child welfare agencies and, at the same time, demonstrates the complexities and challenges inherent in such a process.

Setting the Context

1

FROM EVIDENCE TO OUTCOMES IN CHILD WELFARE

Aron Shlonsky and Rami Benbenishty

Introduction

This introductory chapter is written from the position that the use of evidence in child welfare policy and practice is a moral imperative; that to formulate, recommend, decide on, or even deliver social services requires a commitment to using the very best evidence at our disposal. In all likelihood, few would argue this point. However, major philosophical and practical differences of opinion abound with respect to how evidence is defined, gathered, and utilized in policy and practice. Rather than taking a view that what constitutes evidence is in the eye of the beholder, we seek instead to expand the number of questions asked while refining their scope. We strongly believe that there are specific methods that best answer specific questions, and stringing together such multiple and specific questions and their answers provides an evidentiary overview that is far better suited for decision-making in the complex world of child welfare. Indeed, weaving together these often disparate strands is the essence of decision-making expertise. We begin with a brief overview of evidence-based practice (EBP); touch on some of the criticisms of EBP; argue that the EBP remit includes policy and practice questions not often considered a part of the EBP approach; and explore the use of evidence within and across multiple contexts.

The Evidence-Based Practice (EBP) Revolution

The term *evidence-based practice* (EBP) emerged in formal usage in the early 1990s with the advent of "evidence-based medicine" or EBM (Guyatt, 1991), and the idea was then translated from medicine more broadly into the helping professions (Gambrill, 1999; Gibbs, 2003). As originally developed by Sackett and colleagues (1997), EBP consists of both an underlying practice model and a set of specific steps. The original model envisions a Venn diagram consisting of three circles that overlap in the middle. The circles represent best evidence, practitioner expertise, and client values and expectations. EBP is the union, or intersection, of these three constructs (Gibbs, 2003; Sackett, Richardson, Rosenberg, & Haynes, 1997). An important advance to this early model, by Haynes, Devereaux, and Guyatt (2002), frames clinical expertise as the optimal integration of current best evidence, client preferences and actions, and client clinical state and circumstances, with the overlap conceptualized as clinical expertise (Figure 1.1). That is, clinical expertise only occurs when these three constructs are optimally combined. In some cases, evidence may be strong and perhaps it is weighted accordingly when decisions are made. In other cases, there may be little or no valid evidence but strong client preferences, in which case preferences would figure more prominently in decisions.

This underlying framework translates into a series of specific, practical steps to ensure that each element of the model is systematically implemented (Table 1.1). While the process of EBP has been described elsewhere (Gibbs, 2003; Shlonsky & Gibbs, 2004), the general progression requires that individual practitioners pose a question that can be answered using scholarly databases, query these databases to locate potentially relevant studies, appraise found studies for their quality, establish study applicability with respect to client context, and evaluate whether the intervention was helpful for a particular client or group of clients. Some scholars claim that the term *evidence-based* is somewhat

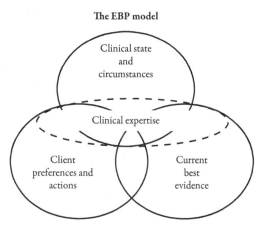

FIGURE 1.1. The Evidence-Based Practice Model
Source: Haynes, Devereaux, & Guyatt (2002)

TABLE 1.1

STEPS OF EVIDENCE-BASED PRACTICE

1.   Become motivated to apply EBP;
2.   Convert information need (prevention, assessment, treatment, risk) into an answerable question;
3.   Track down the best evidence to answer the question;
4.   Critically appraise the evidence for its validity (closeness to the truth), impact (size of the effect), and applicability (usefulness in our practice);
5.   Integrate critical appraisal with our practice experience and the client's strengths, values, and circumstances;
6.   Evaluate effectiveness and efficiency in exercising steps 1–4 and seek ways to improve them next time;
7.   Teach others to follow the same process.

Source: Gibbs, L. E. (2003). Evidence-based practice for the helping professions: A practical guide with integrated multimedia. Pacific Grove, Calif.: Brooks/Cole-Thomson Learning.

misleading, instead preferring the term *evidence-informed* (Chalmers 2005; Gambrill, 2010). Although the terms *evidence-based practice* and *evidence-informed practice* (EIP) differ by one word, both originally refer to the same exact set of steps and processes for integrating current best evidence with client context (Shlonsky, Noonan, Littell, & Montgomery, 2011) and will be treated as such in this chapter.

Within this conceptual model and its steps, evidence is generally defined as information from empirical studies. While some would argue that this definition ignores other forms of important information, we argue that the term *current best evidence* is clearly inclusive of all sources of information. The real issue involves the type of evidentiary question being asked and how to weigh each source of information in terms of its quality and applicability.

The search for evidence is driven by a question, and the question is driven by the evidentiary need (Table 1.2). For instance, a question about whether a program is effective at treating a given condition would best be answered by a systematic review of effectiveness studies (a prevention question would be similar), where more weight is given to studies with lower risk of bias (e.g., well-conducted randomized controlled trials, or RCTs). But for other types of questions, RCTs and other designs measuring treatment effect may not provide the right type of evidence. For diagnostic and prognostic questions, establishment of the psychometric properties of standardized or other measures rely on study designs that do not involve randomization in order to establish their reliability and validity.[1] Such information is crucial in terms of establishing whether and to what extent a problem exists in a community or an individual (e.g., childhood depression), predicting

---

[1] Tests of diagnostic tools can (and where possible, should) use randomization to measure their performance with respect to a reference standard.

TABLE 1.2

TYPES OF EVIDENTIARY QUESTIONS

1.	Effectiveness: Is one treatment or intervention more effective than another or no treatment/intervention at ameliorating or diminishing a problem or condition experienced by a client?
2.	Prevention: Is one treatment or intervention aimed at preventing or stopping the initial occurrence of a problem or condition more effective than anther or no treatment/intervention?
3.	Risk/Prognosis: The likelihood or probability that a client will experience undesirable consequences within a given interval of time.
4.	Assessment: Whether a client has a problem/condition/strength or whether a client has benefited from a given treatment.
5.	Descriptive: dynamics of a given population (e.g., population trends), satisfaction with services, needs assessment, other information that describes a population, problem, or intervention rather than the effectiveness of an intervention, the quality of an assessment, or the modeling of risk.

Source: Adapted from Gibbs, L. E. (2003). Evidence-based practice for the helping professions: A practical guide with integrated multimedia. Pacific Grove, Calif.: Brooks/Cole-Thomson Learning.

what might happen in the future (e.g., whether a child will be maltreated after an investigation), and for measuring change on these very constructs over time. If the tools used to measure key constructs are of poor quality, even the very best RCT will be of little use for generating evidence of effectiveness. Most importantly, however, an appraisal of evidence might not start or end with an effectiveness question.

Evidence does not appear magically out of a vacuum, nor does its availability mean we instantly realize how to interpret and use it. The first questions should not ask, "What is effective for this problem?" Rather, beginning questions should seek descriptive information: What is the problem we are dealing with? How did it come into being? What is the prevalence of the problem? How is it related to other problems? How does it affect individuals? The community? Broader society? What is known about individuals and communities who experience this difficulty? What has been tried before? Even questions such as "Who stands to benefit from interpreting the problem in this way?" may be important to ask.

Sackett et al. (1997) would call these background rather than foreground questions and prompt us to ascertain what we need to know before we ask, "What is effective?" Although background questions are given short shrift in many descriptions of EBP, we would argue that such questions are among the most important of all and that they fit, in a sense, as a lead-in to the basic EBP model. This background "descriptive" information is key to understanding how to pose the more detailed questions that logically follow and, in a departure from the original Gibbs (2003) model, basic epidemiology is the primary focus of the background question category. That is, descriptive information, systematically gathered, can provide the background information needed to adequately understand individual problems and their expression. For instance, in child welfare, a good deal of valuable information on children, families, and communities can be found in child welfare management information systems, and this source of locally relevant data has been mined extensively to guide policy and practice (Dettlaff et al., 2011; R. Gilbert et al., 2012; Goerge, Wulczyn, & Harden, 1995; Webster, Needell, & Wildfire, 2002; F. Wulczyn, 2009; F. H. Wulczyn & Goerge, 1992).

Bringing it all together at the individual level, current best evidence can be used as an entry point (Figure 1.2) to gather information about the etiology, prevalence, and longer term outcomes of child maltreatment, providing the understanding necessary for posing questions more specific to the client at hand (#1). Information on prevalence, likely service response, and outcomes might be gleaned from academic sources (e.g., Cochrane and Campbell Collaboration libraries, databases such as Medline, Psycinfo, CINAHL, Social Services Abstracts, and others), government reports and websites, and other official sources. Internal agency data from evaluations and management information systems might also yield good information specific to the community or area in which the client lives. A risk assessment tool modeling the likelihood of future maltreatment might then be used to guide the choice of service intensity, ensuring that scarce and potentially coercive services are reserved for clients at highest risk (#2). A clinical and/or contextual assessment is then used to elicit key client strengths and needs (#3), which includes the extent to which the evidence maps onto the clinical state and circumstances of the client (3a) and fits with client preferences and values (3b, 3c) as movement is made toward the selection of services. At this point, the process could begin again when current best evidence is sought for a related problem, perhaps starting (#4) with other assessment tools (e.g., depression inventories, child behavior indicators) and, once applied, the effectiveness (#5) of various service options (e.g., cognitive behavioral therapy for depression; parent management training), and then again integrating context with the evidence. Clinical expertise is the optimal integration of these sources of information (best evidence, client state and circumstances, and client preferences/values), resulting in decisions that are both based in evidence and take client context into account. Practice settings that encourage the documentation (preferably electronic) of key demographic and case information about their clients, the interventions employed, and the outcomes achieved are, in fact, creating evidence relevant to their clients and agencies (Benbenishty & Astor, 2007; Epstein, 2010), and results of searches can become a part of ongoing knowledge development and utilization efforts.

Thus, there is a dynamic tension within the individual practice setting as reflected in the intersection of evidence, circumstances, and preferences. That is, the link between evidence and action is not automatic and is mediated by a deliberative process that considers the evidence in context. Evidence in its various forms is "food for thought." Mediating processes are needed to make sense of evidence and apply what's relevant in a certain

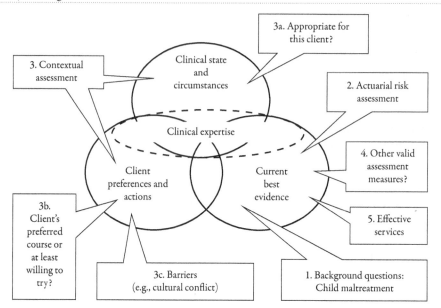

FIGURE 1.2. Cycle of Evidence-Based Practice.
Source: Model adapted from Haynes, Devereaux, and Guyatt (2002).

context, and these processes can be learned. But there is also a dynamic tension between the activities of individual practice and the context in which that practice is situated.

An Expanded Evidence-Based Practice Framework

In reality, many of the decisions taken by child welfare practitioners and the choices they make with regard to their prevention and intervention efforts are dependent to a large extent on the agency, community, and policy contexts in which they work. These contexts are shaped by the features of place: history, geography, population, various communities of practice, and the culture of the agency itself. No single intervention is free of the context in which it is implemented, making descriptive questions that unearth the specific context incredibly important. In an expanded EBP framework, the core elements of practice (e.g., transparency, collective decision-making, client self-determination) remain the same, but contextual factors are added to the more standard individual model at the center (Figure 1.3). First introduced in Regehr, Stern, and Shlonsky (2007), this model includes some of the ecological and historical factors that influence not only the implementation of services but also how we perceive clients and the problems they face. The model presents the practitioner's direct practice embedded in multiple nested contexts including organizational, community-level, political, and sociohistorical.

Practitioners in public agencies are fully aware of the impact of context on their practice. They know that the agency determines to a large extent their caseload; working

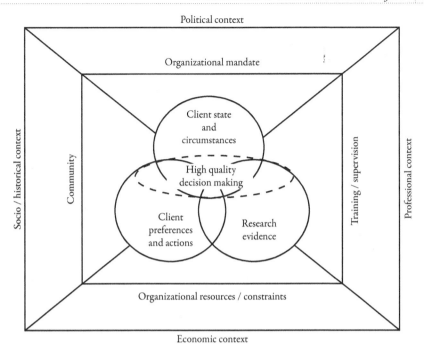

FIGURE 1.3. Expanded evidence-based practice model.
Source: Regehr, C., Stern, S., & Shlonsky, A. (2007). Operationalizing evidence-based practice: The development of an Institute for Evidence-Based Social Work. *Research on Social Work Practice*, 17, 408–416.

conditions; client eligibility criteria for services; the resources allocated to clients; the supervision, training, and supports practitioners receive; and many more aspects of their daily practice. It is easy to imagine how expert practitioners who meet clients with the same challenges and preferences in one agency may select different types and modes of interventions than their colleagues in another location because the agency context predetermines some of their choices.

Furthermore, the agency is embedded within larger community, state/provincial, and national economic, cultural, and sociopolitical contexts (Gilbert, Parton & Skivenes, 2011; Kamerman, Phipps, & Ben-Aryeh, 2010; Wulczyn et al., 2010). Some of these broader influences on child welfare practice are easily apparent: Definitions of neglect are closely associated with the economic status of a country (see, for example, discussion on definition of *neglect* in India by Segal (1992) and in South Africa by Pierce and Bozalek (2004), the role of adoption in child welfare is determined to a large extent by the religious and cultural context of each country, and corporal punishment is seen as abuse in certain places and periods but not in others (Durrant, 2012; Gershoff et al., 2010). In the United States, for instance, corporal punishment in school (e.g., spanking with a paddle) is legal in some states and not in others (The Center for Effective Discipline, 2013).

The impact of larger contexts is immediately apparent when they change. For example, changes in some state laws and regulations regarding eligibility for services for those leaving care after the age of 18 have immediate implications for child welfare managers and practitioners in some states and not in others (Courtney et al., 2011). In Israel, a shift toward more community-based approaches had an immediate impact on reducing the availability of out-of-home placements for maltreated children and the need to develop services for children who were reunified with their parents because of the policy demand to shorten out-of-home placements (Dolev, Schmid, Sabo-Eliel, & Barnir, 2008). In former Eastern Bloc countries (e.g., Romania) changes in regime and ideology had a dramatic impact on the child welfare system, including the adoption of the UN Convention for Rights of the Child as the underlying practice and policy principles and the dismantling of most residential care facilities, so typical of the former child welfare system (Unicef, 2004).

Some of the effects of the larger contexts in which child welfare agencies are embedded may escape awareness just because they are so robust and all- encompassing. Take for example the availability (or lack thereof) of health insurance among working-poor families in the United States. Managers and practitioners in Australia, Canada, Israel, and Scandinavian countries may not even include in their considerations concerns about access to health care for urban youth formerly in foster care, assuming that they have universal access in their respective health systems. In the United States, on the other hand, the interplay between current and former youth in care and the health system is a major source of concern (Schneiderman, Smith, & Palinkas, 2012). Similar examples can be found in the role that schools and after school programs play in providing complementary services in different countries. There may even be contextual differences within countries. For instance, in Canada day care is highly subsidized in Quebec, whereas families must spend enormous sums of money for day care in Ontario. Analogous differences in the availability of day care are evident between regions in Germany, and especially between the former East Germany and West Germany.

Historical events and professional dominant discourses at certain historical points in time and place may also influence individual and organizational decisions. For instance, the situations and preferences of individual clients may be shaped by historical events (e.g., well-publicized child fatality due to leaving a child with maltreating parents), current political and ideological beliefs (e.g., professional discourse may view domestic violence from a feminist perspective, which makes sense on political and ideological levels, but may translate to a more limited set of available services for women with children who choose to stay in abusive relationships (Friend, Shlonsky, & Lambert, 2008; Shlonsky, Friend, & Lambert, 2007)), and prevailing, and perhaps competing, professional theories and discourses (e.g., a "children's rights" perspective may lead to different conclusions compared with a "best interest" focus).

In the realm of our current focus on evidence, it is clear that practitioners operate within embedded contexts that may demand, require, support, or disregard the need to use evidence. In some countries, such as the United States, the demand for empirically supported treatments has now become central to the operation of child welfare services and agencies, and funding for private and not-for-profit organizations is dependent on demonstrating that agency practices are based on programs formally recognized by the federal government as evidence-based (US Department of Health and Human Services, Administration for Children and Families, 2012). In the UK, evidence is in the policy discourse, and many efforts are made to prepare practitioners to use evidence on "what works" (Munro, 2011). Other countries, such as Israel, while touting the importance of EBP, do very little to generate evidence or to support interventions showing evidence for effectiveness. Furthermore, child welfare agencies even within the same country may differ substantially in their emphasis on the effective use of evidence due to differences in the structural, organizational, and personal attributes of management (see Schmid, Chapter 9, this book).

In sum, the very type of intervention considered is strongly related to the need and availability of resources, and these are strongly related to historical, political, social, and economic factors in the client, practitioner, community, and agency.

The Child Welfare Agency as the Center of Evidence-Informed Practice

Much of the current literature on EIP focuses on individual practitioners looking for evidence that can inform their work with clients. This is especially evident in training books, such as Gibbs (2003), that are oriented toward helping students formulate the right questions about their practice, search for evidence, and integrate this evidence into their judgments and decisions regarding their interventions with clients. These are important foci, as individual practitioners are directly engaged with clients and have responsibility for providing the best services suited to their clients' needs and preferences.

In contrast to this sole focus on the individual practitioner, the expanded model of EBP situates the individual practitioner and her clients within multiple contexts affecting this interaction. This wider lens suggests that the focus of our efforts to understand and use evidence should be shifted. In this book we focus the evidence-based perspective on the child welfare agencies in charge of providing services to children and families. We use here the term *child welfare agency* in a very general sense: to identify a meaningful organizational unit that encompasses a number of practitioners working within the same context. Here again, an organizational unit, such as a government child welfare department of a county, may consist of several lower level nested organizational units, such as branches and community outstations. Nongovernmental organizations providing a range of statutory and nonstatutory family support services may be small and focused on one area of service or may be multiservice agencies contending with a wide range of client needs and providing services through multiple organizational units. More conceptual work needs to be done in the future to further elucidate differences between various types and sizes of service units or agencies. While some scholars are working to evaluate agency-based EBP approaches (Aarons, Hurlburt, & Horwitz, 2011; McCracken

& Marsh, 2008; Mullen, Bledsoe, & Bellamy, 2008), the link between individual practitioners and broader child welfare policies and legislation can be seen as one of the less
developed areas of research.

There are several important reasons to engage in this exploration of the meaning
of EIP on the agency level. Most child welfare practitioners are working in agencies
located within specific settings, and with limited resources, all of which constrain
their work with families and children and at the same time provide the resources
needed for interventions. Thus, a practitioner who engages in a process of EIP is likely
to arrive at the conclusion that a number of different interventions or modalities are
suited for different groups of families and their children. Realistically, however, the
practitioner's choices are guided, constrained, or augmented by available personnel
and agency resources, as well as by the types of referrals available in the particular
community.

Furthermore, an individual practitioner may have identified a program that has evidence to suggest its relevance to a client family. However, without agency support, the
practitioner may not have access to that particular program. While it is important to con-
vey this information to clients (Gambrill, 2001), the reality is that certain services may
simply be unavailable. The implementation of many empirically supported treatments
requires considerable investment of resources in order to purchase these programs, train
staff, and implement with fidelity. In most cases, child welfare agencies need to make
choices between several evidence-based interventions. They must make best use of limited financial resources to purchase such programs, and create the organizational infrastructure, such as training, support, and supervision, required for their implementation.
Consequently, they are, in a very real sense, making decisions that are often considered
the domain of the practitioner and are, practically speaking, facilitating the process of
EIP at a level once removed from the practitioner.

Implications of the Expanded Model

INTERVENTION RESEARCH

The role that embedded contexts play in influencing practice and the use of evidence
in child welfare has direct implications for the interaction between those who generate
evidence and for the many others who consider using evidence in their practice. For those
generating evidence, it is essential to identify and document the multiple contexts that
are potentially relevant for the validity of this evidence, and especially to its generalizability to a particular child welfare context. Currently, documentation pertaining to services
labeled as "evidence-based" focuses more on client demographic and problem characteristics and on internal validity (i.e., the study design used to test the interventions). Very
rarely does a manualized program offer in its documentation a larger perspective on the
context in which the program was developed and tested. In this global market of social

interventions, however, these larger contexts cannot be assumed to be similar across the many settings in which a program is to be implemented.

A relevant example of the need to more fully explicate contextual elements is the use of the term *minority* in describing a target population. Clearly, even within the same country or geographical area, there may be large differences between the characteristics, needs, and resources of families and children from various minority groups. For instance, although in Israel Arab minority families share many circumstances and needs, there are major differences between the minority groups of Bedouin, Druze, Muslim, and Christian Arabs. In fact, even within the same minority immigrant group there are many relevant differences between first, second, and later generations (Lorenzo-Blanco, Unger, Baezconde-Garbanati, Ritt-Olson, & Soto, 2012; Marmot et al., 1975; Wengler, 2011) and the circumstances surrounding immigration (e.g., asylum seekers versus opportunity seekers). In many places there are also important differences between immigrants based on their legal status (citizen versus permanent resident versus nonlegal status) and how transient they may be (e.g., Latin American seasonal farm workers in the United States). Simply stating that an intervention addresses minority families and children is insufficient for examining its relevance to the local client population.

In addition to explicating the larger contexts in which empirically supported interventions were developed and tested, it is essential to document the organizational context of the settings in which the empirically supported treatment was carried out and empirically tested. For instance, it is common practice in clinical trials for funders and developers to select sites that have a reasonable chance of completing the trial successfully. In some cases "evaluability" and "feasibility" studies are conducted in advance to determine which sites have the minimal conditions required for participation in complex, long-term, and expensive trials. This is wise in terms of creating a controlled environment in which a new intervention can be reasonably tested. Still, the inevitable outcome of this process involves a selection bias in that the choice of settings is quite unique and hardly representative of the many other settings in which the evidence is expected to be utilized.

Such selection processes are almost inevitable in efficacy studies, but they are also potentially in operation in effectiveness trials that do not use a random selection process as an intervention is scaled up. It is therefore important to document in detail how the agencies were approached, whether some agencies declined to participate, the selection criteria used (including *informal* criteria such as "someone we could work with"; a manager that is interested in empirically supported treatments; stability of leadership; good reputation in the community, etc.), and any other consideration used to select sites for an experiment. If these "details" are left out, it is unlikely that future consumers will be able to adequately assess the important ways in which their site might differ from the original test sites.

We recommend, therefore, documenting contexts as if they were recorded by an observer from a different country. Such a perspective of "looking from the outside in" may help researchers adopt a perspective that can shed light on the subtle assumptions and shared knowledge (considered trivial by insiders and puzzling by others) crucial to the success of an intervention in a different context. Presently, there are no agreed-on reporting guidelines, though there is some work under way to extend the CONSORT Statement[2] to include items relevant to complex social interventions.

However, even such tools cannot possibly document all aspects of the context in which an intervention was delivered; there are so many nested contexts that attempts to document all of them in detail are unrealistic. To illustrate, a "trivial" detail, such as how long it takes to travel to a family in a home visiting program, may make all the difference in the world for attempts to implement such a program in a remote area in which roads are unpaved and treacherous. Nonetheless, it is important to identify and theorize about which aspects of the context "make a difference"; to explore the many gaps in our knowledge relating to the differences in context and its corresponding effect on generalization. For instance, using severe corporal punishment may have similar deleterious consequences for children in many different countries and cultures. Being a single parent, on the other hand, may be a risk factor for certain outcomes in some countries and not in others. Certain interventions may prove robust across contexts, such as parent training, whereas there are questions as to whether some programs, such as multisystemic therapy (MST), may transfer as well (Littell, Popa, & Forsythe, 2005; Sundell, Ferrer-Wreder, & Fraser, 2013). Developing a conceptual framework that identifies which contextual factors may be most relevant in considering the implementation of evidence-based programs in child welfare will make an important contribution to translational science and to practice.

There is clearly a place for thoughtful consideration and knowledge development regarding how various contexts may be relevant for each policy, program, or intervention technique. Some of the answers may be derived from international comparative studies that will help identify context-specific effects and common patterns across most contexts. Furthermore, over time, the cumulative empirical knowledge about successes and failures in transporting empirically supported treatments and lessons learned from implementation in various settings will enrich our understanding of the role that different contexts play.

Child Welfare Agencies: The Need for Evidence

A shift in focus to the agency level requires new ways of thinking as to what evidence is needed to inform child welfare practice and policy and what roles child welfare agencies should play in creating and using such evidence. In contrast to many discussions that

---

[2] The CONSORT Statement is a minimum set of recommendations for authors reporting on their randomized controlled trials. The use of the recommendation promotes complete and transparent reporting and aids critical appraisal and interpretation (http://www.consort-statement.org/home/).

focus only on evidence-based *interventions*, we emphasize the need for evidence required to inform practice at multiple levels (e.g., practitioner, agency, state) and across contexts. We suggest that in order to have evidence inform practice, agencies need to answer a series of questions about their clients, interventions, and outcomes, and on the inter-relationships between these domains within the practice setting. The following are some broad domains of questions child welfare agencies may need to pose in order to have their practices and policies informed by evidence.

CLIENTS

For agencies to be engaged in the process of EIP, they need to know who their clients are on many relevant dimensions, such as:

- Demographics;
- Needs, concerns, problems;
- Personal and social circumstances that contribute to their needs and strengths;
- Preferences and value systems.

These last three dimensions, while seen as important by practitioners, have been paid very little attention by researchers studying the effectiveness of interventions. That is, the process of considering client preferences and values as part of the decision-making process around the choice of interventions is rarely studied in social care.

Although some agencies work with more homogeneous groups of clients than others, all child welfare agencies should expect variability in these client characteristics. It is important, therefore, not only to attend to central tendencies but also to identify variability on key characteristics, so that the needs and circumstances of smaller subgroups are not overlooked.

Furthermore, a simple description of the distribution of each of the clients' characteristics may not tell the whole story. The agency client group may consist of several clearly distinguishable *clusters* of clients, each requiring a different approach, and a search for a different set of potentially effective interventions. Consider, for instance, the characteristics of children in foster care. Children and youth range in age, reason for placement, strengths and difficulties, family supports, and placement history. It is most likely that these children form distinct groups that have much in common internally and are very different compared with others. For example, infants in care have much in common and they are very different from adolescents in care. Among adolescents in care there may be several distinct groups, such as those who have been in care for many years, and a group who have been placed for the first time as adolescents. This latter group may exhibit more delinquent behaviors, whereas the former, children who may have been drifting in care for much of their lives, may have a very different set of needs, resources, strengths, and difficulties.

INTERVENTIONS

Child welfare agencies employ individual practitioners who engage with many children and families. In most agencies, each of these practitioners employs a range of interventions, some more structured than others. The agency as a whole may not have a detailed picture of the range and distribution of the various interventions chosen, services rendered, and resources provided. In order to provide services and conduct interventions based on evidence, it is essential to know what is actually being done by the agency.

Similar to the need for gathering information about client characteristics, the agency also needs to know how frequently specific services are provided, interventions implemented, and resources delivered. Furthermore, it is important to identify "strategies," groups of services, resources, and interventions that may be packaged together in different configurations. A review of these patterns may reveal that service delivery is deliberate and based on thoughtful analysis of clients' problems, circumstances, needs, and preferences. Alternatively, evidence pertaining to the structure of services may draw attention to gaps and areas in which current practices do not reflect the best available knowledge. That is, are certain resources provided exclusively to clients with certain attributes and not to others? Are certain groups of children allocated to particular services (such as out-of-home care) more than others? Are there certain services delivered to all clients, irrespective of their different attributes? It is important to note that finding out that the provision of certain resources is not distributed equally across clients groups may be "good news," indicating thoughtful choices and differential responses driven by professional discretion. Uneven distributions can also offer opportunities for exploring the effectiveness of services.

Evidence of associations between clients' characteristics and the type of intervention they receive should be examined very carefully: do they reflect a lack of awareness or hidden biases? Or perhaps such differential responses reflect good professional discretion based on evidence about the relative effectiveness of certain interventions with different groups of clients. To illustrate, consider a finding in a recent study that child protection teams in hospitals more often report maltreatment of children already known to child protection services than children who are not already known (Benbenishty, Jedweb, Lavi-Sahar, & Lerner-Geva, 2013). Does this pattern reflect stigma and bias, or perhaps reliance on evidence indicating that children already maltreated are at higher risk for future maltreatment (O'Donnell, Nassar, Jacoby, & Stanley, 2012)?

OUTCOMES

Systematic information on client outcomes is arguably the most important evidence for child welfare practitioners, agencies, and policymakers. Yet measuring client outcomes without considering their unique characteristics and attributes is insufficient. As we have indicated above, identifying how well clients are doing as a group is important, but understanding variance in outcomes may be essential evidence for improvement efforts. In other words, it is crucial to identify whether and to what extent client outcomes are associated with differences in client characteristics, intervention types, and delivery methods. This information is central to the identification of client groupings that are not achieving hoped for outcomes, which services and interventions are associated with client progress, and which matches between clients and interventions are producing the best outcomes. Moreover, this type of outcome information is very different from performance information on outputs (i.e., units of service delivered). A mere focus on compliance-driven output monitoring and evaluation systems is unlikely to improve actual child and family outcomes.

The Role of the Child Welfare *Agency* in Creating and Using Evidence

The unique web of contexts and concerns in which each agency is embedded requires that agencies interested in building their practice on evidence create *local* evidence that is relevant to their circumstances and needs. This is not to say that outside evidence is not useful; it can and should be a guide. But a more fully informed agency would match existing evidence to local context and use ongoing monitoring and evaluation systems to guide the implementation of effective services.

MATCHING EXISTING EVIDENCE TO AGENCY LOCAL CONTEXT

Child welfare settings that have evidence about their clients, interventions, and outcomes are better positioned to find and utilize effective services. The search for services is informed by detailed knowledge about clients, their circumstances, and desired outcomes. Armed with such information, the search for evidence is more focused and relevant.

EVIDENCE ON IMPLEMENTATION, INCLUDING ONGOING MONITORING AND EVALUATION

The proactive role of the child welfare agency does not end when an evidence-based intervention has been identified and implementation commences, and indeed it can be argued that implementation includes the proper selection of interventions. Even interventions shown to be effective in multiple studies and implemented with fidelity, or that have been adjusted to fit the specific agency, may not work in a given context. There is a need to examine whether these outcomes were actually achieved as expected. The rich emerging literature on implementation clearly indicates that even fairly straightforward, manualized programs and services require extensive planning, training, coaching, adaptation, and monitoring in order to maximize client outcomes and create sustainability (Fixsen, Naoom, Blasé, Friedman, & Wallace, 2005). Furthermore, given the dynamic nature of the organizational settings in which services are delivered, stability in the service environment and the agency client base cannot be assumed. Agencies need to continuously monitor changing client demographics as well as the outcomes associated with potential demographic shifts. Monitoring and evaluation provides an indispensable social biofeedback mechanism (Benbenishty & Astor, 2005, 2012) that allows agencies to understand the changing environment and react accordingly. In general, this requires a comprehensive, clinically driven and integrated information system that pulls together data from across the agency for use in guiding decisions by front-line workers, supervisors, managers, and administrators (Benbenishty & Oyserman, 1995). Done well, these systems can inform critical thinking about ongoing decisions as well as monitor outcomes for quality improvement and evaluations. Done poorly, they can take time away from clients and lead to, or solidify, a culture of compliance and thoughtlessness (Munro, 2011).

How Evidence can be Created at the Agency Level

We suggest that child welfare agencies use systematic means to document central aspects of their work including client demographics, case level characteristics, type of services delivered (including dose and frequency), staff skills and competence, and a range of high quality tools that measure specific child and family outcomes. In order to address the wide range of questions that agencies pose, it is important to use multiple means to gather evidence. Clearly, all settings will not have the capacity to generate every type of evidence. Nevertheless, we advocate that all child welfare agencies develop capacities to generate at least some form of valid knowledge that informs important aspects of their practice; knowledge that helps them develop and refine local practices and policies, assess the relevance of evidence created elsewhere, and monitor client progress over time.

For individual practitioners, some of the answers to questions regarding individual client characteristics and outcomes are easily obtained during the processes of engagement and assessment. On the agency level, on the other hand, it may prove quite challenging to obtain a detailed picture of the client population, interventions employed, and outcomes. The question should drive the method, and this may prove challenging. For instance, agencies may commonly employ qualitative methods such as focus groups and in-depth case studies in an attempt to better understand their client population. Notwithstanding the potential contribution of such methods, a well-executed epidemiological approach can provide a more systematic and less biased view of the whole range of client characteristics, as well as the clustering of various client characteristics into distinct groups.

The analysis of data generated by other systems, such as census data covering the agency's jurisdiction, may also be very useful. Analyses of such available data directly relevant to the agency may provide important evidence on the unique characteristics of the agency's current clientele, and may also shed light on important changes to come.

Still other methods relate to analysis of agency records either in paper files or as stored in management or integrated agency information systems. For instance, Benbenishty demonstrated how a computerized integrated information system can be designed and implemented in a foster care system, providing valuable evidence about clients, interventions, and outcomes (Benbenishty, 1989; Benbenishty & Oyserman, 1991, 1995). Epstein (2010) advocates clinical data mining that takes advantage of the clinical data available in agency records, both paper and electronic. Quantitative or qualitative data mining can provide meaningful insights on an agency's clients, interventions, and outcomes. Although unstructured agency files are notoriously inconsistent in terms of content and quality, Epstein details methods to help minimize some of these limitations while using information already collected. Advances in database technology can often be used to bring together multiple and disparate sources of information in meaningful ways, opening the door to the development of low-cost, customized monitoring and evaluation systems (Ontario Commission to Promote Sustainable Child Welfare, 2012).

The advantage of implementing an information system that tracks key elements of service provision and outcomes is that it can be augmented with systematically gathered evidence from other sources, such as specific surveys or other instruments used to collect information about the implementation and outcomes of new services or policies being tested. These data can also be linked with external data from other service providers such as education, health, and corrections, making research and quality improvement efforts less costly and manageable than it would be if new data collection methods had to be invented every time an agency had a question. More commonly occurring research questions can be transformed into ongoing performance indicators, allowing agencies to monitor quality and progress rigorously and efficiently.

Systematic gathering and evaluation of single case studies has also been proposed for years as a method to study outcomes and provide evidence on the effectiveness of interventions (Bloom, Fischer, & Orme, 1982). Over the years, disenchantment appears to have developed in terms of the feasibility of this approach (Mullen et al., 2008). Nevertheless, as Barth and Lee (Chapter 4, this book) and others (Orme & Cox, 2001) note, recent developments in conceptualization of the value of ongoing feedback on client's outcomes coupled with technological developments may enhance the willingness of practitioners to employ single case studies, perhaps doing so systematically on a series of clients. This may lead to more widespread use of this method of generating evidence.

Agencies may also generate knowledge through surveys conducted among their clients. For instance, client preferences may be assessed through surveys administered to agency clients. Needs assessment surveys are an important tool in planning agency interventions to address the needs of their community. To illustrate, in Uganda the government and international aid organizations required information on the nature and extent of children's vulnerabilities. Based on a national needs assessment survey, a series of vulnerabilities were identified and targeted for future services and policies; these vulnerabilities included maternal death, disability, child labor and pregnancy before age 17, living apart from siblings, having nobody to talk to, and never visiting a living parent (Kalibala, Schenk, Weiss, & Elson, 2012).

Client satisfaction is a type of often-used outcome that, in isolation, is easily dismissed because of its well-known social desirability bias (i.e., satisfaction measures are prone to positive responses and may have little correlation with more objective outcome measures). However, there are ways such information can be conceptualized and gathered so as to be relevant for agency self-assessment and policy development. Chaffin and associates (Chaffin, Bard, Bigfoot, & Maher, 2012) provide an interesting example. They examined the implementation of the SafeCare home-based model among American Indians as part of a larger randomized controlled trial. The study included measures of consumer ratings of cultural competency, working alliance, service quality, and service benefit. The use of such indicators provided evidence that a manualized, structured, empirically supported model was culturally acceptable for American Indians. Similar surveys could be conducted by agencies implementing empirically supported programs developed with populations that are culturally different from the agency's clients.

Some agencies, especially larger ones, are also able to initiate outcome studies using a variety of designs, including methods such as single case series, pre-post designs, or even well-controlled studies such as RCTs. No matter the size or focus of the agency, though, the point is that process and outcome data are crucial for ensuring that clients are receiving the types of services that are likely to be effective for contending with the wide range of challenges they experience. Simply providing a service that is considered "effective" without measuring whether it is actually of benefit is inadequate and does not reflect the principles of evidence-informed practice.

Individual Practitioners within Agencies

Our emphasis on the agency-level processes involved in EIP does not detract from the professional and ethical responsibility of each individual practitioner working in the agency. Here, we are close to the views expressed by Gambrill (2006), emphasizing that ethical conduct requires that practitioners use evidence to inform their decisions. Practitioners making decisions at the front line should employ their critical thinking skills to implement the process of EIP by systematically searching and appraising the literature, understanding the literature's important but sometimes limited applicability to specific individuals (while not being dismissive of them), and generating their own systematic evidence to continue to improve agency-level decision-making and policies.

There is an ethical imperative to engage in a multiway interaction between the agency and policy context and the individual practitioner, ensuring that front-line practitioners can be effective contributors and users of evidence rather than being seen as submissive recipients of information, policies, and procedures. In fact, practitioners are invaluable participants in continuous quality improvement processes used to create or redesign child welfare practices and policies. To illustrate, many protective service practitioners are required to use structured risk assessment instruments to guide their professional judgments of potential risk and decisions on how to respond to such risk. Many of these standardized instruments are required by the agency, are structured, and have predetermined algorithms connecting between a set of case facts, risk assessment scores, and subsequent recommendations. These instruments may reflect the best evidence in the area of risk assessment, and as such should guide individual practitioners assessing risk of maltreatment recurrence. Nevertheless, even in this highly constrained use of evidence in practice, practitioners still have the duty to employ professional discretion (Shlonsky & Wagner, 2005). They have the capacity to use this discretion to "override" the assessment and make a different recommendation. In order to do this, practitioners should be asked to provide detailed arguments explicating how the nature of a specific case suggests a different approach than implied by the existing instrument. A compilation of such arguments, especially as they are gathered from many individual practitioners in a child welfare agency, may help develop new agency-level insights. For instance, individual practitioners may realize that a standardized instrument is not sensitive to a particular cultural nuance in the agency's clientele. Addressing such cases can then generate new guiding rules and corresponding local adjustments to the tools—and all based on evidence gathered by individual practitioners.

Front-line workers are the first to recognize how certain policies may discriminate against their clients, how changes in clientele make well-established practices less relevant, and how (alongside positive outcomes documented for the client population at large) negative side effects may be evident in some client groups. These individual professional observations should be carefully cultivated, examined, and, when viable, incorporated into the dynamic and ever-expanding repository of evidence that helps shape practice, policies, management decisions, and intervention selection for the agency as a whole.

This process is of special importance in agencies that are implementing evidence-informed programs developed elsewhere. Workers may be the first to recognize misalignments between the assumptions and requirements of the new program and the circumstances of clients, prevailing cultural practices, and historical, legislative, and other barriers. They may point to a lack of required administrative structures and supports, the need for enhanced and focused training, and potential mismatches between the intervention and the characteristics of their individual clients (e.g., the extent to which parents are able to read to their children). In fact, as Mildon, Dickinson, and Shlonsky contend (chapter 5, this book), implementation science puts special emphasis on attending very carefully to the information provided by individual practitioners and finding ways to integrate it into the evolving implementation.

Evidence-Informed Policy

The process of integrating "grass-roots" evidence into the overall EIP approach does not end at the agency level. Agencies operating under common (e.g., state or country level) policies and legislation may provide evidence that can help shape and modify these, particularly if groups of agencies engage in shared endeavors aimed at generating and using evidence. As more agencies critically examine the evidence they generate through their internal processes, they will be better able to identify policy assumptions and practices that are working for and against children and families. Agencies, for instance, may be able to point out how certain policy-based eligibility criteria may be discriminating against certain groups of children and families or inadvertently providing incentives for bad practices.

At the broader level, policymaking can and should be informed by evidence. However, the broader view requires an adjustment of perspective. While a more detailed treatment of evidence-based policymaking is beyond the scope of this chapter, some key ideas are important to consider. In general, evidence-based policymaking involves the use of evidence for groups of clients or populations (Gray, 1997). The essential features of the model remain the same, but its application is at a higher level. In our expanded EBP model, decisions would more explicitly consider the economic, historical, political, and professional contexts, and the implications of adopting the intervention at a population level. The values and needs of the client are substituted with values and needs of the population (Gray, 2004). Thus, the decision to make available, promote, and/or require a given program or intervention is weighed with respect to such things as its cost, proportion of the population targeted (prevalence/incidence), proportion of the population who will likely benefit (effect size), public sentiment toward expenditure, political climate, and the like.

Sometimes, movement toward larger policies can be quite progressive. For example, in Australia, the commonwealth government made a decision to adopt a public health approach to child protection, explicitly developing a policy that uses universal services to drive primary prevention efforts in order to stop child maltreatment before it starts (Australian Government Department Families, Housing, Community Services and Indigenous Affairs, 2009). Yet even such bold moves face severe challenges. Although this is a federal policy, each state is responsible for funding and running its own child protection systems, and the policy was not introduced with an influx of federal funding for preventive services. In addition, the types of preventive services being offered may or may not be effective; high-quality, national data that can be used monitor the uptake of the framework is limited; and it is notoriously difficult to maintain public attention for long-term social service reforms.

While the implementation of empirically supported programs and practices can be successfully facilitated in a number of ways (Durlak & DuPre, 2008; Fixsen et al., 2005; Mildon et al., chapter 5 this book), the use of research in public policy development occurs through a number of core strategies. Walter, Nutley, and Davies (2005) identify five key mechanisms they contend underpin these: dissemination (one-way, tailored presentation of research to policy-makers); interaction (two-way collaborative approaches between researchers and policy-makers); social influence (persuasion by influential experts and peers); facilitation (enabling through technical, financial, organizational, and emotional support); and incentives and reinforcement (use of rewards and control to influence behavior). Although single mechanisms are often used, combinations set within an effective practice may be more likely to lead to progress (Nutley, Walter, & Davies, 2009). In the complex world of policymaking, values may always be more influential than evidence (Gray, 2004). The evidence can be strong and the correct decision may appear to be clear, but context may win out at the end of the day.

Conclusion

The complexity of child welfare services warrants a complex response: one that embraces a wide range of evidence, used in different ways and for different purposes, to contend with the vastly different contexts encountered in such work. This introductory chapter has attempted to present how evidence fits into this complexity, and the many strategies that can be used to inform and guide the provision of high-quality child welfare services. The EIP revolution is upon us, offering a myriad of opportunities with respect to the availability of knowledge and the technology used to store, process, translate, and exchange it. Again, it bears mentioning that all evidence is not created equal—that different types of questions require different types of evidence, and there may not be a single right answer. Multiple sources of information, gathered rigorously, must be used to generate the complex patchwork of evidence needed to made informed choices about the type, scope, and frequency of services, and the manner in which they are provided to individual children and families. As the field matures, the questions will move from "What works?" to "What has a good chance of working for whom and in what circumstances?"

We should not shy away from this complexity. EIP is intuitively appealing because we can acknowledge that human beings are complex creatures living in quickly evolving social systems. Embracing this truth means living with uncertainty, and living with uncertainty means that we must critically think about the evidence we encounter, generate, and use.

2

THE DECISION-MAKING ECOLOGY

Donald J. Baumann, John D. Fluke, Len Dalgleish, and Homer Kern

Introduction

The ways in which decisions are made impact the use of evidence-informed services at all levels of the child welfare system, including decisions made by administrators, program managers, workers, and families. That is, the environments in which decisions are made, as well as the psychological process of decision-making result in actions that produce expected and actual outcomes. In this chapter we review some of the general decision-making literature and noteworthy decision-making literature related to child welfare and then present a framework called the decision-making ecology/general assessment and decision-making (DME/GADM) model. This framework describes the influences and constraints that are operating in child welfare decision-making. The framework addresses the crucial role of welfare assessment, but also describes more comprehensively the factors that influence decisions outside of the assessment process. The implications for evidence-informed approaches are presented, with the prospect of improving the uptake and use of these approaches.

Over three centuries ago, beginning in the Age of Reason, philosophers championed rational thought. Despite the writings of Freud and others in the late 19th and 20th centuries, the notion of rational thought and especially rational decision-making remained firmly entrenched in academia through the mid-20th century. According to two popular theories of the time, social exchange theory (Homans, 1958) and attribution theory (Jones & Davis 1966; Kelly, 1973), humans calculated the costs and benefits of various options before making a decision (the former) and weighed personal and situational forces before determining the cause of someone's actions (the latter). Both were formidable models of rational thought.

During this same period, the psychological landscape was changing. Simon (1956, 1959), who later received a Nobel Prize for his efforts, was demonstrating that reason had its limits, proposing a new "bounded rationality" model of decision-making that described the consequence of imperfect information and limited human information processing abilities. Tversky and Kahneman (1974) were suggesting that reasoning is even more limited than we had believed. These authors provided us with ample demonstrations of certain types of errors in decision-making, suggesting that humans applied a number of heuristics—mental strategies that speed decision-making—under conditions of uncertainty that often led to error. They also framed behavioral based prospect theory, for which Kahneman received the Nobel Prize (Kahneman, 2002), and cumulative prospect theory, which behaviorally reweights rationally based decision expectations for rare and adverse events. At this same time, even the unconscious was making a comeback, stripped of its psychoanalytic trappings (Bowers, 1984). By the later part of the 20th century and the early part of the 21st century the idea of the rational decision-maker had given way to a less rational one. Even so, the exchange can hardly be viewed as stable, given the recent findings and debate over how error prone the use of heuristics is (Gigerenzer, 1991, 1993, 1994, 1996, 2005; Kahneman & Tversky, 1996).

A number of other important theoretical and empirical decision-making frameworks have also been advanced in the sciences. These have included foundational work in the field of judgment and decision-making by Hammond (1955) and Edwards (1954, 1961). The field has also benefited from input from many diverse fields such as economics (e.g., Simon, 1959), artificial intelligence (e.g., Weiss, Kulikowski, Amarel, & Safir, 1978), psychology (e.g., Tversky & Kahneman; 1974), engineering (e.g., Triantaphyllou & Mann, 1995), medicine (e.g., Hunink et al., 2003), and even meteorology (e.g., National Research Council, 1989). These contributions can provide insight and understanding about decisions made by child welfare protective services. Yet, the child welfare field has struggled to benefit from the knowledge gains and progress regarding decision-making research. Instead, it has focused on correcting errors through building risk and safety instruments and systems rather than understanding the sources of errors (Munro & Hubbard, 2011).

In child welfare cases, risk and safety instruments can improve the likelihood of identifying cases that may be at risk of subsequent harm (Shlonsky & Wagner, 2005). Nevertheless they fall far short of being accurate, and this is not merely a function of inadequate implementation. Even the best risk assessment tools implemented under ideal conditions are only able to achieve approximately 70% accuracy for re-maltreatment or re-reporting. For situations where maltreatment has not occurred previously the accuracy is considerably less (Fluke, Shusterman, Hollinshead, & Yuan, 2008). Furthermore, the single best predictor of a re-maltreatment is a prior maltreatment. Because the population of children who are maltreated or at risk for maltreatment is small compared to the population who will not be maltreated or re-maltreated, the error associated with these instruments in the aggregate yields very large false positive error rates. That is to say, a very large number of children and families are rated as being at risk for re-maltreatment when in fact they are not. So while predictions that are made using risk and safety assessment instruments, when well implemented and used consistently, are better than chance, decision-making error is still quite commonplace (Munro, 2008). Finally, these instruments tell us little about how to intervene and in particular provide no guidance regarding one of the most difficult decisions; whether to place a child in out-of-home care. The underlying question in decision-making research related to child welfare is whether decision-making error can be reduced, and if so, how? The problem is much more complex than risk and safety assessment alone.

Three child welfare models in the literature are noteworthy, however. The first is an early decision-making model by Stein and Rzepnicki (1983). This model outlined the broader systems goals of child welfare (e.g., safety and family preservation), pointing out some key processes, including decision-making, and important domains of information (e.g., family, agency, courts, law, etc.). The model broadly sketched the landscape but got little traction empirically. The second, a systems approach by Munro (2005), regards human error as the starting point for understanding decision-making. It takes into account individual factors such as skills and knowledge, resources and constraints such as analytic versus intuitive judgment, and the organizational context in which decisions are made such as changes in thresholds.

The Munro model is compatible with the one we present here. As indicated, the decision-making ecology (DME) was first described in the mid-1990s (Baumann et al., 1997). Like Munro's model, it also takes human error as the starting point for understanding decision-making and suggests that decisions need to be understood within their context.

A third model formulated by Benbenishty and Davidson-Arad is oriented to explaining placement decisions. This judgments and decisions processes in context (JUDPIC) model focuses on multilevel decision-making factors, particularly risk factors at the case level and worker attitudes toward placements. Tested using scenarios, the framework supports the idea that worker attitude concerning placement is a moderating influence on the assessment of risk and that this has a direct relationship statistically to the likelihood of placement (Davidson-Arad & Benbenishty, 2010; Shapira & Benbenishty, 1993).

In the discussion that follows we first present the DME framework along with a description of the decision-making continuum and a presentation of the general assessment and decision-making (GADM) model that explains the psychological process of decision-making. We then conclude with illustrative applications of the concepts.

Decision-Making Ecology Framework

The DME framework presented here represents an effort to advance the field of child welfare decision-making using the knowledge gained from the decision-making sciences. It is a framework for organizing decision-making research in child welfare and places the topic squarely in the context of actual protective-service operations in this field. This is done because decisions take place within an agency culture where a systemic context combines with the case decisions made by the staff of the agency.

With respect to evidence-based practices, this is relevant because decision-making behavior has the potential to make important contributions in the area of implementation and service choices. For example, at the organizational level decision-makers are often confronted with the possibility of adverse events such as fatalities and may respond in a manner that is disproportionately conservative with respect to the actual likelihood that such events will occur. Similarly, policy decision-makers may also view negatively many individual decisions to use interventions that are designed to maintain children in their homes. Providing clarity around more likely outcomes for these cases in the presence of well-implemented evidence-based practices may help modify the way that these decision-makers reach their decisions.

The DME/GADM model has been successfully applied to the problem of disproportionality (Baumann et al., 2010; Fluke, Chabot, Fallon, MacLaurin, & Blackstock, 2010; Rivaux et al., 2008) the substantiation decision (Fluke et al., 2001), the decision to place children into care (Graham, Fluke, Baumann, & Dettlaff, 2013; Fluke et al., 2010), and the decision to reunify children with their families (Wittenstrom, Fluke, Baumann, & Graham, 2013).

As shown in Figure 2.1, the systemic context for decision-making includes a set of influences displayed as ovals. A decision block is depicted as a diamond that incorporates the type of decision (intake, placement, etc.), the psychological processes, and perceived consequences. Finally outcomes shown as a rectangle are the actual manifestations of the decision and are the actual immediate or longer term consequences of the decisions. As indicated by the reverse arrows in the figure, the context can change over time. Further, observed patterns in this model can be ascertained empirically and presented in probabilistic form. As a result, feedback from decisions and outcomes that are improved as a result of successful interventions constitute one form of evidence that can change the context of the model.

Influences cover the range of case, external, organizational, and individual decision-maker factors that combine in various probabilistic ways to influence decisions and outcomes. These influences can be divided into dimensions that represent their important features, and in this context include such information as the real and perceived availability of evidence-based practices. The main objective is to frame the model through the incorporation of data that address the range of critical factors so that decisions can be understood as a part of an entire context.

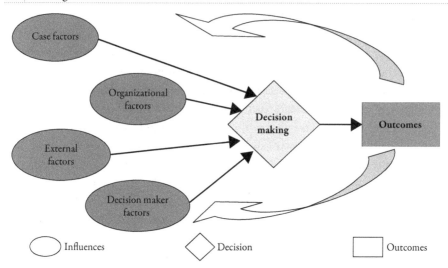

FIGURE 2.1. Decision-making ecology.

For example, case information regarding an incident of maltreatment is necessary for a caseworker to make informed assessments and decisions, yet decisions may depend on external factors, such as law translated into policies that govern what constitutes an appropriate response. Furthermore, the translation of such standards by organizational management, and their use by staff, will vary as a function of individual decision-maker factors, which include knowledge and skill. Further, this extends to the actual and perceived costs and benefits (outcomes) of the decision to the decision-maker, the client, and the agency. These outcomes in turn can influence the other factors in the form of feedback.

Consider first some evidence on case factors. In two studies (Rivaux et al., 2008; Dettlaff, et Al., 2011), researchers were able to show that both the substantiation decision and placement decision were affected by race, risk, and poverty in predictable ways. Findings concerning decision-maker factors (Baumann et al., 2010) suggest that the individual propensity for disparate placement[1] decision-making (i.e., those whose rates may be consistently lower or higher by race or ethnicity) can be made more equitable by improving caseworker skill, particularly in the area of cultural awareness. Consider, too, organizational factors. The presences of a lower proportion of African Americans or Hispanics on one's caseload (exposure) also accounts for disparate placement decisions. Finally, consider external factors. Fluke and his colleagues, using data from the Canadian Incidence Study, provide support for the possibility that the lack of community resources was one of the sources of placement disparities among aboriginal children (Fluke et al.,

---

[1] A *disparate placement decision* is when the odds (or ratio) of a child placement involving one racial or ethnic group is not equal to the odds (or ratio) of a child placement of another racial or ethnic group. Disparities can be calculated for any number of decisions.

2010). These findings illustrate that possible sources of decision-making error can be empirically identified within the DME.[2]

The diamond in Figure 2.1 represents case decision-making. The three features of decision-making in child welfare are: (1) the range of decisions made by the caseworker, supervisor, or even judges, referred to as a decision-making continuum;[3] (2) the psychological process of decision-making; and (3) the outcomes, or consequences, of the decision. The latter is represented by the rectangle on the right side of Figure 2.1 with arrows indicating that decision-making has consequences for children (e.g., recurrence), the workers themselves (e.g., distress), and the agency (e.g., public scrutiny). The continuum and process are represented in figures that follow.

DECISION-MAKING CONTINUUM AND TRAJECTORIES

The key feature of the decision-making continuum shown in Figure 2.2 is that it runs through the episodes, or stages of service, involved in cases processed by child welfare agencies. In fact, one way to think about caseworkers' jobs is that they are coordinators of a decision-making continuum.

This continuum starts at intake ("Do I initiate an investigation or not?") and ends at case closure, when all children in a family are deemed to be safe from maltreatment in the

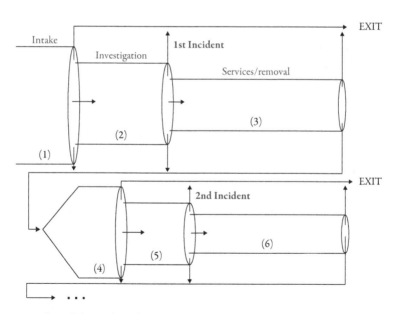

FIGURE 2.2. Flow of clients through the decision-making continuum.

---

[2] We are using *errors* in a broad sense to refer to biases such as those referenced at the outset of this paper as well as in a more strict sense to refer to false positive and negative errors such as those used in signal detection theory through receiver operating characteristics and the like.

[3] By *continuum* we refer to a sequence or progression of events. These events do not have values ranging from low to high or bad to good.

foreseeable future. It is not uncommon for a very large number of minor decisions to be made leading to each of the major or key decisions.

The relative size of the cylinders in Figure 2.2 can be viewed as representing case volume and the length of the cylinders as duration. The episodes are shown at the top of the continuum and cover caseworker decisions that range from intake (1) through service provision (2) and removal (3) for the first incident and consequently labeled as 4, 5, and 6 for the second incident. Through this continuum, children or families may follow different paths that are sometimes referred to as trajectories, the frequencies of which may characterize the decision-making proclivities of a given child welfare system. In addition to children and families moving through all or part of trajectories, the decision-maker may only be involved in part of the continuum. In systems that have greater specialization, workers may only meet an existing case at intake, during investigation, or in service provision, whereas caseworkers in systems with less specialization may see the child and or family throughout the life of the case.

THE PSYCHOLOGICAL PROCESS OF DECISION-MAKING: THE GENERAL
ASSESSMENT AND DECISION-MAKING MODEL

The psychological process of decision-making has three important features. First, it is useful to make a distinction between an assessment and a decision. As shown in Figure 2.3, an assessment involves a judgment of a situation given the current case information.

This assessment may be about the amount of risk or the strength of evidence (e.g., concerning parenting behavior, parent mental health issues, etc.) or the overall level of concern. Each of these can be an estimate along a dimension ranging from low to high.

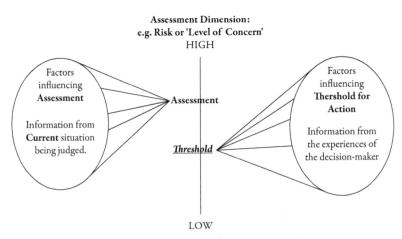

If the **Assessment** is *ABOVE* the *Thershold*, then ACTION is taken.
If the **Assessment** is *BELOW* the *Thershold*, then NO ACTION is taken.

FIGURE 2.3. A general model for assessing the situation and deciding what to do about it—Dalgleish.

A decision addresses whether or not to take a course of action. So the GADM model's alternative title could be "A General Model for Assessing Situations and Deciding What to Do About Them." In this model, we assume a threshold for action that turns an assessment of a situation into a decision-about action.

Thus, a second important feature of the psychological process of decision-making is a decision threshold. The theoretical base for the threshold concept is signal detection theory (Swets, Tanner, & Birdsall, 1955), and more recently Dalgleish (1988, 2003) proposed the GADM model in the child welfare field that makes the important distinction between assessment and action.

A decision threshold refers to the point at which the assessment of the case information (e.g., level of concern) is intense enough for one to decide to take major actions that form the basis of the continuum of decisions described above (e.g., intake, placement, reunification, etc.). This decision threshold is a personal "line in the sand." It is influenced by the experiences and history of the decision-maker, which is where the psychological aspects of the decision-making process are most active. These are both their actual or vicarious experiences and the conscious or subconscious interpretation of external factors and organizational factors in the DME. In fact, a decision-maker's own internal factors might be at odds with these external or organizational factors. A third psychological feature in the process of decision-making is a shift in this threshold. A shift in threshold refers to a change in level of concern deemed to be sufficient for action; a threshold shift would be involved if various features of the DME changed the basis for the decisions that fall along the decision-making continuum. An individual factor influencing a threshold shift might be experience. For example, a new worker might tend to render more affirmative decisions to be on the "safe side." Conversely, an experienced worker may know of—and be wary of—the consequences for children placed in the fostering and adoption system. One organizational influence that would alter the threshold would be a policy that dictates which cases would be accepted or should be attended to immediately (e.g., age and injury requirements for cases accepted and prioritized). Factors such as these would change the thresholds of the individuals and also impact the volume of cases moving through the decision-making continuum. Finally, conditions and contexts may change as a child and family move through the continuum necessitating adjustments to the initial decisions, however certain consequences of the initial decisions may be more or less irrevocable. For example, a placed child who has been reunified may have lasting emotional issues as a result of the placement. Similarly, when a threshold is not reached and the child does not advance to the next stage along the continuum, re-maltreatment may occur.

Applications: The Decision-Making Ecology and Thresholds along the Continuum

The DME model can be applied at each of the key decision points of the decision-making continuum; at intake (Dalgleish, 2003), at removal (Dalgleish, 1988), and at reunification

(Dalgleish and Newton, 1996). Consider the intake and the removal decisions. The threshold for each requires adequate information to make an assessment. The threshold may be higher for removal, compared to that required at intake, and this is reflected in the size of the cylinders in Figure 2.2, which indicate that as one moves further along the continuum there are fewer children who share that trajectory in the system. Furthermore, at the right end of the decision-making continuum, one might expect not only a higher level of information needed to make an assessment but also different types of information as well. This extends to the identification of what might be effective services and especially evidence-informed treatments and practices.

Consider the distinctive foci of the decision-making continuum; an intake worker may primarily contemplate information about the *allegation*, whereas an investigator making a removal decision may additionally consider the amenability of the situation to service intervention, given the nature of the risk. For reunification, Dalgleish and Newton (1996) found that information about the sustainability of change in the family was a factor influencing the assessment of risk. Thus, qualitatively different case information is needed to make an assessment at different stages along the decision-making continuum. It is possible that the assessment and the threshold for a decision can be the same, particularly when risk levels are very high or very low. However, other influences in the DME can alter the decisions along the decision-making continuum. For example, lowered appropriations or the passage of legislation limiting the length of time a child may remain in foster care (external factors) might cause the agency to alter its policy (an organizational factor) on the permanency planning for children in care. This would result in a threshold shift toward reunification, even under the same assessment conditions that might have existed prior to the policy change.

THE DECISION-MAKING ECOLOGY AND OUTCOMES

A final feature of the DME is the outcome of these decisions. Outcomes are represented by the rectangle in Figure 2.1. The large reversed arrows in Figure 2.1 indicate the assumption that, to the degree that the consequences of decisions can be presumed, perceived, or known, thresholds may shift through the influence of the four factors driving the DME: case, organizational, external, and individual decision-maker.

In the DME, outcomes are viewed from three perspectives having to do with consequences to the client, to the decision-maker, and to those external to the agency. All affect the factors in the DME, and thus the decision thresholds. The more familiar perspective involves outcomes to the client. Safety, permanency, and well-being are the best examples. However, another more immediate consequence is to the decision-maker. In decision theory this is typically considered the more immediate utility of a decision. First, it can affect changes in decision thresholds. Consider, for example, how a decision to close a case that results in a child fatality would affect the thresholds of decision-makers throughout the agency or even across agencies. Second, these consequential decisions (among other factors in the DME) can affect whether or not a worker stays with the agency (Baumann,

Kern, McFadden, & Law, 1997). Finally, consequential outcomes that are external to the agency can include public anxiety media exposure and legislative scrutiny. Child fatalities often generate all three.

Outcomes are also interrelated and may impact one or more of the DME decision influences. For example, a serious recurrence of maltreatment impacts the child, the family, and the caseworker who may have closed the case. Both the family and caseworker could be held accountable in one sense or another, and all involved parties would experience the event itself in a negative way. Possible scrutiny by those external to the agency would bring additional pressure to bear by holding the agency accountable as well. This might well involve legislative and or policy changes (external or organizational factors) that would change thresholds for taking action. Even in the absence of actual events, the decision-maker's perception that such outcomes could occur undoubtedly influences thresholds.

The decisions that lead to these consequential outcomes are fraught with uncertainty because the decision-maker cannot avoid the possibility of error. If action *is* taken, the decision-maker might be wrong, and if action *is not* taken they might be wrong as well. Hammond (1996) called this conundrum the "duality of error." Table 2.1 below reflects these errors. It shows the four possible outcomes for the decision to remove the children from their home and place them in care: Two types of correct outcomes and two incorrect ones. The box in the upper left-hand corner shows a correct decision to remove the child from the home. The box in the lower right corner shows a correct decision to not remove the child from the home. The box in the upper right-hand corner shows that errors resulting in false positives can result in an unwarranted placement in care because the child was safe. The box in the lower left-hand corner indicates that a lack of action can result in harm to the child. One or the other of these errors is unavoidable, that is, the theory implies that from a statistical perspective we can anticipate individual decision-makers will make each of these types of errors at an average rate. Moreover, the consequences of these errors may be considered as symmetrically bad and they sometimes are (McMahon, 1998).

TABLE 2.1

OUTCOMES FOR DECISIONS TO TAKE ACTION OR NOT: THE FOURFOLD TABLE

	Should Have Taken Action	Should NOT Have Taken Action
Decision: **YES—** Remove	**Hit** Correct outcome	**False Alarm** Error Damned if you do False positive
Decision: **NO—**Not Remove	**Miss** Error Damned if you don't False negative	**Correct No** Correct outcome

That is, a false positive error where the child is mistakenly placed in care may be considered as dreadful as a false negative error where the child is not placed and is re-harmed. However, they are often asymmetrical depending on who is affected by the error. For a resilient child an unwanted temporary placement may be just disturbing compared with being seriously physically re-harmed. Further, agencies place greater emphasis on one source of error over another, moving away from one kind of error over another and willing to indulge the opposite kind of error (Mansell, 2006). Presumably, values resulting in an asymmetrical error will lead to the development of policy, resources, and practices that are aligned promoting the more "desirable" type of error. This practice could extend to the development and utilization of specific evidence-supported approaches that are consistent with the asymmetry and emphasizes the special role of the agency in as a learning organization that can systematically process the information from many practitioners and generate such feedback.

Applications: Training in Threshold Placement and Threshold Differences

Individual caseworkers may value these consequences differently. To demonstrate this and roughly identify threshold placement, a decision-maker could answer this question: "Given that you can't avoid the possibility of error, which one do you want to avoid the most?" At one level the decision is nearly as simple as that. However, it might be difficult for the decision-maker to articulate why he or she prefers to avoid one error over another. The number of stakeholders involved in the decision helps explain this dilemma. In child protection they include: the child; the family; the caseworker; the caseworker's work unit, supervisor, and agency; other professionals; the courts; and society in general. For each of these stakeholders, and for each outcome, there are sets of consequences. Which raises the question: "Do the various people working in child protection differ in the values they place on consequences?" The answer is "yes."

A memorable example came to one of the authors (Dalgleish) during a workshop on thresholds for people working in multidisciplinary child-protection teams, although such examples are not unique in the literature (Gold, Benbenishty, & Osmo, 2001; Benbenishty, Osmo, & Gold 2003). After going through the process of making the consequences explicit for different stakeholders, a family physician said that he wanted to avoid "false alarms" (false positives) because of the harm to families falsely accused of child abuse. This was vehemently challenged by a social worker from a public children's hospital who wanted to avoid "misses" (false negatives) because she had seen many dead and injured children.

In terms of the GADM model, the physician's threshold was high, and he may have required a higher level of risk and thus greater concern before he took action. The social worker's threshold was low, and thus lower levels of risk generated high levels of concern requiring her to take action. To make things equal in this example, let us assume that they

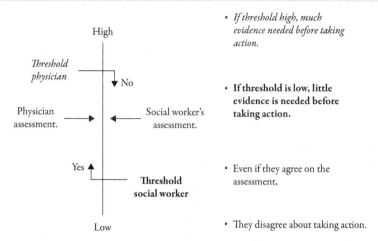

FIGURE 2.4. Applications of the threshold concept—decisional conflict.

are both told about a case and given the same case information. Assume also that they have been well trained in an assessment tool and have jointly assessed the case to have moderate levels of risk.

Figure 2.4 indicates why the physician would not want to take action and the social worker would. They do not differ in their assessment of the case but they do differ in their decision to take action or not. In the GADM model this is called "decisional conflict." Alternatively, though less commonly (Rossi, Schuerman, & Budde, 1999), two people might have the same threshold for action but differ in their assessment of the case factors and the integration of the case-factor information into a summary assessment of risk. The GADM model refers to this as "judgmental conflict." Judgmental conflict is easier to resolve because it requires both people to review the case factors and agree on which ones to include in their assessment, as well as the relative importance of the case factors. Decisional conflict is much more difficult to resolve because it depends on the relative value decision-makers place on the consequences of the possible outcomes as discussed above.

Summary and Implications

In this brief chapter, we have attempted to present a case for the usefulness of the DME combined with the GADM. We began by making the point that the field of child welfare has been slow to take advantage of decision-making frameworks—a dilemma that has impeded our efforts at understanding decision-making and its contexts. Developing a clearer understanding of errors is a particular concern as addressing these errors is pivotal in child welfare policy development.

We also presented what we have learned thus far using this framework. For example, we have learned that the DME can be applied to a number of contexts, including the substantiation, removal, and reunification decisions—all of which are key decision-making points along the decision-making continuum. It is also applicable to the context of social problems such as disproportionality since disparate decisions at key decision points can increase overall disproportionality. Indeed, key factors in the DME, such as case, individual, organizational, and external factors, are found to increase or decrease disparities and allow us to better understand them.

Consider that evidence-supported practice might be improved by using training programs that target specific errors and how they can be mitigated. For example, one potential source of bias uncovered by Dettlaff and his colleagues (Dettlaff et al., 2011) and by Rivaux and her colleagues (2008) is the fundamental attribution error. This error appears to lie behind some of the observed racial differences in decisions to substantiate maltreatment allegations and place children in care. Some child welfare workers may attribute poverty to the person, rather than to the client's situation, lowering their threshold for these decisions (i.e., more likely to substantiate and/or place in care). More explicit and experiential training with regard to poverty and risk may be beneficial in improving self-awareness concerning this fundamental attribution error.

The DME also contains the GADM model, which helps to explain the psychological process of decision-making more fully. In that regard, three psychological features were described. The first was the distinction between the psychological process of assessment and that of deciding to take a course of action. The point being that, although the assessment (e.g., of case factors) might be the same, individuals may differ in the action they decide to take. The second feature is known as a decision threshold, which we again note varies among individuals based on their various experiences with factors in the DME. The final important psychological feature is that this threshold can shift. Mansell (2006) provides a good example of such a shift. He describes threshold changes in the New Zealand Child Welfare system as a function of the degree to which family preservation or child protection is emphasized by policymakers over time, and then translated to outcome concerns related to child safety in dynamic balance with the costs of services.

Implications for evidence-informed approaches are manifold. Starting at the case level family members, workers, supervisors, and the courts must make critical life-changing decisions such as placement on the basis of many factors. Thus the successful introduction of an array of evidence-supported services depends on the combination of the assessments of the case, but equally important is the context in which services are provided. Assuming these case-level agents are aware of evidence-supported practices, decision-making issues extend to timely availability of services, their location, confidence in the provider, an understanding of their potential efficacy, acceptability to the family, complexity, cultural relevance, and feedback regarding service provision, outcomes, and so forth. While these concerns are most often associated with implementation issues (see

Barth & Lee, Chapter 4, Mildon, Dickerson & Shlonsky, Chapter 5, this book), agents are likely to make different decisions based on this knowledge.

Asymmetry in ascribing value to different types of errors is also likely to play a role. For example, given that an evidence-supported approach is likely to result in keeping a child in their home, if there is an asymmetrical balance at the decision-maker or agency level that emphasizes the value of not committing false negative errors, the service may not be utilized as expected (frequency, dose, etc). Figuring out how particular evidence-supported approaches to assessment are most likely to support the mitigation of different types of errors may be crucial from the perspective of defining or developing and reinforcing a framework of values.

Finally, at the policy level it is important to note that certain evidence-supported approaches to assessment may be more or less effective at different decision points in the continuum of child welfare services. Thus, the application of an approach to assessment to a decision where there is no evidence that it will support that decision may result in poor decision-making. Some approaches may be suited to work most effectively when applied to a specific decision, as well as with specific types of families (see Casillas & Fluke, Chapter 8, this book). This has implications for designing an empirically supported array of approaches, used at different times and in different ways, and consideration must be given to the resources that are required for such an undertaking. Knowing the source and magnitude of errors and the factors in the DME that may mitigate them allows for the development and execution of policies that have greater clarity, precision and more accurate targeting of scarce resources. If, for example, it is known that the amount and mixture of cases on a worker's caseload affects his or her decisions, different caseload mixes can be structured as part of on-the-job training. For instance, exposure to African American clients (Baumann et al., 2010) for all caseworkers, regardless of their race or ethnicity, improves decisions and implies that such exposure should be a part of training. This is a very challenging proposition, however, since few benchmarks exist for most child welfare decisions, in part because it is very difficult to operationalize and observe appropriate measures of decision errors. While examples are few (one exception is Mansell et al., 2011), efforts to develop and operationalize decisional standards are crucial for improving services in complex child welfare systems.

It is clear that decision-making will be an important ingredient in the implementation of evidence-supported practice in child welfare. The answers to key questions, such as how practitioners will decide when and under what circumstances these practices will be most effective, must be found. However, the most common dialogue regarding decision-making research has tended to focus solely on the role of assessment, where the assumption appears to be that good assessment leads to appropriate decision actions. However, this is a very limited view of the process and ignores our increasing understanding of nonrational decision-making behavior. As illustrated by the examples in this chapter, the growing body of research and theoretical perspectives are beginning to help us understand how the characteristics of decision-makers and the circumstances that they operate within influence their decisions. We think the DME/GADM synthesis provides a focus for developing insights and formulating hypotheses as a component of implementation research, which by clarifying the decision-making context can play a pivotal role toward successful implementation of evidence supported practice in child welfare.

Beyond Empirically Supported Interventions

INNOVATIVE STRATEGIES FOR A COMPLICATED WORLD

3

THE TRANSPORTABILITY OF EMPIRICALLY SUPPORTED

INTERVENTIONS

Knut Sundell and Laura Ferrer-Wreder

EMPIRICALLY SUPPORTED INTERVENTIONS (ESIs) are normally based on research about risk and protective factors and their relation to desirable and problematic outcomes. Manipulating risk/protective factors associated with targeted outcomes can improve lives and prevent problems or lessen their severity (e.g., Ferrer-Wreder, Stattin, Lorente, Tubman, & Adamson, 2004). In an initial trial of an imported ESI outside of its home country, the association between targeted risk/protective factors and the subsequent outcomes is an empirical question to be tested ideally before but certainly during the trial. Does the relationship between risk/protective factors and outcomes exist in the new context? Do such relationships work in a comparable fashion in the new participant group relative to the original validation sample? Such a line of inquiry offers the opportunity not only to disseminate potentially beneficial programs and practices but also holds the promise of deepening the global knowledge base on risk/protective factors as well as outcomes of great public health importance (e.g., mental health, antisocial behavior).

The spread of evidence-based practice to new domains and new nations is fueling a need for more ESIs and high-quality intervention outcome studies. Accordingly, the ESI knowledge base in many countries is rapidly growing. Yet, the number of promising ESIs is still relatively small in comparison to the need. Thus, the import of existing ESIs from other cultural contexts appears to be warranted. For instance, of the 134 Swedish outcome studies of behavioral and social interventions conducted between 1990 and June 2010, 41% involved the evaluation of ESIs originating from other countries (Socialstyrelsen,

2011). With a successive increase in the number of imported ESI outcome studies, there are several empirical examples of failures to replicate the original benefits of some ESIs.

This chapter describes possible reasons for these failures to replicate previously demonstrated intervention benefits and reviews contextual variables that may promote a successful ESI transfer. The chapter closes with a suggestion of how to include culture in intervention outcome studies, particularly effectiveness trials of imported interventions.

Mixed Findings from International Replications

There are ESIs that have been shown to produce benefits in international replications. Examples of such interventions are well represented among the US Blueprints model and promising programs (BMPPs; http://www.blueprintsprograms.com). Examples of BMPPs exported from the United States to other countries and verified in randomized controlled trials (RCTs) include: functional family therapy in Sweden (Hansson, Cederblad, & Höök, 2000), multidimensional treatment foster care in Sweden (Hansson & Olsson, 2012; Kyhle Westermark, Hansson, & Olsson, 2011), and the Incredible Years in England (Gardner, Burton, & Klimes, 2006), Canada (Taylor, Schmidt, Pepler, & Hodgins, 1998), Norway (Fossum, Mørch, Handegård, Drugli, & Larsson, 2009), and Sweden (Axberg & Broberg, 2012).

However, other international trials have failed to replicate original benefits or produced mixed results. One example is the American-developed multisystemic therapy (MST), an intensive family and community-based treatment for adolescents with serious adjustment difficulties that can include criminal behavior, violence, substance abuse, and serious emotional disturbances. MST does have an extensive evidence base in its home country (Schoenwald, Heiblum, Saldana, & Henggeler, 2008). As of 2012, MST had been imported to several countries and had undergone controlled evaluation. Although MST intervention benefits were replicated compared with a control group in Norway (Ogden & Hagen, 2006), the Netherlands (Deković, Asscher, Manders, Prins, & van der Laan, 2012), and the United Kingdom (Butler, Baruch, Hickey, & Fonagy, 2011), the same benefits relative to a control group were not demonstrated in Sweden (Andrée Löfholm, Olsson, Sundell, & Hansson, 2009) or Canada (Leschied & Cunningham, 2002).

Another example of an intervention with mixed international replication trials is the Australian parenting training program Triple-P, which has been successfully exported from Australia to Germany (Hahlweg, Heinrichs, Kuschel, & Feldmann, 2007), Hong Kong (Leung, Sanders, Leung, Mak, & Lau, 2003), Japan (Matsumoto, Sofronoff, & Sanders, 2010), Switzerland (Bodenmann, Cina, Ledermann, & Sanders, 2008), and the United States (Prinz, Sanders, Shapiro, Whitaker, & Lutzke, 2009). However, data from another controlled trial in Switzerland (Eisner, Nagin, Ribeaud, & Malti, 2012; Malti, Ribeaud, & Eisner, 2011) and one in Canada (McConnell, Breitkreuz, & Savage, 2011) did not produce significant effects.

The Strengthening Families Program (SFP 10-14) is an American-developed family-focused universal drug prevention program. The results of a recent randomized controlled trial conducted in Sweden with a universal version of SFP 10-14 yielded no statistically significant differences between youth taking part in SFP 10-14 relative to adolescents in a treatment as usual (TAU) control group (Skärstrand, 2010).

Another example of difficulties in transporting ESIs within Europe is represented by the Dutch Örebro Prevention Program trial (ÖPP). ÖPP is an evidence-based Swedish-developed parent intervention aimed at encouraging parental rule-setting concerning children's alcohol consumption (Koutakis, Stattin, & Kerr, 2008). When this intervention was exported to the Netherlands and evaluated in a randomized controlled trial (RCT), ÖPP in itself did not decrease the onset of drinking. However, ÖPP in combination with a student intervention was found to be effective (Koning et al., 2009).

There are four possible interconnected reasons for the inconsistent results in transportability research on ESIs in different countries. One has to do with differences in the research design across trials. A second reason deals with ambiguities in the cultural adaptation process. A third potential reason is that the ESI has not been implemented with fidelity or was implemented without a cogent implementation plan (e.g., Fixsen, Naoom, Blasé, Friedman, & Wallace, 2005). A fourth source of variation may lie in political, sociodemographic differences or cultural contexts that might moderate the effects of an ESI in a new context.

RESEARCH DESIGN

Several aspects of research design have been related to variations in intervention-related effect sizes. First, there normally are different results from randomized and nonrandomized experiments; in some cases the nonrandomized trials produce greater effect sizes, and in other instances the opposite is the case (Shadish, 2011). Efficacy trials with well-controlled evaluations normally produce larger effect sizes than effectiveness trials that are evaluated as part of ordinary services (e.g., Curtis, Ronan, & Borduin, 2004; Lösel & Beelmann, 2003; Petrosino & Soydan, 2005). The same goes for passive versus active control conditions, with greater effect sizes often shown for comparisons involving passive control conditions such as a wait-list control or placebo, compared to other active interventions such as TAU (Grissom, 1996; Hrobjartsson & Gøtzsche, 2001; Magill & Ray, 2009; Shadish, 2011). Furthermore, the strategy for handling drop-outs is a factor that might influence the observed intervention effect sizes. The earlier strategy of only including participants who are followed-through with an intervention or treatment (i.e., treatment on the treated, TOT) normally produces greater effect sizes relative to an intention to treat analysis (ITT), which includes dropouts in the analysis (Wright & Sims, 2003). Other aspects of research design of importance are how the intervention group is defined, the length of the follow-up time, and key measures describing intervention success.

Andrée Löfholm, Brännström, Olsson, and Hansson (2013) reviewed 13 randomized controlled evaluations of multisystemic therapy for antisocial youth. Of these RCTs, 10 are from the United States and one each from Norway, Sweden, and Canada. Results illustrated heterogeneity across the outcome evaluations. No two studies used the same design according to the aspects mentioned above. For instance, the control conditions included individual therapy/counseling, cognitive behavioral therapy, TAU within juvenile justice system, TAU within child and adolescent mental health care, and TAU within the child welfare system. In TAU, the most common alternative was that the comparison group received a mixture of various interventions that could include individual or group treatment with different emphases and theoretical bases, placements in out-of-home care, and nonplacement interventions. No information was available about what interventions the individuals in the TAU condition actually received, and while the dose, duration, and breakdowns were often described for the experimental group, no such information was available regarding the TAU condition. As in a systematic review by Littell, Popa, and Forsythe (2005), a meta-analysis on eight of the 13 RCTs indicated no significant overall difference between MST and the control condition on recidivism. However, two other meta-analysis (Baldwin, Christian, Berkeljon, & Shadish, 2012; Curtis, Ronan, & Borduin, 2004) identify significant overall effects of MST. The different conclusions seem to depend on the inclusion and exclusion of studies.

The conclusion of Andrée Löfholm and colleagues is that the estimated treatment effects suggested that the various control conditions seemed to contain a greater variation in change-producing mechanisms than experimental conditions, supporting the hypothesis that content of TAU conditions could affect outcomes. One interpretation is that the lack of effect in the Swedish trial might be because the Swedish TAU condition was more effective relative to American TAUs. For example, a comparison of Child Behavior Checklist (CBCL) change scores from the Swedish, Norwegian, and two American MST evaluations showed that the average decrease in CBCL T scores for the Swedish MST group was similar to that of the Norwegian MST study and larger than or equal to that of American studies (Sundell et al., 2008). This cross-study comparison of change scores indicated that the Swedish MST treatment was effective. The Swedish and Norwegian TAU groups, however, decreased their CBCL scores considerably more than did the two American TAU groups. This indicated that the Swedish TAU, and to a somewhat lesser extent also the Norwegian, was more potent relative to its counterparts in the United States. Thus, the mixed findings across international replications of imported ESIs may in part be due to variations in research design (e.g., type of control group) across trials.

CULTURAL ADAPTATION

When an ESI is imported to a new culture, certain adaptations and modifications are normally needed. The difficulty in the cultural adaptation process involves making the determination of when an adaptation is necessary as well as when an adaptation may have compromised intervention effectiveness. In an imported ESI trial, a relatively straightforward and first adaptation may involve language. If nothing else, the intervention manual needs to be translated when it comes to different languages.

In some imported ESI trials, translation is not enough and other changes are necessary. An illustration of this point can be found in the Swedish parent management training program titled COMET (Kling, Forster, Sundell, & Melin, 2010). COMET includes behavioral parent-training components developed by Barkley (1997), Webster-Stratton (1996), and Bloomquist and Schnell (2002). Based on pilot testing of COMET with Swedish parents, it was decided to downplay time-out (normally an essential part of parent management training) because it was found to be offensive to many of the Swedish parents. Two subsequent RCTs comparing COMET to a wait-list control group showed that COMET evidenced the expected intervention benefits relative to the control group (Enebrink, Högström, Forster, & Ghaderi, 2012; Kling, Forster, Sundell, & Melin, 2010). Thus, it seems that this adaptation, although quite significant, did not reduce COMET's effectiveness.

Several adaptations were made in the Swedish trial of SFP (Skärstrand, Larsson, & Andreasson, 2008). As mentioned, SFP 10-14 is a school-based, family-oriented drug prevention program. Prior to the implementation, two reference groups were formed, one with researchers and one with teachers, to investigate a potential interest in an alcohol prevention family program and to identify possible barriers to participation. Furthermore, two sixth-year classes in two schools in Stockholm were chosen to participate in a pilot study. On a regular basis throughout the pilot study there were meetings with the group leaders, the teachers, and the research team. In addition, after each session the group leaders and the teachers completed checklists, which contained questions about the content of each session including: Was there enough time to do all the activities? Were the necessary prerequisites present for the session? How well did the parents/children respond to the activities? Following the completion of the first seven sessions, a focus group was conducted with attending parents. As a result of all these preliminary studies, several adaptations were made to the Swedish edition of SFP 10-14, which were discussed and agreed with the program's first author, Dr. Virginia Molgaard.

One major change in the Swedish version concerned the program format. From discussions with the two reference groups, it was clear that the most appropriate setting for a family program in Sweden would be public schools, using the class teacher as one of the leaders for the youth sessions. Consequently, the youth sessions were held during the daytime on an ordinary school day. Instead of having a family session after every youth meeting as in the United States, the choice was to have a total of two family sessions in the schools but after school time: one in the seventh session to finish part one of the program, and one in the last session of the second part of the program. The attendance rate of parents in these sessions was higher (47% at the first session and 27% in the second) than in American evaluations of SFP 10-14 (38%; Spoth, Redmond, Trudeau, & Shin, 2002; 17%; Spoth, Greenberg, Redmond, & Shin, 2007).

Another difference between the original SFP 10-14 and the Swedish version was the size of the groups. The former is designed for 8 to 13 families and three facilitators (two for youth sessions and one for parent sessions). The Swedish version included a whole school class of 25 to 30 students and all parents who were interested in participating. Two or three facilitators implemented the youth sessions. Facilitators also conducted the two parent sessions. In addition, more emphasis on alcohol and other drugs as well as an extra session were added to part two of the intervention with the students.

An example of an activity change in the Swedish adaptation of SFP 10-14 involved the closing circle. In the original SFP 10-14, the parents form a closing circle and recited a saying related to the program (i.e., a creed) at the end of each session. This was considered to be to culturally inappropriate for a Swedish context and was thus omitted.

All material, including manuals and manuscripts for the videos were translated into Swedish. The quality of the Swedish videos was improved by using a professional film team and trained actors. The videos were shot in real-life settings, not in a studio. Altogether, 11 videos plus one demonstration video were made compared with 12 in the original SFP 10-14.

The adaptation of SFP 10-14 to a Swedish context conformed to many of the recommendations for the international dissemination of SFP 10-14 published by its program developer. A major component involved a recommendation for locally determined "surface structure" changes but an explicit stance against "deep structure" changes to SFP 10-14, based on evidence from SFP 10-14 trials with American ethnic subgroups (Kumpfer et al., 2008). The terms "surface and deep structure" were developed by Resnicow et al. (2000) who posited that the deep structure of an intervention refers to an intervention's causal model, which specifies the empirical and theoretical relations between intervention activities, theory-based mediators of change, and ultimate outcomes. Resnicow et al. (2000) also posited that the surface structure of an intervention consists of how intervention messages link to participants' life experiences. Relevant surface structure is thought to increase participants' intervention acceptance and comprehension.

In the Swedish SFP 10-14 trial, although there were some additions to the lesson content, the Swedish researchers appeared to avoid major changes to SFP 10-14's deep structure (e.g., deleting lessons, combining lessons, taking away content from individual lessons), but did make "surface structure" changes to program materials and altered the program delivery format. Nevertheless, the distinctions between "deep" and "surface" changes are not always easy to make. In the present case, the changes in parent participation may be seen by some as surface, whereas others would consider these changes to be quite deep, directly relevant to the program logic regarding the interaction between parents and their children.

Other recommendations followed in the Swedish trial included the use of culturally competent group leaders and implementation of SFP 10-14 with fidelity (Kumpfer et al., 2008). Other recommendations that were not pursued in this trial include an a priori examination of key mediators of intervention change and outcomes (i.e., "gather needs assessment data on etiological precursors"; Kumpfer et al., 2008, p. 230).

As previously described, the Swedish SFP 10-14 trial showed no intervention-related benefits compared to a TAU control group in a cluster randomized controlled trial (Skärstrand, 2010). The intervention trial design, in the Swedish case, conformed to other SFP 10-14 trials, in that it was a traditional randomized controlled trial with multiple assessments. As in other effectiveness research studies, the design of this Swedish SFP trial did not allow for a determination of whether intervention effectiveness was compromised by the adaptations or if the adaptations were insufficient and more changes were necessary in order to yield SFP 10-14 benefits among Swedish families.

Another illustration of the varying need to adapt imported ESIs to new implementation contexts can be found in the Swedish MST trial (Andrée Löfholm et al., 2009). One aspect of the program delivery format was initially changed in this trial. As mentioned, MST is an intensive family- and community-based treatment for adolescents with serious adjustment difficulties. When MST was implemented in Sweden, the Swedish vacation legislation caused a major change in the program delivery format of MST during the first year of implementation. Because Swedish employees are assured four weeks continuous summer holidays, in reality no treatment occurred between mid-June and mid-August. Thus, the concept of 24/7 (i.e., treatment available 24 hours a day, seven days a week) was compromised.

In summary, the process of adapting and quality-assuring an imported ESI is complicated. The line between deep and surface structure changes can sometimes be blurred, such as when changes in program delivery format may inadvertently cut into the deep structure of an intervention (e.g., aspects of intervention dosage or fidelity). Recent Swedish trials of some imported ESIs illustrate the need for greater systematic attention to the role of culture in the adaptation of imported ESIs.

IMPLEMENTATION

Implementation fidelity involves adherence to the program curriculum and competence in using the intervention (Berkel, Mauricio, Schoenfelder, & Sandler, 2011). Fidelity is a key variable among implementation markers and has been found to modify intervention benefits (Durlak & DuPree, 2008). If an imported ESI is implemented with poor fidelity, the intervention might fail to be as effective as suggested by the original research.

For example, the previously described Swedish MST randomized clinical trial used services usually available for conduct-disordered youths in Sweden as a control condition. In most cases, youths in both treatment and control conditions decreased their problem behavior, showed improved relations within the family, and improved their social skills. None of these improvements were statistically different between the groups (Andrée Löfholm et al., 2009). In other words, both treatments worked equally well. In MST, treatment adherence is measured monthly by caregiver report on the MST

Therapist Adherence Measure (TAM). The interviews are used to ensure that therapists are faithful to the model in their work with individual families. The implementation of MST was supervised by MST Services, Inc., the organization that disseminates MST technologies throughout the world. TAM scores were more than a full standard deviation below the mean reported in the United States. This raised the possibility that MST may not have been implemented with sufficient fidelity in Sweden to provide a fair test of its effectiveness.

An alternative interpretation is the questionable validity of TAM in a Swedish context. There were no significant correlations between TAM scores and outcomes. The comparably low TAM did not seem to be mirrored by relatively low effect sizes on all measures for the MST group. This is in contrast to other studies of MST showing significant relationships between fidelity and outcomes (e.g., Schoenwald, Chapman, Sheidow, & Carter, 2009; Schoenwald, Sheidow, & Chapman, 2009).

Another factor that may explain a significant MST effect in Norway and a nonsignificant effect in Sweden is that the implementation of MST in Norway was guided by the Ministry of Child and Family Welfare, implemented nationally and sponsored by a research unit to support and evaluate the quality of the implementation. In contrast, the Swedish implementation was guided by local initiatives without a national supporting framework. This may have influenced the success of implementation efforts in those aspects of implementation captured by the TAM as well as those aspects of implementation not measured by the TAM.

SOCIAL SERVICE SYSTEMS, SOCIODEMOGRAPHIC AND CULTURAL CONTEXT

Exporting ESIs across cultures and within cultures with varying access to resources and development presents numerous challenges and rewards. A notable challenge in the effort to import/export ESIs globally involves better understanding and incorporating knowledge of how social services are organized cross-nationally. As has been demonstrated, variations in standard social services may alter the outcome of whether or not a newly imported ESI can be considered more effective than TAU or not.

For example, in some countries intensive case management is a service for persons with severe mental illness. Those persons are allocated a nurse, social worker, or other clinician as a case manager who carries a small caseload of between 10 and 20 patients. The case manager takes primary responsibility for keeping contact with patients, assessing their needs, and ensuring that these needs are met. A systematic review of intensive case management with this population included data from 29 RCTs conducted in several countries, demonstrating substantial heterogeneity with respect to implementation procedures and outcomes between studies (Burns et al., 2007). Metaregression showed that intensive case management worked best in societies where the use of hospital care by individuals with severe mentally illness was high, but was less successful when hospital use by these individuals was already low. The interpretation was that where community services are good, hospital care was used sparingly and only when absolutely necessary (Burns et al., 2007). Under such circumstances, a case manager may find it difficult to have an impact on hospital use, if that is the outcome by which this type of intervention was judged as useful. When community services are poor, it is fairly easy for patients to spend long periods of time in hospital, and a case manager in this type of intervention may find it easier to reduce the need for hospitalization. Thus, low levels of hospital use can be seen as a proxy for good community services, which has been shown to modify the effects of case management interventions for individuals experiencing severe mental illnesses (Burns et al., 2007).

The importance of considering the existing services relative to the value added from the introduction of a newly imported ESI can be illustrated by the American-developed Nurse-Family Partnership (NFP). To date, NFP (Olds, 2002) has not been implemented in Sweden, but a Swedish NFP trial might have difficulty in demonstrating the full array and magnitude of intervention benefits relative to TAU. In Sweden, there is universal maternity care for pregnant women and child health centres for children until the age of six, which is used by almost 100% of Swedish parents (Magnusson, 1999). Those services offer, to a certain degree, similar information and training as NFP. Thus, the effects of NFP might be expected to be the same as TAU in Sweden.

Another argument against the import of such an intervention to a Swedish context is connected to the prevalence of the primary target group, young single mothers living in poverty. In Sweden, only 0.65% of mothers are teenagers, compared to 5.21% in the United States (UNICEF, 2001). Although the intervention itself may have empirically validated ingredients, the prevalence of the target group is small and this Swedish group would also most likely already be receiving several standard child welfare services that have elements of NFP's programmatic active ingredients. While it is an untested empirical question, an intervention such as NFP may be particularly useful in contexts in which services as usual for families are not easily accessible and are of less than ideal quality. Yet, in those contexts where this is not clearly the case, NFP might have challenges demonstrating effectiveness relative to TAU. As a matter of fact, preliminary results in a German RCT indicate that although self-rated maternal competences increased significantly in a NFP treatment group as compared to a TAU, analogous changes were not observed on quality of interaction with the child or measures of child development (Jungmann, Kurtz, Brand, Sierau, & von Klitzing, 2010; Jungmann, Ziert, Kurtz, & Brand, 2009; Kurtz, Brand, & Jungmann, 2010).

Another illustration of this point comes from the area of correctional systems for juvenile offenders. In Sweden and Norway, youth offenders are almost entirely responded to through a child welfare approach (Ginner-Hau & Smedler, 2011). The standard procedure for prosecutors or criminal courts is to refer the offending youths to the child social services without any legal sanctions imposed on the young person. This system makes in-home services quite frequent (Sundell, Vinnerljung, Andrée Löfholm, & Humlesjö, 2007). Consequently, delivery of services via the home would not be such a novel feature as it is in interventions such as MST as implemented in the United States, where youth offenders are often institutionalized and processed within a juvenile justice system, which itself is a demonstrated risk factor for future incarceration (Lipsey, 1999).

Beyond important variations in TAU, different sociodemographic contexts might also moderate the relevance and potency of an ESI in a new delivery context. For example, staying within the area of youth antisocial behavior and criminal offending, a cumulative stressors model (e.g., Rutter, 1979) would point toward the importance of high rates of neighborhood poverty as a detractor to youths' motivation for rehabilitation, either through low social cohesion and informal social control or via negative parenting, which may have importance for the relation between poverty and youth psychosocial symptoms (e.g., Grant et al., 2003). Other contextual stressors may include relatively high crime and substance abuse in given neighborhoods, which may provide ample opportunities for sustaining antisocial attitudes and role models. Rehabilitation from antisocial behaviors might depend on the number of stressors that a youth faces (Jaffe, Caspi, Moffitt, Polo-Tomás, & Taylor, 2007). ESIs might be found to be more or less effective depending on the prevalence and severity of stressors mentioned above. This variation could be partially a function of how risk/protective factors, both internal and contextual, differ. For example, these factors may pattern themselves in a given cultural context, and connections between risk/protective factors and outcomes of interest may differ in unique ways across contexts. If variations in these relations differ in meaningful ways, the effects of an imported ESI may be compromised, although the ESI may be quite useful in its original validation context.

Many ESIs have an explicit intervention model, sometimes also called a theory of intervention change, causal model, logic model, or an intervention's "deep structure" (Fairchild & MacKinnon, 2009; Resnicow et al., 2000). An intervention's deep structure is a model of how a given intervention works. There is a specification of particular relations between the targets for intervention change (i.e., mediators) and outcomes. When considering the generalizability of an intervention's deep structure across nations, there is the question of mediators and outcomes. Just focusing on outcomes, one can question whether these ultimate targets for intervention change are at a comparable level cross-nationally. If they are not, the ability to demonstrate intervention effectiveness can be compromised in an imported ESI trial in which base rates of outcomes vary from the home country relative to the new intervention context.

An illustration of this point can be made with national variations in adolescent substance use, which is often the target of change for several well-known ESIs. In many countries in Europe and North America cannabis is a widely used substance among adolescents. However, both lifetime and current prevalence estimates vary greatly among 31 countries, in a nationally representative, self-report, classroom survey with 47,000 15-year-olds (ter Bogt, Schmid, Gabhainn, Fotiou, & Vollebergh, 2006). The lifetime prevalence of cannabis use varied between 2.5% in the former Yugoslav Republic of

Macedonia (both males and females) and was highest for males in Switzerland (49.1%) and females in Greenland (47.0%). Overall, cannabis use was associated with perceived availability of cannabis (peer culture) and the presence of communities of older cannabis users (drug climate). Variables of no statistical importance were such socioeconomic indicators as per capita private consumer expenditure and percentage of youth unemployment.

Therefore, an intervention program targeting risk factors such as perceived availability of cannabis and the presence of communities of older cannabis users will probably have a small effect in countries with a comparably low prevalence of cannabis use and a larger effect in countries where prevalence is higher.

Cultural aspects might also be important for alcohol consumption among adolescents. Koning and colleagues (2009) suggested that the reason why the Swedish ÖPP trial was not effective on its own in the Netherlands (as opposed to Sweden) was that parents may be less effective in deferring the onset of adolescent alcohol use in countries such as the Netherlands, which has a lower legal drinking age and a more lenient alcohol policy than in Sweden. Thus, the etiology of alcohol misuse and abuse in the Netherlands may work through a different pathway relative to the etiology of alcohol problems among Swedish youth.

Culture is complex and can be conceptualized in a variety of ways (Super & Harkness, 1999). Furthermore, most countries consist of numerous subcultures, and there might be larger differences within countries than between them. The value of adapting established interventions for new cultural groups has been debated, and attempts at culturally tailoring interventions have been described in several subfields within intervention science (e.g., mental health therapy and prevention programs, substance use prevention programs; Bernal, Jiménez-Chafey, & Domenech Rodríguez, 2009; Resnicow et al. 2000). However, our global understanding of many of the phenomena we seek to improve through interventions is limited. Also, from a global perspective the exact effects of cultural differences across nations are mostly unknown and have not been the focus of systematic large-scale research when it comes to import/export of ESTs to new nations. Nevertheless, incorporation of the perspective of culture into imported ESI effectiveness trials is clearly needed (Castro, Barrera, & Holleran Steiker, 2010; Ferrer-Wreder, Sundell, & Mansoory, 2012).

The *Planned Intervention Adaptation* (PIA) Protocol

There are several theoretical models available to guide the cultural adaptation of ESIs in domestic and international contexts (e.g., Bernal et al., 2009; Castro et al., 2010; Kumpfer et al., 2008; Resnicow, et al., 2000; Schoenwald et al., 2008). Typically, the models prescribe a series of steps or a progression in a decision-making process as one adapts, implements, and evaluates an ESI in a new context. Most models for the cultural adaptation of ESIs share the problem of not having an extensive evidence base to support their use. Fixsen and colleagues (2005) made a relevant observation connected to the present discussion when they stated that "implementation outcomes should not be assumed any more than intervention outcomes are assumed" (p. 6). This statement could be expanded to include the cultural adaptation of interventions. Theory development in the cultural adaptation of interventions has far outstripped systematic and controlled empirical work in this area. Yet, future progress in this field depends on theory-driven research with respect to how to go about conducting and testing the effects of culturally oriented intervention adaptations.

The Planned Intervention Adaptation (PIA) protocol has the potential to make a contribution to the emerging intervention cultural adaptation field. Briefly summarized, the PIA protocol is a generic (not program-specific), a priori tool for determining the need, and if warranted, the scope and nature of intervention adaptations that may improve an imported ESI's utility with a new cultural group.

PIA is a research framework, and at its core is the idea that intervention adaptation should be guided by formative research. Also, central to PIA is the creation of two editions of the same intervention (i.e., the same ESI is adapted to differing degrees). This then leads to a competitive experimental test of two editions of the same ESI, with the overall aim of empirically testing the relation between intervention adaptations, to differing extents, and intervention effectiveness.

PIA is based on Resnicow and colleagues' (2000) intervention adaptation model (e.g., See also Ahluwalia et al., 2002; Harris et al., 2001) and represents an elaboration of this framework to the specific situation of testing the effectiveness of an imported ESI (Ferrer-Wreder et al., 2012). Programmatically, generic intervention adaptation models for imported ESIs are not common in the cultural adaptation literature (Castro et al., 2010; Ferrer-Wreder et al., 2012). Thus, PIA is designed to fill this gap in theory development. As in the case of other models of intervention cultural adaptation, PIA also suffers from a lack of empirical support. However, a description of PIA even in the absence of a direct evidence base may be useful at this point because it provides a detailed illustration of the feasibility of launching systematic and theory-driven research on the cultural adaptation of imported ESIs. It is important to note that PIA incorporates elements suggested in other models in this area (Castro et al., 2010; Kumpfer et al., 2008, See Ferrer-Wreder et al., 2012 for a comprehensive treatment of the similarities and differences between PIA protocol and other relevant adaptation models) and thereby serves an example of the types of ideas and techniques advocated in several of the available models.

The PIA protocol is most relevant to a situation in which an existing ESI is imported to a new country (see Table 3.1). For reasons of programmatic sustainability and appropriate intervention development, it is recommended that the PIA protocol be used in a collaborative manner in which program developers as well as intervention scientists and

TABLE 3.1

PLANNED INTERVENTION ADAPTATION (PIA): A PROTOCOL FOR CULTURALLY
TAILORING AN IMPORTED EMPIRICALLY SUPPORTED INTERVENTION

Phase I	Phase II
Step 1: Select a promising empirically supported intervention (ESI) for importation. Program developers and program stakeholders in the new context decide to work together to adapt and test the selected ESI. A *Formative Research Participant Pool* is created. *Adaptation as Usual* (e.g., translating surveys and intervention materials) takes place.	**Conduct an Effectiveness Trial of the Imported ESI with Three Experimental Conditions:** • ESI_{Min} = A minimally adapted edition of the imported ESI—From Phase I Step 1 (language changes and minor surface structure changes only to intervention) • ESI_{Full} = A fully adapted edition of the imported ESI From Phase I Steps 1–5 • Treatment as Usual or other Control Condition
Step 2: Create three subsamples from the *Formative Research Participant Pool* with subsample 1 completing back translated instruments and those already in use in the new implementation context. The instruments are then changed on the basis of the psychometric analysis that examined the cultural equivalence and appropriateness of the evaluation instrumentation.	**OUTCOME OF PHASE II: Effectiveness Trial Results Assist in Additional ESI Adaptations** • The effectiveness trial's study results may point to the need for additional changes to the ESI and another effectiveness trial or point toward the need for a larger scale dissemination trial with the edition of the intervention found to be most effective (e.g., ESI_{Min} or ESI_{Full}).
Step 3: Subsample 2 completes revised instruments from Step 2. Researchers then test the generalizability of the ESI's theory of program change (i.e., connections between theory-based mediators of intervention change and ultimate intervention outcomes) in subsample 2 (i.e., a deep structure inquiry). **Step 4:** Subsample 3 takes part in focus groups designed to examine the ESI's materials and activities for cultural relevance and appropriateness (i.e., a surface structure inquiry).	

(continued)

TABLE 3.1
(CONTINUED)

Phase I	Phase II
Step 5: Deep and Surface Structure Inquiries Guide Adaptations Made to the Imported ESI	
New stakeholders and program developers make changes to the imported ESI according to the results of the formative research studies (Steps 1–4). A minimally adapted and fully adapted editions of the ESI are pilot tested, which informs another round of intervention refinement.	

other program stakeholders (e.g., policymakers, program participants, practitioners, or end users) in the new intervention context work together to implement the protocol. The responsibility to carry out this protocol should ideally not be the sole responsibility of any one stakeholder group on its own.

PHASE I—PRE-INTERVENTION TRIAL STUDIES

Phase I begins ideally by making a collaborative agreement between the ESI's program developers and program stakeholders in the new implementation context to carry out the PIA protocol. If relevant, translation and back translation of study surveys and program materials should also take place. The rest of the steps in Phase I involve a series of modest-size formative, preintervention trial studies that will inform the adaptation of the imported ESI to the new implementation context and prepare the imported ESI to be tested in Phase II. It is estimated that Phase I studies would take approximately one year to complete.

The Phase I studies are based on a sample of participants who are similar to those individuals who will ultimately take part in the imported ESI. Adequate sample sizes should be used in order to meet the test assumptions of the statistical tests to be used and to generate reasonably detectable effect sizes. The PIA protocol is ideally suited for an effectiveness trial that sets the stage for a larger scale dissemination trial. Thus, practically feasible but adequate sample sizes are what is strived for. The participant samples in Phases I and II of the protocol are similar to one another, in a demographic and etiological sense, but should be recruited separately and at different points in time. The sample is randomly divided into two smaller subsamples. Step 2 in Phase I consists of Subsample 1 completing the newly translated study surveys. The evaluation team would then conduct validity and reliability analyses on Subsample 1's survey responses and modify the study surveys accordingly using well-established statistical methods used to test the cross-cultural structural equivalence of psychological surveys or observational methods (e.g., Byrne & van De Vijver, 2010). This would be particularly important if the study measurement to be used in the evaluation of the ESI had not been previously used in the new implementation context.

Step 3 in Phase I of the protocol involves a preliminary inquiry into the imported ESI's deep structure. In this step, Subsample 2 would complete the revised study surveys generated from Step 2 in a cross-sectional study design. The evaluation team would then test relations between the ESI's targets for change and the intervention's intended outcomes.

Step 3 is not a common part of the intervention cultural adaptation research literature, although it has been recommended on several occasions (e.g., Castro et al., 2010; Kumpfer et al., 2008). Step 3 addresses the question whether the imported ESI's "active ingredients" work in a different cultural context where the relationship between risk/ protective factors and the targets for change may not be the same as they were in the original validation samples. Step 3 is specifically taken in order to test the potential generalizability of an imported ESI's deep structure in the new implementation context. If archival descriptive data sets exist in the new implementation context that provide information comparable to that which would be generated in Step 3, then this is also a potential way to make this a preliminary test of the imported ESI's deep structure (Kumpfer et al., 2008).

Step 4 in Phase I involves recruiting a smaller group of participants from Subsample 2 to take part in a focus group that would prescreen the surface structure of the imported ESI in order to determine whether intervention materials and activities were acceptable and culturally relevant. Testing the cultural relevance of an intervention's surface structure through qualitative expert panels and/or participant focus groups or interviews is not a novel suggestion in the intervention cultural adaptation field. However, we view this step as most useful when it is integrated into a theory-based and more comprehensive (dealing with both surface and deep structure aspects of an intervention) adaptation model that includes the experimental design features like those described below in Phase II of the PIA protocol.

The results of the Phase I should provide empirical evidence to guide deep and surface structure changes to an imported ESI prior to its implementation in a controlled effectiveness trial. In Step 5, program stakeholders in the new implementation context and the imported ESI's developers work together to determine the nature and extent of needed changes to the imported ESI and create an empirically informed adaptation of the imported ESI. The products of Phase I should include a minimally adapted edition of the ESI with only language and minor surface structure changes made to intervention (program and training materials) and a fully adapted edition of the imported ESI that is empirically informed by Steps 1 through 5. A small-scale pilot test of the newly generated interventions should also inform more finalized intervention editions (minimal and fully adapted) that are then tested in Phase II. Thus, Phase I of the PIA protocol sets the stage for Phase II.

PHASE II—EFFECTIVENESS STUDY

Phase II of the PIA protocol involves the use of an experimental research design to test the minimally and fully adapted editions of an imported ESI versus a control condition (e.g., TAU or wait-list). Variables that primarily should influence the choice of control condition is the control condition in the original outcome study, including whether there exists a true TAU and whether its effects are known. The participants in the intervention trial could complete relevant surveys pre- and posttrial and at a 6-month follow up. Intervention related changes could be determined either through more traditional outcome analyses or with structural equation modeling of mediation-outcome and moderation-outcome effects (Fairchild & MacKinnon, 2009). While more complicated than traditional outcome analyses, mediation-outcome/moderation-outcome analyses would allow for an additional test of the imported ESI's deep structure by examining relations between targeted mediators of intervention change (risk/protective factors) and ultimate outcomes targeted for change in the respective intervention groups. While there certainly can be a choice in the approach to the analyses in Phase II, what is arguably most critical is the comparative nature of the experimental design used in Phase II. Such a design allows for a determination of the relation between intervention adaptations and changes in intervention effectiveness (Castro et al., 2010), this is a design feature that has been lacking in many recent trials of imported ESIs.

The PIA protocol is a synthesis of several practices already incorporated into other intervention cultural adaptation models (e.g., collaboration building between program developers and new stakeholders, needs assessment, and pilot testing; Ferrer-Wreder et al., 2012). The cultural adaptation of imported ESIs is an evolving research literature. Advances in this area are most likely to come from the conceptual and empirical prioritization of conducting systematic, planned research on the cultural adaptation of interventions, rather than following a particular formula or sequence for the adaptation of imported ESIs. While we view PIA as a promising model, it is one of many potentials ways to put culture, adaptation, and intervention utility at the forefront of intervention effectiveness research.

Conclusions

The spread of evidence-based practice throughout the world has resulted in an increased need for ESIs and corresponding trials of imported ESIs. Some of the controlled trials of imported ESIs have indicated that a number of factors can influence whether successful transport from one country to another is possible. These factors or modifiers include variations in aspects of research design and the degree of adaptation initiated in an imported ESI trial, as well as wider contextual variations. These variations may have led to what is now a disparate effectiveness/dissemination trial evidence base on the effects of imported ESIs.

Following from these observations, there is a need to continue to launch effectiveness trials of imported ESIs in new contexts. It is important that future imported ESI trials incorporate research design features that allow for an examination adaptations made and the intervention benefits evidenced in new cultural contexts. In an imported ESI context, the connection between culture and intervention effectiveness is unavoidable and should be the subject of substantial research attention (Castro et al., 2010). Arguably, carefully controlled effectiveness research is warranted before an ESI is recommended widely for dissemination in a new cultural context. Also, it is important for future research to explore what, exactly, constitutes a new context. There may also be substantial lessons learned from domestic intervention adaptations for ethnic subgroups, especially if the new context also has ethnic or other important subgroups. Additional explorations should include the identification of specific aspects of adaptation that are unique to each research context and should remain conceptually and practically separated.

The disparate evidence base on imported ESIs may serve as a catalyst for building theories about the variables that constitute a successful transportation of imported ESIs, as well as spur the building of empirical knowledge about this topic. This type of work is in its beginnings (e.g., Castro et al., 2010; Kumpfer et al., 2008; Schoenwald et al., 2008). Progress in this area has been limited, at best, due to a lack of systematic research on cultural and other contextual factors that may be related to intervention benefits and a resultant lack of systematic evidence about the theoretical models used to drive cultural adaptation of ESIs.

The transportation of ESIs from one cultural context to another has the potential to help move the theory and methodology of intervention science forward. For instance, the dilemmas and potential progress to be made in this area have focused the wider field of intervention science on issues of adaptation and implementation, as well as the need for operationalizing the concept of TAU. Therefore, questions about the importation of ESIs can inform wider progress in intervention science on how to best navigate tensions between adaptation and fidelity. Advances in the intervention cultural adaptation field may also contribute to the development of standards for intervention evidence (e.g., adequate outcome analyses and research designs in effectiveness trial contexts). Implementation science in general and the field of cultural intervention adaptation in particular hold the promise of disseminating useful interventions across the globe and deepening what is known about positive and problematic development cross-nationally. While a great deal of theory-guided empirical work needs to be conducted on this topic in the future, the potential for knowledge advancement and innovation in the international, imported ESI field appears promising.

Acknowledgments

Text in this chapter is also reported in the Sundell, K., Ferrer-Wreder, L., & Fraser, M. W. (in press). Going Global: A Model for Evaluating Empirically-Supported Family-Based Interventions in New Contexts. *Evaluation & the Health Professions.*

4

COMMON ELEMENTS AND COMMON FACTORS APPROACHES TO EVIDENCE-INFORMED CHILDREN'S SERVICES

Stacking the Building Blocks of Effective Practice

Richard P. Barth and Bethany R. Lee

A Common Elements and Factors Approach to Children's Services

Professionals in the children's services generally agree that greater adoption of science-informed practices is a reasonable path for improving existing services. The route to greater implementation requires thinking broadly about the assortment of ways—in addition to adoption of a complete manualized evidence-supported treatment program—that evidence from randomized clinical trials can be used to guide effective services. Certainly it is important to note that adapting evidence-based practices to international contexts will require a still greater acknowledgement of the need for adaptations to be effective. This challenge is deepened for services provided to children and families to provide child protection from abuse, as this area of practice has had less attention than mental health services.

Child and family services have endeavored to become more science-informed at least since 1883, when Anna Dawes, in a paper given at the International Congress of Charities and Correction at the Chicago World's Fair, stated, "What is needed, it seems to me, is some course of study where an intelligent young person can...be taught the alphabet of charitable science" (Lehninger, 2000, p. 11). This chapter endeavors to provide a framework for intervention that further builds the language of treatment science by elaborating the concepts of *common elements* and *common factors* and broadening the use of evidence beyond just manualized evidence-supported treatments (MESTs).

An evidence-supported treatment is one that, generally, has enough scientific evidence behind it to allow for a reasonable conclusion that the treatment is likely to provide some benefit to clients who are appropriate for the intervention and willing to engage in it. These have also been called evidence-supported interventions by Mildon and Shlonsky (2011), who point out that there are multiple perspectives on just what comprises an ESI but argue that the child protection field is moving toward providing referrals to services that are demonstrably effective. (At present, many of the MESTs involved with child protective and child welfare services are delivered by contract agencies rather than directly by governmental departments.) These include PCIT (parent child interaction therapy), which has been used with birth parents and foster parents (Chaffin, Funderburk, Bard, Valle, & Gurwitch, 2011; Timmer et al., 2006); SAFE CARE, which has been used with families referred for child neglect (Chaffin, Hecht, Bard, Silovsky, & Beasley, in press); The Incredible Years (Linares, Montalto, Li, & Oza, 2006), which has also been used with biological families; and versions of multidimensional treatment foster care (originally designed for use in juvenile services) that have been implemented with children in foster care supervised by a child welfare agency (Fisher, Kim, & Pears, 2009; Westermark, Hannson, & Vinnerljung, 2008) as well as in a less intensive version developed explicitly for foster care, known as KEEP (Chamberlain et al., 2008; Price, Chamberlain, Landsverk, & Reid, 2009). Triple P (Positive Parenting Program) has also shown evidence for reducing maltreatment and placements into foster care (Prinz, Sanders, Shapiro, Whittaker, & Lutzker, 2009). MESTs are programs that have been evaluated as effective and have a clearly defined rationale, set of activities (usually ordered in a logic that arises from the conceptualization of the treatment developer), and means for checking that fidelity to the manual was evident. Most programs that have undergone the rigorous evaluation required to be identified as evidence-supported have manuals, although these manuals can vary in form and length (i.e., they can range from relatively brief outlines of topics to cover in treatment to comprehensive manuals with hundreds of pages of instruction).

This chapter introduces various paths for promoting within the child welfare service system the use of practices that have some research evidence. It should be noted that child welfare services engage relatively few MESTs; this is because much of child welfare services are more about decision-making than treatment (Barth, 2008). However, child welfare workers do make referrals to programs that are hopefully grounded in some evidence. In addition, child welfare professionals do engage in multiple practices that could be guided by evidence, including engaging clients, conducting home study assessments, and family decision-making processes. Although these practices may not have MESTs, this paper will discuss alternate methods for building practice on empirical evidence.

In the process of considering how to promote effective practice, we will also discuss the basis for children's services intervention, the foundation of values and practice frameworks, and the place of specialized knowledge pertaining to specific issues with child welfare clients (e.g., issues that arise from having been adopted, or having experienced trauma, or having a chronic health or mental health condition). The analysis begins by discussing the significant limitations that are every day becoming more evident regarding the use of MESTs in children's services. We will then reconceptualize effective practices to include the common factors and common practice elements models. Finally, we will integrate these ideas into a comprehensive framework for considering the use of evidence in children's services.

Manualization of Treatments

Manualized treatments originally developed as an outgrowth of clinical research—certainly as early as the 1960s (see Fraser, Richman, Galinsky, & Day, 2009 for a full discussion). The lack of manuals thwarted efforts to understand what really went on (and what went wrong) when programs did not succeed and prevented replication when they did succeed. The path to becoming an evidence-based practice almost always, now, leads through the manualization of the intervention, and is considered a key step in readying the treatment for independent testing in clinical trials.

Manualization certainly occurs in many different ways. Some manuals use hundreds of pages to, basically, script a 12- to 16-week intervention. Others are much more thematic and describe what would be considered a "service" that may last 6 months or more. These would include the manuals for such programs as multisystemic therapy or Family Connections, which train practitioners to think in terms of a broad array of factors and settings that will determine the content and course of the intervention. More focused manuals dictate what a practitioner is to do, when, and in what way. Trauma Focused Cognitive Behavioral Therapy (TF-CBT), for example, is a highly manualized, specific collection of practice elements that are introduced in a prescribed sequence with an approximate duration. These include: psycho-education, stress-management, narrative therapy, exposure therapy, cognitive restructuring, and parental treatment.

IMPLEMENTATION ISSUES WITH MESTS

Although MESTs are undoubtedly expanding in use in the United States and around the world (see Sundell & Ferrer-Wreder, Chapter 3, this book), practitioners have identified many barriers to implementing MESTs including the logistics of training as well as the correspondence between various treatments and clients' needs (Chorpita, Bernstein, & Daleiden, 2011). For example, Powers, Bowen, and Bowen (2010) reviewed 51 school-based interventions that were judged to be effective and found many implementation obstacles including high start-up costs, challenging training and staffing requirements, and a lack of easily accessible information about the programs. Hennessy and Green-Hennessy (2011) looked at mental health interventions listed in the National Registry of Evidence-Based

Programs and Practices and found that among 91 evidence-based mental health programs there was still a very wide range of implementation support available, with more than half the implementation materials and trainings being proprietary (rather than publicly available). Thus, workers' ability to provide evidence-based practices depends, at minimum, on the decisions of their agencies to (1) adopt a program; (2) purchase training expertise and materials; and (3) enter into an agreement to pay for fidelity monitoring and ongoing supervision along with those materials.

A crucial limitation of many discussions about evidence-based practice in children's services is inattention to what happens if the practitioner—whether in the CWS agency or in the agency to which a referral has been made—lacks the tools or time to implement a specific treatment that might be recommended by an analysis of the best available practice for their client. For workers that contract with child welfare to provide mental health services and other family supports, this can occur because the practitioner has not been trained, has not had sufficient supervision and support to make the training stick, or lacks the conditions that are necessary for implementing with fidelity. The challenges of creating these conditions should not be underestimated. The initial investment required to develop a workforce with expertise in multiple evidence-supported interventions may be prohibitive, and coordinating multiple manualized treatments within a single agency can create a complicated infrastructure of different forms, fidelity efforts, contracting, and monitoring tasks (Chorpita, Becker, & Daleiden, 2007).

Even if therapists were trained to faithfully use every evidence-based treatment identified in published randomized clinical trials, only about two-thirds of their caseload would be covered by practices matched to their clients' problem area, age, and gender (Chorpita et al., 2011). When interested in finding treatments that match by ethnicity and service delivery setting, therapists could match only a very small number of clients to evidence-based treatments. Clearly, a narrow adherence to MESTs alone is not adequately comprehensive to improve usual practice in children's services.

A complete approach to evidence-based practice must also take implementation of the selected method into account, as implementation fidelity is typically associated with improved outcomes (Chapman & Schoenwald, 2011; DePanfilis, Filene, & Smith, 2010). One assumption of MESTs is that the detailed guidance provided in manuals will result in high-fidelity interventions. However, "flexibility within fidelity" (Kendall, Gosch, Furr, & Snood, 2008) suggests that manualized treatments do not need to be rigidly implemented.

Suveg, Comer, Furr, and Kendall (2006) suggest that it is far better for practitioners to become familiar with treatment manuals and associated theoretical principles, in order to apply the treatment in a way that is both flexible and individualized but also consistent with the MEST's principles. In the researchers' case study of an 8-year-old girl with cognitive delays, social phobia, selective mutism, and generalized anxiety, a modified CBT program was formulated based on her individual needs, and was found to be highly successful (Suveg et al., 2006).

Recent findings from a large randomized clinical trial of youth referred for depression, anxiety, or conduct problems indicate that the flexible use of the procedures is likely to be what is most important to the achievement of outcomes. Weisz et al. (2012) compared standard manualized treatments—CBT for depression, CBT for anxiety, and behavioral parent training for conduct problems—with modular treatment integrating the procedures of the three separate treatment manuals and usual care. The study demonstrates that the modular treatment outperforms usual care and the strict reliance on manualized interventions. The modular treatment produced significantly steeper trajectories of improvement than usual care and standard treatment on multiple measures of behavior problems. Youths receiving modular treatment also had significantly fewer diagnoses than usual care youths post treatment. In contrast, outcomes of standard manual treatment did not differ significantly from usual care. They conclude that the modular approach may be a promising way to build on the strengths of MESTs, improving their utility and effectiveness with referred youths in clinical practice settings.

RECONCEPTUALIZATION OF EFFECTIVE PRACTICES

Given that the number of MESTs is in the high hundreds and continues to grow (e.g., Chorpita & Daleiden, 2009), and that the implementation drawbacks of manualized treatments—such as their high implementation costs (Kazdin & Blase, 2011)—limit their widespread adoption in children's services, new conceptualizations are necessary. An expanded view of effective practices that involves two principal concepts—*common elements* and *common factors*—shows promise for meeting the prerequisites of being effective and accessible to practitioners and yielding greater opportunity for creating positive outcomes for clients.

Based on work by Chorpita and colleagues (e.g., Chorpita, Daleiden, & Weisz, 2005; Chorpita et al., 2007), a *common elements* framework conceptualizes clinical practice in terms of generic parts that cut across many distinct treatment protocols, and has focused heavily on identifying specific clinical procedures common to evidence-based practices (cf. Garland, Hawley, Brookman-Frazee, & Hurlburt, 2008). The *common elements* approach differs from the important but broader *common factors* approach, which has been championed by Duncan, Miller, Wampold, and Sparks (e.g., Duncan, Miller, Wampold & Hubble, 2010; Sparks & Muro, 2009). The common factors approach asserts that the personal and interpersonal components (e.g., alliance, client motivation, therapist factors, and goals) common to all therapeutic interventions are critical to treatment outcomes. While common factors may be important to all client interactions in a general way, common elements refers to specific treatment choices involving these same clients. Table 4.1 provides examples of the kinds of practices that are associated with common elements and common factors.

These two approaches and their potential contributions have generally not been discussed along with other MESTs in the children's services literature and, rarely, in any

TABLE 4.1

EXAMPLES OF COMMON ELEMENTS AND COMMON FACTORS

Name	Definition	Approach
Activity selection	Working with youth to select enjoyable activities that can enhance mood	Common Element
Attending	Teaching parent to identify opportunities to build relationship with youth	Common Element
Engagement with caregiver	Working with caregiver to build understanding of treatment and problem-solve barriers to involvement with services	Common Element
Praise	Teaching caregiver to encourage positive behaviors from youth	Common Element
Response cost	Building caregiver understanding of how to use consequences to extinguish undesired behaviors from youth.	Common Element
Relationship/Rapport building	Promoting a trusting relationship between youth and provider	Common Element/ Common Factor
Monitoring/ Providing feedback	Identifying goals and measuring progress in a systematic way	Common element/ Common Factor
Empathy	Recognizing and sharing feelings experienced by client	Common Factor
Warmth, positive regard	Demonstrating acceptance and support toward a client	Common Factor

mental health or child welfare literature (cf. Barth et al., 2012). What these approaches have in common is that they are both emerging as a complement to the dominant children's services discussions of evidence-based practice and MESTs (as identified through treatment clearinghouses that review and rank treatments such as the Substance Abuse and Mental Health Services Administration National Registry of Evidence-Based Programs and Practices [SAMHSA, 2011]). The next section will further describe each of these models and their potential application within children's services.

IDENTIFYING THE PRACTICE ELEMENTS

The idea of dismantling interventions into their components has been forwarded simultaneously in North American social sciences by two groups: Bruce Chorpita with his common elements approach, and Dennis Embry and colleagues, who have proposed evidence-based kernels as units of behavioral influence. Although the common elements approach has gained greater traction and implementation in child mental health practice, we will briefly overview the evidence-based kernels, which has the potential for broader application.

Embry and Biglan's (2008) evidence-based kernels have two key features: each kernel has been shown through experimental design to influence a behavior and the kernel is an indivisible component of an intervention. Interestingly, they propose evidence-based kernels that cover a very diverse field, including kernels like "sin" taxes on cigarettes or alcohol, use of a mystery shopper in retail settings, and dietary supplements like Omega-3 fatty acids and zinc. Each of these kernels has been shown to change behaviors, in addition to more commonly considered treatment activities like time-out, praise, and motivational interviewing, which they also identify. They have proposed a searchable database repository to catalog these evidence-based kernels and increase the use of effective practices.

Common (Practice) Elements Approach

The common elements approach identifies elements found in several evidence-supported, effective manualized interventions. Rather than overload workers with lengthy manuals, the common elements approach allows practitioners to " 'borrow' strategies and techniques from known treatments, using their judgment and clinical theory to adapt the strategies to fit new contexts and problems" (Chorpita et al., 2007, pp. 648–649). A practice element becomes the unit of interest rather than the entire treatment manual. Treatment elements are selected to match particular client characteristics, allowing for practitioners to establish therapeutic alliances, utilize their clinical judgment, and still follow protocols for evidence-based treatments.

Common elements researchers Chorpita et al. (2007) summarize the understanding of this approach, which is also referred to as the distillation and matching model (DMM): "what the common elements approach really attempts to do is to guide clinical decision making by providing a dynamic snapshot of the entire treatment literature at a given point in time, and by encouraging a new level of analysis for treatment monitoring and implementation that can potentially increase compatibility and utility in certain contexts. This is intended to translate into improved decision making both in selecting and implementing treatments" (p. 651).

The matching aspects of the approach are based on a detailed analysis of identifying treatment components that are common to addressing a specific problem (e.g., depression, anxiety, disruptive behaviors). Focusing on the building blocks of treatment represents a departure from the traditional notion of discrete, intact protocols that are delivered with all their treatment elements without a specific strategy for matching those elements to the needs of the clients and to information that arises during treatment. Unlike many treatment manuals, modular approaches to practice guided by a common elements framework can offer a high level of flexibility in regard to topic, pace, pairing, and sequence (Weisz & Chorpita, 2010).

In looking specifically at child mental health treatments, Chorpita and Daleiden's (2009) approach to this task was composed of two questions: What features characterize successful treatments? What strategies are common across effective interventions? In order to identify the common practice elements, trained coders reviewed 322 randomized clinical trials that tested interventions for major mental health disorders for children and teens. Over $500 million was invested in these research studies, which included 30,000 youth and were conducted over a span of 40 years.

The coding process for the 322 randomized clinical trials first consisted of frequencies of practice elements from "winning" treatment groups in randomized clinical trials. (Note: a winning treatment is one that performs significantly better than the comparison group, whether that is a second evidence-based practice or treatment as usual.) A practice element is defined as, "a discrete clinical technique or strategy used as part of a larger intervention plan" (Chorpita & Daleiden, 2009; p. 569). These element frequencies were then tallied to see what practice elements were most commonly found in effective interventions. Forty-one specific "practice elements" (e.g., relaxation, exposure, time-out) were identified that were found in at least three of the winning treatment groups. At the time of this writing, 35 of these have been turned into practice guidelines that can be used by practitioners for assistance in implementing these common elements.

The common elements approach is a framework that has gained a foothold largely within children's mental health, meaning that the elements are organized around specific mental health diagnoses. The approach is much broader, however, and offers an opportunity for any subfield of human services that has a body of intervention research that can be coded for its common elements. The opportunities for application of this approach to child welfare services are many.

Current work underway at the School of Social Work at the University of Maryland includes identifying the common elements of "family engagement" and "placement prevention." These are routinely needed efforts in child welfare services and there is sufficient rigorous peer-reviewed evaluation literature to provide the basis for developing a common elements approach. Other practices central to child welfare services may have farther to go to develop a common elements approach—because they have not been well articulated, well tested, or both—but could benefit from the approach indicated above. The value placed on better articulation of these common practice behaviors—should this articulation work be done—would likely contribute to our ability to test the fidelity of each approach against best practice standards.

Incorporating a modular approach to treatment using a common elements framework offers possible advantages over traditional manualized interventions in isolation. For example, treatment manuals are often geared toward specific child mental health disorders. Yet some children may have multiple issues to address, prodromal symptoms, or need services that do not match the length or intensity specified in a treatment manual (Chorpita et al.,

2005; Chorpita, Becker, & Daleiden, 2007) or for which no evidence-based treatment exists (Schiffman, Becker, & Daleiden, 2006). For practitioners, learning common elements and how to adapt them to maintain client participation in treatment and to adjust along with evidence of client progress—rather than master a diverse collection of treatment manuals—may improve service delivery (Chorpita et al., 2005, 2007).

As a paradigm, the common elements approach has limitations. For example, the studies that are the basis for determining common elements typically do not allow determination of the effect size of each common element on its own; rather, evidence for the common elements is based only on their inclusion in interventions that have demonstrated efficacy (Chorpita et al., 2007). Similarly, although common elements are identified through empirical research conducted with diverse samples of youth, few studies conducted adequate subgroup analysis to understand whether some youth in the research sample benefited more than others. The problem of differential effects for subgroups is also a consideration for MESTs as well. Third, although the common elements approach allows for a high level of flexibility when there is a high degree of complexity or interference; recognizing this, the developers of the common elements approach agree that following a treatment manual as prescribed may still be the best option for many clients whose conditions closely match those of treatment research participants (Chorpita et al., 2007). Hence, the common elements approach is not intended as a model to replace MESTs, but as a complementary way to pursue effective practices when an MEST is not available or appropriate.

TOOLS TO SUPPORT THE COMMON ELEMENTS APPROACH:
THE PRACTICEWISE EXAMPLE

Tools are currently being developed to assist practitioners in the selection and delivery of common elements. PracticeWise is probably the most developed of these, primarily focusing on children's mental health. The website, www.practicewise.com, states that it seeks to "bring science and evidence seamlessly into the process of clinical care" through the various tools and guides provided. PracticeWise offers the following subscription-based resources: (1) PracticeWise Evidence-Based Services Database (PWEBS); (2) PracticeWise Practitioner Guides; (3) PracticeWise Clinical Dashboards; and (4) Modular Approach to Therapy for Children (MATCH). PracticeWise is a proprietary website, and it claims that the resources that are generated by the subscriptions are primarily reinvested in improvements of the database and expansion of the practice guidelines.

PracticeWise Evidence-Based Services Database

PracticeWise Evidence-Based Services Database (PWEBS) allows users to specify client (e.g., target problem, age, gender, ethnicity) and treatment (e.g., setting, format) characteristics, among other search criteria, to identify the practice elements that comprise the interventions that have demonstrated positive outcomes in studies that have included youth with those specified characteristics. For example, a search for elements appropriate for a 15-year-old male exhibiting disruptive behavior problems yields goal setting, praise, problem solving, and social skills training as the top four most frequent practice elements.

Common Elements PracticeWise Practitioner Guides

After developing a treatment plan that has been partly informed by the PWEBS search, practitioners may use the practitioner guides, a set of clinical guidelines for how to implement the practice elements. Each two-page practitioner guide reflects a synthesis of the literature regarding the standard content related to the element and provides step-by-step instructions to facilitate implementation (e.g., communication skills includes creation of communication hierarchy, discussion of speaker and listener skills, and turn-taking as the speaker). The practitioner guides provide a roadmap to users for what content to cover related to the element, but they can be easily customized to individual clients. For example, the practitioner guide may specify an activity practicing relaxation strategies; however the practitioner working with the youth can choose to customize the practice session to fit the time frame available or the youth's needs and interests.

The practitioner guide summarizes the common elements of evidence-based treatments for youth, clearly identifying the treatment objectives and how to implement each element. These handouts guide practitioners in performing the main steps of the technique and cover elements such as psychoeducation, modeling, social skills, time-out, and, engagement with caregiver. A clinician with significant experience with a particular element may choose to review the guide for additional ideas or may adhere more closely to the guide if the practice element as delivered by the clinician previously has not been effective.

Match

Another tool within PracticeWise is the Modular Approach to Therapy for Children (MATCH). Formulated for practitioners working with children ages 7 to 13 with anxiety, depression, traumatic stress, and conduct problems, modular evidence-based treatment uses flow charts to assist in putting practice elements together. The MATCH interactive system helps organize selection of practice elements and practitioner guides, child worksheets, caregiver handouts, and recording forms from CBTs and behavioral parent management training. Practitioners can find their way through these comprehensive flow charts based on the symptoms and individual needs of each child and family.

Clinical Dashboards

After a treatment plan has been developed and the clinician begins implementing the practice elements, the clinical dashboard provides a way to monitor treatment progress

(Chorpita, Becker, & Daleiden, 2007). The clinical dashboard offers a visual summary of individual client progress and tracks achievement of treatment goals or other progress measures on a weekly/session basis. Based in Microsoft Excel, this monitoring tool also documents which clinical practice elements were used, and when they were delivered with each client. Practitioners are encouraged to use standardized measures (e.g., Child Behavior Checklist, Youth Self-Report, Children's Depression Inventory) as well as idiographic measures that reflect the specific treatment goals of the individual client and can be regularly monitored by the youth and/or adults in the environment (e.g., frequency of school attendance, number of prosocial peer interactions, subjective mood rating). The practices checklist marks the practice elements covered at each treatment session. Practitioners can display up to five progress measures of a client at a time, using any measures of their choice (e.g., test score, treatment goal).

Using software designed for the purpose of monitoring progress on a few goals, practitioners can view client progress in a clear line graph format, and also customize their dashboard to write in additional practice elements. Using the clinical dashboard, practitioners, supervisors, and clients have access to historical progress and treatment data at a glance. Regular collection of data provides a means of monitoring progress, and the graphical presentation of progress and treatment data together allows for inferences to be drawn regarding the effectiveness of selected practice elements.

Mere mention of this process may bring out concerns about the failure of single-subject research to be implementable in the real world practice of many practitioners. In the past, there was little value placed on providing this level of monitoring of clinical practice for the provider or feedback to the client. As will be referenced later in this chapter, as we discuss common factors, measurement feedback systems now have growing support from outcome studies to indicate that checking in with clients about their current experience of their outcomes and their alliance to treatment appears to have an independent benefit. Along with some technological advances in the utilities of case-tracking programs, the perceived benefit to clients may increase the proportion of workers who seek to find a way to routinely engage clients in such measurement efforts.

Common Factors (Client-Directed, Outcome-Informed) Approach

The common factors approach had its earliest articulation by Saul Rosenzweig (1936), who asserted that different psychotherapeutic approaches contained common unrecognized factors critical to positive treatment outcomes. The commonalities in therapeutic encounters were similarly identified in E. Fuller Torrey's memorably titled book, *Witchdoctors and Psychiatrists* (1986). He asserted that the effectiveness of therapeutic interventionists (be they psychotherapists in Western culture, witchdoctors and spiritual healers in other places in the world) is determined by four key ingredients. These were identified as having a shared worldview, the personal qualities of the provider, the client's expectations, and the client's increased sense of mastery (Torrey, 1986, p. 78).

Although also written about by social workers (e.g., Cameron & Keenan, 2010; Drisko, 2004), common factor concepts have not yet been embraced by the profession, or, more generally, in the area of children's services. The fit of the common factors approach with the movement toward evidence-based practice has not been much discussed. The name "common" or "nonspecific" factors was originally given to features of the psychotherapeutic exchange that were universal to the therapy experience, not related to the specific therapy model or approach and highly determinant of the outcomes. For example, the therapist's personal qualities, therapeutic alliance, and the client's hopes and expectations are considered common factors, as they may have influence on the therapeutic outcome regardless of the intervention techniques employed. These nonspecific factors are often considered to be less critical in manualized interventions because their structure assumes that clinicians cannot stray far from best practice.

Much of the empirical evidence supporting the common factors approach has been assembled through meta-analyses. In comparing results across diverse psychotherapeutic models, outcomes show little variation by unique model, suggesting that the bulk of therapeutic change is due to therapist actions (e.g., fostering therapeutic alliance, reviewing treatment progress, and engaging in a client-centered relationship) that are common across all generally accepted approaches. In assessing meta-analytic findings, advocates of the common factors approach have suggested that unique factors of a treatment contribute less than 15% of the outcome (Wampold et al., 1997), or even as low as 1% of the variability in outcomes (Ahn & Wampold, 2001; Norcross & Wampold, 2011). Results from a meta-analysis of 27 component studies (where a complete treatment was compared to a treatment without a theoretically important component or with an additional theoretically supported component) found no significant difference in outcomes that were related to the inclusion or exclusion of specific treatment components (Ahn & Wampold, 2001). This appears to support the argument that the key ingredient of an effective therapeutic intervention is the training of the practitioner to develop a therapeutic alliance and that the specific practice components are not nearly as important.

This does not, of course, undo the argument made by cognitive-behavior therapists that a well-trained practitioner who has exceptional skills in engaging clients and creating a therapeutic alliance *and* in the use of an evidence-based intervention would have the best chance of a positive outcome (e.g., Raue & Goldfried, 1994). It is very plausible that many of the therapists examined in these studies did not employ the strongest evidence-based interventions. The common factors approach places the greatest emphasis on the therapist's relational skills above and beyond the actual treatment techniques employed (although the approach does recognize that a credible treatment model is also critical to success).

Critics (e.g., Siev, Huppert, & Chambless, 2009) have taken issue with the results of meta-analyses that appear to discredit the value of specific treatment models. Several reasons have been cited. One is the way studies were selected. Specifically, only experimental studies in which both groups received active treatments were included; wait-list control or no treatment conditions were not included. As such, the effectiveness of the common factors is entangled with the unique treatment techniques; no studies have been conducted that assess the common factors as a stand-alone treatment. It is possible that specific treatment techniques must be combined with the power of the common factors to create a necessary condition for change (Anderson, Lunnen, & Ogles, 2010). Even if the critique were correct that the contribution of MESTs is not as large as that of common factors, Rubin (2011) points out that the amount of variance explained by specific evidence-supported treatments would still substantially increase the number of clients who would have a successful outcome.

In sum, the meta-analytic work that arguably demonstrates the greater impact of the common factors over specific evidence-based practices has set off a volley of analyses and counteranalyses by treatment researchers. From our perspective, the merits of the common factors approach are not contingent on a precise determination of the power of MESTs because these are complementary methods. Although much of the research evidence used to establish the common factors has been based on studies of adult samples, application of this approach to children's services will be illustrated in the following sections.

CLIENT DIRECTED, OUTCOME INFORMED

Duncan, Miller, Wampold, and Hubble (2010) contend that effective therapy arises from allegiance to a treatment model, monitoring of change, and creating a strong therapeutic alliance. They have endeavored to elevate the use of common factors and "practice-based evidence" to a higher level of impact by structuring a system called "client-directed and outcome informed" (CDOI; Duncan et al., 2006). A central element of the CDOI approach that may end up being one of its greatest strengths is this effort to consistently measure the therapeutic alliance and the level of client symptoms. Repeated and systematic use of fairly simple tools (described later) may significantly enhance client and practitioner attunement to client needs. These tools solicit feedback from clients on their level of functioning as well as feedback to therapists on the therapeutic alliance. Being client-directed and outcome informed is based on the concept and the experience that continuous feedback within a practice-based evidence approach, "individualizes psychotherapy based on treatment response and client preference" (Anker, Duncan, & Sparks, 2009, p. 702). The authors highlight the findings that systematic feedback minimized therapy dropout and improved the effectiveness of treatment; therapists also consistently reported benefiting from the feedback (Anker et al., 2009).

The CDOI approach to therapy is a treatment strategy that uses common factors. According to Duncan, the leading voice in the CDOI method, CDOI services, "contain no fixed techniques or causal theories regarding the concerns that bring people to treatment" (Duncan, n.d.). Instead, he values the client's voice, social justice, and effective recovery coming from therapeutic partnership. The CDOI keys, in treatment, are that client and clinician can work together to enhance the most successful factors across theories, use the client's ideas and preferences to guide technique, and use reliable and valid measures of the client's experience of the alliance and outcome (Duncan, n.d.).

COMMON FACTORS TOOLS FOR SOLICITING FEEDBACK

Instead of simply offering a generalist argument for focusing on the therapeutic alliance and the importance of client feedback, the common factors approach has developed tools that help the therapist monitor the therapeutic alliance and progress toward intermediate outcomes. Although the use of the CDOI measurement tools has not been experimentally studied in child and youth services, there is growing evidence that the use of such tools improves positive outcomes and reduces the proportion of children getting worse (Lambert & Shimokawa, 2011).

Two crucial tools for feedback in the CDOI approach are the Outcome Rating Scale (ORS) and the Session Rating Scale (SRS). Each scale is a reliable and valid four-item, self-report instrument used at each therapeutic meeting. Both measures are available in full online (www.heartandsoulofchange.com). The unique aspect of these tools is that scoring and interpreting the score is a collaborative effort between client and therapist. Rather than the therapist assigning meaning to a client's feedback, the *client explains the meaning* behind the mark on the scale. This helps identify alliance strengths and weaknesses in therapy from both points of view, rather than a solely "expert-driven" approach (Sparks & Muro, 2009).

The ORS asks the adult client about her current level of functioning personally, in close relationships, in life outside the home, and overall. The ORS is completed at the beginning of each session, as the responses should guide the topics and content of the therapeutic interaction. At the end of the session, the client can complete the SRS. The SRS collects feedback about the therapeutic alliance, specifically the extent to which the client felt heard and understood, worked on issues he wanted to work on, and appreciated the therapist's style, and an overall session rating. For both the SRS and the ORS, clients rate each item from 1 to 10, with higher scores indicating higher functioning or satisfaction. The ORS has not been rigorously tested with parents involved with child maltreatment, but these parents often suffer from depression and other mental health problems and are also likely to report that services are not responsive to their needs (Burns et al., in press). Anecdotal evidence suggests that the use of CDOI tools could help to better engage youth and guide child welfare workers in decision-making (Sparks & Muro, 2010); however, the acceptability and effectiveness of using the CDOI tools with mandated populations has not yet been well established.

When working with children, practitioners can employ the same helpful, client-focused feedback tools using versions that have been formatted for children. Vital and sometimes overlooked in therapeutic work with children is the clinician's ability to give youth a voice in their own therapy. The CORS and CSRS are child-specific scales of the ORS and

SRS designed for use with children ages 6–12. Written at a third grade reading level, the tools are used to track effectiveness and therapeutic alliance as reported by children and their parents or caretakers. The CORS shows strong reliability (alpha = 0.84) and validity as compared to a longer youth outcome questionnaire (Pearson's coefficient = 0.61; Duncan et al., 2006). Sparks and Muro (2009) report on efforts to integrate the CDOI approach with Wraparound, a family-driven practice model for youth at risk of out-of-home placement. In anecdotal reports from agencies implementing Wraparound who added the CDOI tools, they found that the data from the tools provided helpful feedback in developing effective plans for service that reflected the family's perceived needs and priorities.

Researchers have found that using client feedback in couples therapy has reliable scientific support for alliance building and monitoring treatment progress for clients and therapists (Anker et al., 2009). Feedback tools (e.g., ORS and SRS) that are not linked with a certain therapy or method can be used in community settings more easily than specific treatment packages. There are two means to collect, store, and interpret CDOI data. One is an end-user software program (ASIST) and the other a Web-based program (Partners for Change Outcome Management System, or PCOMS). Both of these programs can create graphs that illustrate the expected change over time for a client's specific need and allow the practitioner to track the client's actual progress over the course of intervention. SRS scores are also plotted.

Research now shows the extent to which the feedback tools can improve client outcomes. Anker et al. (2009) spearheaded the first randomized clinical trial to measure the effect of CDOI/Measurement Feedback System (MFS) on clients. The study included couples using the feedback measure, ORS, at pre- and posttreatment and follow-up (N = 103), compared to couples receiving treatment as usual (TAU) (N = 102). Results were promising in that those couples using the ORS achieved almost four times the rate of clinically significant change. The feedback condition showed a moderate to large effect size (0.50). Of equal importance is that those couples maintained a significant advantage on the ORS at the 6-month follow-up. Overall, couples using the ORS showed greater marital satisfaction and lower rates of separation or divorce (Anker et al., 2009).

Common Ground between Common Elements and Common Factors

The common factors model and common elements approach share some common ground. In addition to both approaches emerging as a response to the proliferation of individualized development of treatments, areas of agreement between the common factors and common elements are: a "both/and" relationship with MESTs insofar as they do not exclude the use of manualized interventions as long as those interventions do not interfere with treatments that use common factors and elements (including some feedback from clients); an emphasis on client involvement and practice-based evidence; and "flexibility within fidelity" (Kendall, Gosch, Furr, & Snood, 2008). This section will first describe some key areas of overlap and then briefly review the distinguishing characteristics of each approach.

Although manualized practices are more structured than common factors and common elements, all three approaches have value for practitioners. The common elements and common factors provide options when there are no manualized evidence-based practices known to be effective with a specific client or problem area. When manualized interventions exist for a given clinical situation, the common elements approach is not intended as substitute practice (Chorpita et al., 2007). Rather, the decision-making framework expects practitioners to identify compelling reasons for deviating from evidence-based interventions (Chorpita et al., 2005, 2007). Within the common factors field, the acceptance of manualized interventions has been limited (Duncan & Miller, 2006) but many now recognize the value of MESTs as complementary (Morgan & Sprenkle, 2007; Sexton, Ridley, & Kleiner, 2004; Sprenkle, Davis, & Lebow, 2009). Recent research that demonstrates that manualized practices do not interfere with youth engagement (and may promote it in the early stages) should further encourage the use of manualized approaches. Even the more staunch common factors proponents (e.g., Sparks & Muro, 2009) would have nothing against MESTs except when they are chosen without client input or lack the flexibility to shift based on ongoing client feedback. As such, rather than expecting practitioners to choose either manualized practices or common factors/elements, a complementary perspective is supportable.

Successful delivery of common elements relies on common factors. Some of the common elements (e.g., engagement, rapport building, psychoeducation) target common factors (e.g., therapeutic alliance, expectations, hope). As a result, agencies that are beginning to focus their training on common effective practices can begin with common factors and make the transition to adding common practice elements that have an overlap.

The recent development of relatively similar tools for measuring the process of treatment has given the common elements and common factors approaches new reasons to build an alliance (no pun intended). Monitoring progress toward outcomes are facets of both the common factors and common elements models. In the PracticeWise common elements approach, the clinical dashboard is a tool that a practitioner can use to track intervention components and client improvement (Chorpita, Bernstein, & Daleiden, 2008). Within common factors, short instruments like the ORS and SRS provide feedback to the practitioner about progress from the client's perspective. The need to develop routine ways to monitor treatment and develop feedback systems has been identified as critical to the broader improvement of mental health services (Bickman, 2008). Leaders of the common elements and common factors approaches recommend the use of measurement feedback systems in their work, although the extent to which this is now done, or will be done, in practice settings remains uncertain.

Finally, the idea of "flexibility within fidelity" is relevant for both models (Kendall et al., 2008). For common elements, flexibility is inherent in the approach, in regard to the selection, sequence, and pacing of each practice element. However, each element has generally prescribed steps or tasks that should be covered to ensure that it is delivered in a comprehensive way. Yet, the common element approach does not necessarily require that prescribed steps be covered. If a practitioner implements a common practice element the way she always does and the data show progress, then the clinician does not need to implement the common practice element according to the practitioner guide. But, if a practice element is new to a clinician or the clinician is not seeing progress, then we suggest that the clinician check their fidelity to the guide.

Instead of fidelity to the treatment manual, the common elements approach focuses on client progress on the clinical dashboard toward agreed upon goals. Likewise, the common factors approach endorses flexibility in engaging clients. Treatment should be adapted to meet a client's characteristics and preferences, including the therapist's own style or methods. Fidelity for common factors means assessing the client's perspective of the treatment to ensure that the client's goals are being met and, if not, changing course. In this way, fidelity does not mean staying true to a treatment manual, but staying true to the client's goals in the treatment process. Finding the balance between engaging child protection clients—who are among the most difficult of all clients to engage—and moving ahead with treatment planning for children's needs is going to be difficult but provides even greater reason why the most effective forms of engagement are needed.

AN INTEGRATIVE FRAMEWORK

Common elements and common factors make potentially important contributions to providing evidence-informed treatment to parents and children involved with children's services practice. This section will propose an integrative framework for thinking about the role of common factors, common elements, MESTs, and other sources of knowledge within the field. As children's mental health treatments and, arguably, other children's services practices, evolve in the era of evidence-based practice, a model that classifies the varied approaches and concepts seems fitting. Social work has not yet agreed on a single view of evidence-based practice (Rubin & Parrish, 2007), suggesting that an organizing framework that incorporates the diverse efforts toward evidence-informed practice may be a helpful contribution. Each of these approaches can have a role in decision-making about intervention approaches with clients seeking treatment. There are likely many building blocks that can be used to improve children's services practice and the quality of services delivered to clients. The integrative framework identifies some of these components and suggests an order in the hierarchy of evidence-informed children's services practice (Figure 4.1). We loosely use the metaphor of a triangle without claiming that the size of the areas under the stripes in the triangle represents the actual use, or potential benefit, of any of these methods. The rationale for the triangle is that the lower levels on the triangle are the broadest in terms of their application. At the bottom of the triangle are the most general structures that apply to all cases involved with child protection and at the top is the most specific knowledge that may only apply to a few cases. In the middle area are the common

FIGURE 4.1. A framework for conceptualizing the role of various components of evidence-supported social work practice.

factors that can be quite generally held (even in nontreatment cases that primarily involve case management) and, then, the common elements that are clearly indicated for cases involving treatment.

Policy and Value Directives

Children's services practice stands on the platform of policy and value directives that determine such core considerations as ethical conduct, communicating only with those who have a legally supported "need to know" (unless explicit permission is obtained to go beyond this group), legal and agency mandates, and so on. This is the foundation of the pyramid and must be applied with every client.

Practice Principles

Many agencies have practice principles or specific models of care that serve as a next level to help select appropriate interventions. For example, child welfare agencies may require that interventions be "family-focused" or mental health agencies may operate within the framework of "systems of care." These are not evidence-based interventions, per se, but are principles that contribute to the identification and conduct of best practices.

Common Factors

The common factors approach is a more specific way to implement what can be considered common practice principles of engaging clients and attending to the achievement of outcomes. By focusing on the therapeutic relationship and the client's assessment of progress toward goals, the common factors approach remains responsive and flexible. The systematic collection of client feedback is critical to this approach. This relatively new refinement is now considered the tie that binds all the factors together, allowing the common factors to engage the clients, heighten hope for improvement, fit client preferences, maximize therapist-client fit, and accelerate client change (Duncan, 2010a). Although using the Partners for Change Outcome Management System (PCOMS) is not, yet, acknowledged anywhere as an evidence-based practice (Duncan, 2010b), it has promise. A new meta-analysis of the use of client feedback systems suggests that their use reduces by half the proportion of clients who worsen during treatment (Lambert & Shimokawa, 2011).

Common Elements

The common elements approach may represent the next level of evidence-based practice precision. These are specific practice elements that have been identified, as described above, because they were present in successful treatments in randomized clinical trials involving at least one manualized intervention. Developers of the common elements perspective would certainly expect that intervening with any of the common elements would include attention to the therapeutic alliance but not as the sole focus. The common elements approach also prioritizes collecting data from clients about their outcomes—a hallmark of the common factors approach. For that reason, we have left the line between these approaches dotted. Early implementation of the common elements approach in Hawaii, Minnesota, and Maine involves its use as a way to achieve general practice improvement by children's mental health and child welfare practitioners.

Manualized Evidence-Supported Treatments

As previously discussed, MESTs are treatments that have been identified as superior to a treatment as usual condition or a placebo condition in a randomized clinical trial. Many of these interventions are now well recognized in clearinghouses of evidence-based practices used by children's services practitioners (e.g., SAMHSA's National Registry of Evidence-Based Programs: NREPP).

Specific Practice Knowledge

Although not directly discussed in this chapter, work with troubled children and families often requires some specific treatment issues. At the top of the pyramid is a category that we call *specific practice knowledge*, which includes information that may be particularly germane to the culture, circumstances, and characteristics of clients. (We note that there is not a commonly accepted term for *specific treatment knowledge*, as it seems inaccurate to refer to it as "practice wisdom" and it is more than book knowledge of local culture or context.) This category may include sensitivity issues that arise because of a specific chronic condition (e.g., schizophrenia or cystic fibrosis), family circumstance (e.g., divorce or adoption), or cultural heritage (e.g., living in a family that is first or second generation in the United States). This information may improve engagement of clients and increase the feasibility of completing treatment-related activities. We do not argue that this specific practice knowledge is essential to successful treatment but expect that it will contribute to practice effectiveness when used to properly inform the implementation of other science-informed treatments. One of our reviewers very reasonably argued that this underestimates the impact of specific family factors—for example, if a family is Arab or ultraorthodox Jewish—and that this kind of specific knowledge probably comes into play at each level of the pyramid.

In all, this framework outlines how the varied efforts to infuse evidence into children's services practice can be ordered. This model both acknowledges and identifies the many sources of influence that drive practice decision-making. Each of these approaches has a contribution to make in preparing children's services workers to serve clients. Practitioners should be well prepared and adept at navigating each of these layers as they identify treatment and service delivery that will be most effective for each client. The long-standing presence of social work values, policy directives, and specific practice knowledge likely make these levels most familiar to social workers and most prevalent in social work education.

Recently, social work practice and education have begun to integrate MESTs (Rubin, 2011), but the common factors and common elements approaches have largely been ignored by social work and have been the domain of psychologists. Because we are convinced that the common elements and common factors models have value for children's services practice and are more readily integrated than many MESTs, we next describe broader implications for children's services.

Conclusions and Implications for Children's Services

MESTs alone are not likely to be sufficient for incorporating research-based findings into practice for all clients. Thus, children's services practitioners should be skilled in common factors and common elements that will allow them to respond to unique client needs. In this section, we will suggest specific considerations for children's service workers, supervisors, and administrators who are considering how to more broadly integrate effective practices.

An aspect found in both the common elements and common factors approach is the importance of monitoring progress toward outcomes. Agencies are likely to have an increasing interest in outcomes management, in order to respond to growing pressures to achieve quality improvement, accreditation, and reimbursement (Bickman, 2008). On a practice level, children's services personnel need to be skilled in consistently evaluating the impact of their services. Although this is mandated in the Code of Ethics (NASW, 1996), this is not uniformly practiced in a systematic way. Both the common factors and common elements provide tools to quickly and easily monitor client progress. The common elements resources include a charting mechanism to track outcomes visually. The common factors model solicits feedback from clients at each session using short surveys. Either of these methods when used consistently would allow social workers to use data to make decisions: specifically, individualizing services based on the client's response. Being responsive to client's preferences and tracking progress toward client goals could well increase the quality of usual care.

In addition to the direct practice level, the common factors and common elements models have implications for agency managers and, especially, supervisors. Supervision should be focused on helping new practitioners learn effective practice skills and "not least in this process is the supervisor's role as the guarantor of public protection against sub-standard practice and undesirable outcomes" (ABECSW, 2004, p. 3). In the role of ensuring quality services, methods to improve treatment as usual should be welcome. Clinical supervisors should be knowledgeable not just about MESTs, but also the common factors and common elements approaches. During supervision, the common elements clinical dashboard or the common factors feedback ratings can be reviewed to assess the supervisee's skills and struggles. Specific techniques included in the common elements could be role-played between the supervisor and supervisee to expand skills, and the evidence-based database could be queried to identify relevant practice elements for a particularly challenging client. These tools offer additional ways for clinical supervisors to promote high quality usual care.

Agency administrators also need to be mindful of the infrastructure needed to implement and sustain common factors and common elements models. Specifically, access to the common elements PracticeWise materials are currently subscription-based. A financial investment within an agency may be needed to provide access to practitioners or institutional-level licensing. For the common factors model, several software programs are available for implementing an outcomes measurement system with varying costs and sustainability issues. Agency administrators may also want to consider the role of a quality assurance officer in aggregating outcomes across clients to monitor performance within various programs or across the agency's services. The importance of implementing effective practices is a value that must be shared by agency administrators and reflected in the resources made available to clinicians and other staff.

In considering the implementation of any new ideas like the common factors and common elements, agency leaders and practitioners may be resistant to change or devoting the time and attention needed to implement these approaches to effective practices. In a landscape where policy and changing regulations often drive practice, making a sustained commitment to learning and implementing new practice approaches may be a challenge. Further, the increased performance expectations and decreased funding and resources may limit opportunities for adoption of new approaches to practice. Because some aspects may be familiar to child service workers (like empathy and therapeutic alliance in the common factors model; or teaching parents about praise and time-out in the common elements approach), practitioners may dismiss these approaches as not providing any new ideas. This flawed assessment may impede practitioner buy-in.

While much of this chapter conceptualizes social work practice from a primarily clinical perspective, we recognize that social work practice has a rich history of providing first response to child abuse reports, ongoing case management, and macro interventions with communities and large organizations. The frameworks of the common factors and common elements approach could plausibly be adapted to identify effective techniques in macro-level interventions and assessing client feedback and outcomes even when the client is a large group or community, although we have no particular experience with this usage.

NEXT STEPS FOR RESEARCH

Future research on the utility of common elements and common factors as paradigms of social work practice should occur at two levels. While this chapter argues that both common elements and common factors are legitimate alternatives to eclectic treatment as usual, more research is needed to assess whether these approaches are as effective as manualized treatments. Randomized clinical trials comparing the use of common elements and common factors with evidence-supported manualized interventions are needed (e.g., Weisz et al., 2011).

It also remains unclear who are the clients that stand to benefit most from the application of common elements and common factors. Research that clarifies the subgroups of clients for whom common elements or common factors hold the most utility for improving outcomes has yet to be done, but may lead to enhanced delivery of evidence-based interventions for the most vulnerable populations. The advantages or disadvantages of MESTS over common elements and common factors are likely to vary with the problem being addressed or the characteristics (e.g., age and gender) of the clientele. Indeed, both common elements and common factors need to be subjected to rigorous clinical trials research to substantiate their legitimacy among target populations and for specific problems, and perhaps their primacy over or complementarity with current, evidence-supported manualized interventions.

Much additional research is needed to take the common factors and common elements approaches beyond just traditional mental health care. Thus far, the common factors approach has primarily developed in individual adult mental health treatment and more recently with marriage and family therapy. The common elements approach originated with child mental health. Children's services researchers might employ the frameworks to identify and advance both common elements and common factors in child welfare, intimate partner violence, juvenile justice, geriatric psychosocial services, and other family work found in social work settings.

The advancement of common elements and common factors could eventually benefit from systematic reviews to identify efforts to identify common elements or factors associated with traditional social work practice. At the current time, systematic reviews address overall program impacts but refinements could generate information on more specific social work domains such as engaging clients in treatment, placement prevention among children with severe mental health needs, or case management. The identification of these common elements and factors might be further task-analyzed into steps or components that can be observed and taught across social work curricula and in traditional social work practice settings.

Conclusions

Even though this chapter calls for increased attention to the common elements and common factors approaches in improving usual care of children's services practice, these approaches are not without limitations. Notably, these approaches do not unequivocally meet all of the nine ideal attributes of evidence-based interventions as defined by Bond, Drake, and Becker (2010): well defined, reflecting client goals, consistent with societal goals, effective, minimum side effects, positive long-term outcomes, reasonable costs, easy to implement, and adaptable to diverse communities and client subgroups. Nonetheless, they meet a substantial number of these and are especially strong in being well defined, reflecting client goals (which do not have to be seen through the lens of the treatment manual), sensitive to side effects, available at a reasonable cost, easy to implement, and adaptable to diverse communities and client subgroups. The greatest limitation is that the evidence of their effectiveness and long-term outcomes is not yet strong enough to meet the standard test for evidence-based practices (i.e., evaluated as effective in two randomized clinical trials not conducted by the treatment developer).

Nonetheless, the domain of evidence-based practice must make choices about how to invest our efforts to improve outcomes for children and families. Continued reliance on the dissemination of evidence-supported manualized treatments as a primary transformational strategy will not achieve our goals. Refocusing on the training and integration of evidence-supported elements and factors with a practice framework that continues to build on the value of safety, permanency, and well-being for children and that incorporates client preferences will best advance our effectiveness.

Acknowledgments

This chapter builds on a presentation by the first author made at "The Use of Evidence in Child Welfare Practice and Policy" conference at Bar-Ilan University in Jerusalem and in a paper titled "Evidence-based practice at a crossroads: The emergence of common elements and factors" (Barth et al., 2012), available in *Research on Social Work Practice*. The authors are grateful to authors of that paper and the editors of this volume for ideas that helped improve this chapter.

5

USING IMPLEMENTATION SCIENCE TO IMPROVE SERVICE AND PRACTICE IN CHILD WELFARE

Actions and Essential Elements

Robyn Mildon, Nancy Dickinson, and Aron Shlonsky

Introduction

The ultimate goal of services and supports in child welfare service systems is to decrease the prevalence of child abuse and neglect and increase child permanency, safety, and well-being. Over the last decade, thinking about how to accomplish this has involved the identification and cataloging of empirically supported interventions (ESIs)[1] and attempts to disseminate these widely and effectively (Embry & Biglan, 2008). Despite these efforts, there is agreement among researchers and policymakers that child welfare services have been slow to effectively implement ESIs (Aarons, Wells, Zagursky, Fettes, & Palinkas, 2009; Garland, Hurlburt, & Hawley, 2006; Godley, White, Diamond, Passetti, & Titus, 2001; Stirman, Crits-Christoph, & DeRubeis, 2004). Without high-quality implementation, in addition to wide-scale dissemination of ESIs, child welfare agencies and the families they serve are unlikely to realize the full benefits of these programs and practices with respect to improved child outcomes.

---

[1] Throughout this paper, the term *ESIs* will be used as a synonym for empirically supported interventions, empirically supported programs, and empirically supported treatments.

By *implementation* we are referring to a set of planned and intentional activities that aim to put into practice ESIs or empirically supported practices (ESPs)[2] within real-world service settings (Fixsen, Naoom, Blase, Friedman, & Wallace, 2005; Mitchell, 2011). Implementation is a process, not an event, and should be distinguished from adoption, which is defined as the formal decision to use an ESI or ESP in practice (Mitchell, 2011). Effective implementation has more traditionally referred to the full implementation of all components of a program or practice, as planned by the original developer(s). More recently, implementation researchers have systematically started to examine the degree to which core components of a program can be maintained while allowing for local adaptation as a way to accommodate what may be needed at a system, policy or organizational level to facilitate effective implementation and sustainment of the ESI or ESP (e.g., Aarons, et al., 2012).

A variety of issues inherent in child welfare service settings make implementation in this sector a complex and difficult endeavor (Aarons, Hurlburt, & Horwitz, 2011). One issue is the challenging and often co-occurring problems faced by a large proportion of families in child welfare services (e.g., past or ongoing child maltreatment concerns, mental health issues, violence in an adult partnership, homelessness, poverty). These consumer complexities within the child welfare service setting have implications for how ESIs are both conceptualized and implemented. For example, most ESIs developed and trialed in research settings focus on the amelioration of a single issue or problem behavior (e.g., ADHD; substance misuse; bullying), within a particular population (e.g., single racial and ethnic group—in the main White American/European), at a particular time in their developmental history (e.g., first time young moms; Hawley & Weisz, 2002; Mitchell, 2011; Weisz, Southam-Gerow, Gordis, & Connor-Smith, 2003).

The very structure of child welfare organizations may also lead to poor implementation (Glisson & Himmelgarn, 1998). In many places (countries) child protection organizations have hierarchical, bureaucratic structures that are heavy in procedural documentation, rather than lateral structures that focus on active or collaborative learning (Gambrill & Shlonsky, 2001; Regehr, Hemsworth, Leslie, Howe, & Chau, 2004), and these are poorly suited to implementing complex social interventions that rely on honest and timely feedback and that require creative solutions that do not violate model fidelity. Moreover, child welfare decisions are subject to public scrutiny and occur within the interconnected context of law enforcement, service providers, treatment systems, communities, and consumers, a process that often results in risk-aversive—rather than innovative—behaviors. With high documentation demands, high caseloads and workloads, high staff turnover, and high sensitivity to any negative media exposure, opportunities for the types of consultation and supervision needed to create and maintain clinical expertise may be in short supply (Munro, 2011). Without addressing these larger

---

[2] Throughout this paper, the term *ESPs* will be used as a synonym for empirically supported practices.

organizational and practice level challenges, as a planned part of an implementation strategy, interventions, even effective ones, may not work (Mildon & Shlonsky, 2011).

Adapting ESIs to the realities of these clinical and organizational complexities is an important strategy for enhancing implementation, and the application of high quality implementation frameworks and strategies can help guide the implementation process, leading to more effective implementation of ESIs. This chapter will briefly discuss the evidence for the impact of high-quality implementation on program outcomes. Next we will discuss three emerging areas of work, all of which aim to achieve more effective implementation of ESIs in child welfare service settings:

- Improving the "implementability" of ESIs through the attention and use of common elements of interventions and supporting planned and appropriate adaptation of interventions in the service setting;
- Utilizing frameworks of implementation to guide implementation efforts;
- Addressing each of the critical components of implementation and the research evidence for each of these.

Implementation Matters

While the identification of ESIs and ESPs can be helpful when practitioners, agencies, and policymakers are shopping for programs in which to invest, the emphasis on identifying and cataloging effective services has not been matched by a corresponding effort to systematically assess the extent to which an ESI is implemented and to evaluate the impact of this on program outcomes (Aarons, Sommerfeld, & Walrath-Greene, 2009). Only beginning in the 1980s did studies emerge that clearly showed that the quality of implementation had an impact on desired outcomes (e.g., Aarons, Sommerfeld, Hecht, Silovsky, & Chaffin, 2009; Abbott, O'Donnell, Hawkins, Hill, Kosterman, & Catalano, 1998; DuBois, Holloway, Valentine, & Cooper, 2002, Durlak & DuPre, 2008; Grimshaw & Russell, 1993; Lipsey, Howell, Kelly, Chapman, & Carver, 2010; Tobler, 1986).

Despite this, we now have extensive empirical evidence describing the importance of implementation. Durlak and DuPre (2008) conducted an extensive review of implementation studies in the field of prevention and health promotion programs targeting children and adolescents. To answer the question "Does implementation affect outcomes?" the researchers reviewed data from nearly 500 studies that were evaluated in five meta-analyses, as well as data from a further 59 qualitative studies. They found that the magnitude of mean effect sizes were at least two to three times higher when programs were implemented well and with few or no problems in the implementation. The data from the qualitative studies confirmed that full implementation of programs was associated with better outcomes, particularly when fidelity and dosage were used to measure levels of implementation.

Implementation research in the last 15 years has also helped to advance our understanding of the factors that may affect the level of implementation that is achieved (Durlak & Dupre, 2008). Rigorous experimental designs that test the influence of all possible factors that may affect implementation are difficult, if not impossible, to apply to real-world implementation contexts (Meyers, Durlak, & Wandersman, 2012). Therefore, individual or multiple case studies have been the main way researchers have learned about factors that affect the implementation process. Although the external validity of findings may be weak due to this methodology, the literature offers a number of high-quality quantitative and qualitative reports that contribute to our understanding of the implementation process (e.g., Domitrovich, Gest, Jones, Gill, & Sanford DeRousie, 2010; Saunders, Ward, Felton, Dowda, & Pate, 2006; Walker & Koroloff, 2007). This has resulted in the identification of major components that may well affect overall implementation, and constructs within these components that can affect one or more aspects of implementation. For example, Damschroder and colleagues (2009) identified five major domains (e.g., intervention characteristics, outer setting, inner setting, characteristics of individuals involved, and the process of implementation) and 29 constructs within these that have an impact on the level of implementation achieved (e.g., stakeholders' perceptions of the quality and validity of evidence; client needs and resources; the degree to which an organization is networked with other external organizations; characteristics of the organization such as the social architecture, age, maturity, and size; and the culture of an organization including norms, values, and basic assumptions of the organization).

Improving the "Implementability" of Empirically Supported Interventions: Common Elements and Adaptation

While debate persists with respect to what constitutes ESIs (Gambrill, 2010; Littell & Shlonsky, 2010), the child protection field is moving toward providing services that are demonstrably effective. In the main, efforts to do this have focused on identifying and disseminating ESIs. ESIs consist of collections of practices that are performed within known parameters (philosophy, values, service delivery structure, and treatment components) and are put together in the form of a structured manual containing details of procedures and tools (Fixsen et al., 2005).

The ESI approach has challenges with respect to implementation in agencies serving children and families with complex and multiple needs. These include: ESIs can be too constraining of practitioners' practice as a result of rigid manualization and structure (Lyon et al., 2013); there are difficulties in implementing an ESI widely with fidelity and maintaining effectiveness (Embry & Biglan, 2008); in the real world there are often difficulties in accessing adequate training in a variety of ESIs that have been developed (Kazdin & Blase, 2011). In addition, many existing interventions that are treated as ESIs may also have limited effectiveness, modest effect sizes, issues with scalability, limited generalization, and difficulties with maintaining or sustaining the program without adaptation in child welfare service settings (Embry & Biglan, 2008).

As an alternative to manualized ESIs, researchers and program developers have recently turned their attention to the identification and integration of what have been termed empirically supported practices (ESPs) in a number of fields including child welfare. Framed this way, ESPs are effective skills, techniques, and strategies that can be used by an individual practitioner. Such practices describe core intervention components that have been shown to reliably produce desirable effects and can be used individually or in combination to form more complex procedures or programs (Embry, 2004).

This newest wave of intervention research recognizes the benefits to be gained by understanding more about current practice when trying to build effective services across contexts. This approach, known as the "common elements" (Chorpita, Daleiden, & Weisz, 2005a, 2005b) or "kernels" (Embry & Biglan, 2008) approach, explored more extensively by Barth and Lee (Chapter 4, this book), is based on the idea that ESIs are made up of a number of elements that can be identified, specified, and implemented in different ways. It rejects the assumption that these elements can only be organized and delivered in fixed arrangements specified in ESI models and manuals. Chorpita et al. (2005a) define a "practice element" as "a discrete clinical technique or strategy (e.g., "time-out" or "relaxation") used as part of a larger intervention plan" (p. 11). Practice elements are defined by their content, not by duration, periodicity, or location within a manual.

The common elements approach offers a genuine possibility in terms of facilitating more effective adoption and implementation. It is conducive to a high level of adaptability to context and reciprocal adaptation between intervention and context, and these may serve to decrease the substantial barriers to adopting ESIs that exist in provider attitudes, characteristics of client populations, and the characteristics of usual practice (Mitchell, 2011). By breaking interventions down into small elements, practitioners and families are better able to choose the intervention content that best addresses their needs. For example, intervention content and practices can be systematically selected and organized according to the developmental stage of the child and family members.

A second emerging strategy that shows promise for supporting the adoption and effective implementation of ESIs is to identify core elements and adaptable characteristics of ESIs and accompanying systems and organizational solutions for their adaptation (Aarons et al., 2012; Meyers et al., 2012). The argument is that, in general, practitioners need support and guidance when adapting ESIs to new contexts and populations. Such support must rely on the local knowledge that these practitioners have about the setting that is to host the innovation. Multiple implementation researchers state that intervention developers should provide a foundation for adaptation by identifying what can be modified (e.g., surface structure modifications that are intended to boost engagement and retention) and what should never be modified (e.g., an innovation's core components) as part of their dissemination strategy (Meyers et al., 2012). Approaches have been developed to help resolve the tension between the need for fidelity and adaptation (e.g., Aarons et al., 2012; Lee, Altschul, & Mowbray, 2008), and such guidance can foster adherence to an ESI while also enhancing its fit and relevance to the organization and client group.

Whether applying the common elements approach (resulting in the systematic and planned selection and evaluation of ESPs to suit client needs and service context) or the planned adaptation approach (resulting in the systematic and planned adaptation of the ESI model), it is essential to actively support implementation with specific training and technical assistance (e.g., coaching), fidelity monitoring and support, and organizational and systems change if children and families are to fully benefit from the promise offered by empirically supported approaches.

Frameworks of Implementation

Since the beginning of the twenty-first century, implementation researchers have increased their efforts to describe the process of implementation. These can be descriptions of the main steps involved in implementation and/or more refined conceptual frameworks based on research literature and practical experiences such as theoretical frameworks and conceptual models (Meyers et al., 2012).

Frameworks for implementation are structures that describe the implementation process and include key attributes, facilitators, and challenges related to implementation (Flaspohler, Anderson-Butcher, & Wandersman, 2008). They provide an overview of practices that guide the implementation process and, in some instances, can provide guidance to researchers and practitioners by describing specific steps to include in the planning and/or execution of implementation efforts, as well as pitfalls or mistakes that should be avoided (Meyers et al., 2012).

While there is no agreed upon standard in the field, some efforts have been made to synthesize these approaches to implementation. In one outstanding example, Meyers et al. (2012) conducted a synthesis of 25 implementation frameworks. Frameworks were sought across multiple research and practice areas as opposed to focusing on a specific field (e.g., Damschroder et al., 2009 who focused on the health care field). Only frameworks that described the specific actions and behaviors (i.e., the "how to") that can be utilized to promote high-quality implementation were included in the synthesis. The authors argued that systematically identifying these action-oriented steps served as practical guidance for planning and/or executing implementation efforts. They found that many frameworks divided the process of implementation into several temporal phases, and within these phases there was considerable agreement on the critical elements or activities conducted within each. Their synthesis found 14 elements that could be divided into four distinct temporal phases of implementation.

The first phase, "Initial Considerations Regarding the Host Setting," contains a number of elements, all of which describe work that focused primarily on the ecological fit between the program and/or practice and the host setting. Activities here commonly include assessment strategies related to organizational needs, innovation-organizational fit, capacity or readiness assessment, exploring the need for adaptation of the program or practice and how to do it, obtaining buy-in from key stakeholders and developing a supportive organizational culture, building organizational capacity, identifying or recruiting staff, and conducting some preimplementation training.

The second phase is "Creating a Structure for Implementation." Here the focus of the work can be categorized into two elements: developing a plan for implementation and forming an implementation team that clearly identifies who is responsible for the plan and tasks within it. The third and fourth phases incorporate the actual *doing* of the implementation (whereas, the first two phases focus on *planning* for implementation).

Phase three, "Ongoing Structure Once Implementation Begins," incorporates three elements: technical assistance (including training, coaching, and supervision), monitoring ongoing implementation (process evaluation), and creating supportive feedback mechanisms to ensure all relevant players understand how the implementation process is progressing.

Finally, phase four is "Improving Future Applications." Here the element is identified as learning from experience, which commonly involves retrospective analysis and self-reflection including feedback from the host setting to identify particular strengths or weaknesses that emerge during implementation.

The authors highlighted that many of the frameworks included in the synthesis were based on what had been learned about implementation from practical experience and through staff feedback. There were few instances where studies empirically tested the implementation framework that had been applied and modified based on their findings. What was more common was making modifications to implementation frameworks based on: feedback received from the setting about ineffective and effective strategies, considering what others were beginning to report in the literature, and/or by critical self-reflection about one's effort.

Despite the considerable similarity across frameworks, some researchers have made the point that the development of implementation frameworks is shaped by the service contexts in which they are applied (Aarons et al., 2011). In recognition of this, Aarons and colleagues (2011) developed the only published conceptual model of implementation specifically developed with child welfare settings in mind. Rather than describe the specific actions and behaviors involved in the process of implementation, their model focused on factors that are the most likely to have a strong influence on the implementation of ESIs and ESPs in publicly funded child welfare service settings. The authors identified multiple factors, both within the service setting and outside it, likely to have the greatest potential impact on implementation at each of four different implementation phases, including exploration, adoption/preparation, implementation, and sustainment.

For example, during the exploration phase, factors identified within the inner context included the characteristics of individual adopters. The presence of individual adopters can be an important determinant of whether an agency will or will not explore or make use of ESIs or ESPs (Rogers, 2003). These individuals value innovation, are often seen as innovators and early adopters and often engage in ongoing education, follow the research and professional literature, and have good professional networks (Berwick, 2003; Grol, 2001). However, Aarons et al. (2011) highlight that, compared with disciplines such as medicine, child welfare has only recently started to develop a strong research base for adopters to draw on and discussions of the use of ESIs in child welfare are a relatively recent event (Barth et al., 2005; National Association of Public Child Welfare Administrators [NAPCWA] 2005). An example of an outer context factor (outside the implementation site) that can be observed during the exploration phase and that has an influence on implementation in child welfare service settings might be demands from state legislatures for practice change in response to public concerns over issues in child welfare services (e.g., abuse while in state-mandated out-of-home care).

Other frameworks are similar but do not include specific reference to, or strategies for dealing with, child welfare system settings. These include the framework developed by the National Implementation Research Network (NIRN) (Fixsen et al., 2005) and the Getting to Outcomes (GTO) framework (Chinman, Imm, & Wandersman, 2004; Chinman et al., 2008; Wandersman, 2009; Wandersman, Imm, Chinman, & Kaftarian, 2000). Nevertheless, these frameworks contain elements that may be useful and, as is the case with the widely used NIRN framework, may have greater documentation and detailed actions geared toward helping agencies "implement" an implementation framework. Each of these will be described, in brief, below.

As noted earlier, child welfare services have been slow to implement ESIs (Aarons, Wells, et al., 2009) and even slower to study implementation within a child welfare setting. The seminal synthesis of implementation research literature by the National Implementation Research Network or NIRN (Fixsen et al., 2005) has quickened the pace of child welfare's focus on the importance of implementation to support effective services. NIRN's synthesis examined implementation research published since 1970. The selection criteria that generated 743 articles (of which 377 articles were "significant for implementation") included empirical studies, meta-analyses or literature reviews describing well-designed experimental evaluations of implementation factors, and useful frameworks in any domain. Most of the articles focused on such domains as mental health, education, health, juvenile justice, and others, but very few were related to child welfare settings. The NIRN implementation framework that grew out of this synthesis, however, has been supported by the US Children's Bureau as an effective implementation approach, and Children's Bureau–funded Implementation Centers and National Resources Centers are using it in their work with state and local child welfare agencies to improve the uptake of best practices and ESIs (Blasé, Fixsen, Metz, & Van Dyke, 2009). The NIRN model has yet to be tested empirically in child welfare.

The NIRN framework names six functional stages of implementation: exploration, installation, initial implementation, full implementation, innovation, and sustainability (Fixsen, Blasé, Naoom, & Wallace, 2009). These stages are not linear and mutually influence one another during the implementation process, which may take 2 to 4 years to complete. In their 2005 implementation research synthesis, Fixsen and colleagues noted commonalities among successful implementation programs and identified their core implementation components. Using the NIRN model, we can see that successful implementation of ESIs is driven by workforce development, supported by effective leadership practices and organizational conditions. Workforce development includes recruitment of a pool of applicants who have a realistic understanding of the work of child welfare; a competency-based selection process that ensures the hiring of the right applicant for the ESI practice; practitioner training and coaching to improve staff performance; and a performance assessment process that provides ongoing feedback about staff fidelity to the ESI model. These core implementation components, and others, will be discussed later within the context of what we know from research about their effectiveness.

The Getting to Outcomes Framework (Wandersman et al., 2000, 2009) is a results-based accountability approach for change that has been tested with substance abuse interventions. Tested using a longitudinal, quasi-experimental design, programs using a GTO approach performed better with respect to generating necessary improvements in individual capacity to implement substance abuse interventions with fidelity and, as well, overall program performance was better for intervention group programs than it was for comparison group programs (Chinman et al., 2008). The GTO framework uses a 10-step accountability approach to build capacity at the individual and program levels for effective prevention practices. Basically, GTO builds capacity through a series of ten questions that program implementers must address in order to achieve successful implementation (Chinman et al., 2008). These questions are linked to specific steps in the GTO process: questions 1 to 6 are the planning steps; questions 7 and 8 are the process and outcome evaluation steps; and questions 9 to 10 are the steps of using data to improve and sustain programs.

While not developed in a child welfare setting, the Getting to Outcomes (GTO) framework was applied to the selection, adoption, and implementation of solution based casework (SBC), a comprehensive casework practice model in a public child welfare agency that has a growing evidence base (Antle, Barbee, Christensen, & Sullivan, 2010; Antle, Barbee, Sullivan, & Christensen, 2008; Barbee, Christensen, Antle, Wandersman, & Cahn, 2011). GTO questions were applied to the implementation of SBC as summarized here:

1. *What are the underlying needs and conditions that must be addressed by the casework practice model?* Typically, child welfare agencies identify needs that arise from data or reports—and sometimes lawsuits—that highlight some failure in

their attempts to provide for the safety, permanency, or well-being of children that come into contact with their system. This provides the motivation to find more effective ways to practice.

2. *What are the goals and objectives that, if realized, will address the needs and change the underlying conditions?* This planning step helps the agency to specifically identify how the future will be different if they are successful.

3. *Which evidence-informed casework practice model can be used to reach agency goals?* At this step, consultants and university partners can help state agencies choose which casework practice model is best for the state and the workforce that the state can afford.

4. *What actions need to be taken so that the selected program, practice, or set of interventions fits our child welfare agency?* Many aspects of fit are at play during this step, including leadership support, need for infrastructure changes to facilitate the new practice, and training of providers.

5. *What organizational capacities are needed to implement the program?* Assessing organizational capacity for change occurs in two areas: the human capacity (finding champions for the change and assessing staff clinical skills); and the organizational facilitators of and barriers to change.

6. *What is the plan for this program?* At this step, the SBC implementation team developed a plan for training the practice model across the system, as well as a plan for the infrastructure changes needed to support the new practice (e.g., financial and personnel resources, relevant policies and procedures, computer system upgrades, changes in the Continuous Quality Improvement/Quality Assurance or CQI/QA tool, work load changes).

7. *How will the quality of program implementation be assessed?* The question refers to the need to ensure that a process evaluation takes place while the practice model is piloted and implemented across the system. A process evaluation, among other questions, will help to answer whether the practice model is being implemented as it was intended and with fidelity or not, as well as pointing out who adheres to the practice model and who does not.

8. *How well did the program work?* This question refers to an outcome evaluation that can help to answer whether or not the practice model created significant positive changes for children, youth, and families in the child welfare system.

9. *How will CQI strategies be incorporated?* Continuous quality improvement activities, consisting of focus groups, case reviews, and others, enable the agency to examine how adherence to the practice model can be improved.

10. *If the program is successful, how will it be sustained?* In an environment where child welfare leaders typically stay in their jobs for an average of only two years, there need to be short-, medium-, and long-term plans for institutionalizing the practice model.

While these multiphase implementation frameworks and conceptual models, and the elements within these, provide guidance for understanding and navigating the implementation process, to the best of our knowledge there is only one comprehensive tool designed to document progress through implementation stages using a focused, observation-based measure of key milestone attainment. The Stages of Implementation Completion (SIC), developed by Chamberlain, Brown, and Saldana (2011), was developed to measure the progression through the implementation stages of an ESI being rolled out in the context of a randomized controlled trial. Although it is in the early stages of development, process-based measures of implementation phases, such as the SIC, can be useful to implementation researchers and those doing implementation work in order to assess and compare implementation efforts in terms of current status, progression, attaining milestones within each phase, and the speed with which each phase is completed. Process-based measures could also be developed in relation to the effectiveness of an implementation process and the outcomes of implementation (Proctor et al., 2009).

Critical Components of Implementation

As mentioned previously, most research on implementation has not focused on use of implementation frameworks mentioned or described above but instead examine the specific factors that influence the overall success of implementation. These include barriers and challenges inherent in the implementation process as well as factors within the context that have an impact on the degree to which effective implementation is achieved (e.g., Aarons et al., 2011). Despite this shortcoming, several studies have examined the specific steps or components identified within these implementation frameworks. These fundamental features can be referred to as elements or critical components necessary for quality implementation and, although there is substantial agreement about what these critical components might be, concrete research evidence about their effectiveness varies (Fixsen et al., 2009) and is discussed extensively in other reviews (Durlak & Dupre, 2008; Fixsen et al., 2005, Greenhalgh et al., 2004). This section will focus on describing only those critical components that have the strongest evidence in child welfare settings. These are: staff recruitment and selection, training and ongoing technical assistance, and use of ongoing fidelity monitoring with staff evaluation.

STAFF RECRUITMENT AND SELECTION

A competent and committed workforce has been identified as a major driver of effective implementation of ESIs and ESPs (Fixsen et al., 2005), and targeted recruitment and competency-based selection of staff are critical components for making sure the right staff are hired who can implement ESIs and ESPs well (Dickinson & Comstock, 2009). Although staff recruitment and selection has been identified as critical to effective implementation in both the Quality Implementation Framework (QIF) (Meyers et al., 2012) and NIRN implementation frameworks, these practices have rarely been the focus of implementation research. However, what is known from research about recruitment and selection can make important contributions to successful implementation.

Realistic Recruitment

The term *realistic recruitment* describes a process that presents accurate information to potential applicants about the real nature of a job and the organization through a variety of techniques, including the use of recruiters from inside the agency who can realistically describe the job (Wanous, 1992) and realistic job preview videos of unscripted interviews with child welfare workers (Faller et al., 2009). In a summary of 12 studies, job retention was 24% higher for employees who had been recruited using inside sources, compared with those who applied through job advertisements, job fairs, and other impersonal sources (Wanous, 1992). Rather than selling the organization, realistic recruitment presents outsiders with all pertinent information about the work without distortion.

In his recruitment research review, Wanous (1992) describes a number of ways in which realistic recruitment (i.e., telling it like it is) can lead to the retention of staff.

1. *Vaccination*. Realistic expectations can reduce on-the-job disappointment, which often leads to turnover (Faller et al., 2009);
2. *Self-selection*. Realistic information allows applicants to make an informed choice about whether they are suited for the job;
3. *Personal commitment*. Making a realistic choice to take a job without coercion or misrepresentation facilitates greater personal commitment to the job.

The characteristics of applicants who are recruited through such realistic strategies tend to include high levels of self-efficacy, good coping skills, and strong commitment, and these are among the descriptors of workers shown by research to be attracted to child welfare positions and, once hired, most likely to remain in their jobs (Dickinson & Painter, 2011; Ellett, 2000). Durlak and DuPre (2008) also document, in their review described earlier, that self-efficacy is one of four provider characteristics most consistently related to successful implementation (along with perceptions related to the need for, and potential benefits of, the innovation and skill proficiency). As Meyers and his colleagues (2012) note, providers who are recruited to implement ESIs, can develop skill proficiency through training and ongoing support, but the necessary characteristics, attitudes, and attributes that are not amenable to training should be the focus of recruitment and selection activities.

Competency-Based Selection

When an applicant has a clear understanding of the nature of the job for which he or she is applying and chooses to continue with the application, the selection process must focus on hiring the applicant whose characteristics, attitudes, and competencies fit the requirements of the job. Education is one characteristic that has been found to be important under certain conditions. Findings from a meta-analysis of research in business and an analysis of the Nurse-Family Partnership prevention program (Fixsen et al., 2005) support the importance of education and background in practitioner selection. In child welfare, Barbee and her colleagues (2011) refer to their earlier research (Barbee, Antle, Sullivan, Huebner, & Fox, 2009) in calling on agencies to hire MSWs or BSWs with special training in child welfare for front-line and supervisory positions in implementing a practice model that requires complex clinical skills, such as SBC. Other provider characteristics related to successful implementation include openness to change (Barbee et al., 2011), openness to ESIs and ESPs (Aarons, 2004), flexibility, and congruence with agency values and mission (Aarons et al., 2011; Cahn, 2003). Durlak and DuPre (2008) also document that four provider characteristics most consistently related to effective implementation of ESIs and ESPs are self-efficacy, perceptions related to the need for and potential benefits of the innovation, and skill proficiency. Providers with these characteristics are more likely to implement a program or practices at higher levels of fidelity.

The criteria for selecting practitioners should be determined from job analyses that clarify job tasks and expectations, minimum practitioner qualifications, and the knowledge, skills, abilities, and competencies that are important to achieve ESI and ESP outcomes (Bernotavicz, 2008). There is general agreement about the value of selecting practitioners based on generic competencies in the behavioral health field, including assessment, engagement, and interpersonal skills (Bernotavicz & Locke, 2000; Fixsen et al., 2005), and these form the basis of a competency-based selection approach in which each competency is assessed during the interview process through two or more selection components. Selection components typically include a structured interview of questions that measure knowledge and attitudes required by the job, direct observation and assessment of skills in behavioral vignettes or responses to role-play situations, and a written work sample test that approximates a job task that the candidate will be expected to perform (in child welfare the applicant may be asked to read and write an analysis of a typical child welfare case) (Bernotavicz & Locke, 2000; Fixsen et al., 2005). One of few studies on the effectiveness of a staff selection process, described by Fixsen and his colleagues (2005), analyzed the relationship between selection factors and later job performance for married applicants for teaching parents in a teaching-family program (Maloney et al., 1983). Results showed that couples that were hired had higher scores on the selection process than those that were not hired. Hired couples with higher levels of performance on the job 3 to 5 months later also had significantly higher scores on the behavioral vignettes during their interviews and stayed longer on the job than lower performing couples.

STAFF TRAINING AND ONGOING TECHNICAL SUPPORT

The critical components of training and ongoing technical assistance have the strongest empirical support compared to the other components commonly included in implementation frameworks (Fixsen et al. 2005; Wandersman, Chien, & Katz, 2012). All of the implementation frameworks discussed in this chapter highlight the critical importance of preparing staff at multiple levels of the organization for implementation of ESIs or ESPs. While preparation of front-line staff who will deliver the new practices receive the most attention and study, some researchers (e.g. Barbee et al., 2011) speak to the need to train leaders (including community partners) across a state or region on the principles, theories, and general practices of the new model and to train front-line supervisors at a deeper level in order to ensure that they can provide coaching and support to workers in the new practice. While these approaches make intuitive sense, this kind of "dosage" approach to training has not yet been evaluated.

What has been studied more comprehensively is the impact of the components of the training process on practitioner skill development. Research reviews of findings from a variety of disciplines (Fixsen et al., 2005; Grimshaw et al., 2001; Hoge & Morris, 2004; Lyon, Stirman, Kerns, & Burns, 2011) conclude strongly and consistently that single-exposure training models are ineffective methods for producing changes in practitioner skills. Classroom-based training workshops have traditionally been the most widely used method of training. Largely didactic, these trainings can increase knowledge about the intervention in the short run (Sholomskas et al., 2005), but knowledge gained does not last nor does it result in sustained behavior change (Miller, Yahne, Moyers, Martinez, & Pirritano, 2004).

The challenge is to determine which training methods are effective in changing practice behaviors, and a number of rigorous studies have done just that. For example, Miller and his colleagues (2004) conducted a randomized controlled trial evaluating the effectiveness of a motivational interviewing (MI) training workshop and the added value of two training enhancements (feedback and coaching) for helping substance abuse clinicians learn the clinical method of MI. MI proficiency was evaluated from practice samples obtained before and immediately following training and then later at 4, 8, and 12 months. A total of 140 health professionals (counselors, psychologists, social workers, nurses, and physicians) who regularly treated substance abuse disorders were assigned at random to one of five treatment conditions. The 2-day workshop only condition had a format that was about half didactic and demonstration and half direct practice of skills. Participants were observed and coached by the trainers during the trainings but received nothing else until 8 months post training, when they were given feedback on practice tapes. The workshop plus coaching group participated in up to six individual coaching sessions by telephone with an expert training in MI over the course of four months. This group also received personal feedback after the 8-month follow-up. The workshop plus feedback group got personal feedback on their practice tapes throughout the trial and, after 8 months, participants received up to six coaching sessions. The final intervention group—the workshop plus feedback and coaching group—received all interventions. The self-training control group only received a manual and training videotapes and were instructed to learn the method on their own. Results showed that the 2-day workshop resulted in greater learning than the self-training group. Furthermore, the results showed that either feedback or coaching improved MI proficiency over that gained from the workshop. Only the groups that received feedback or coaching (or both) reached the level of proficiency that the authors concluded was required to provide MI within clinical settings, with the largest gains shown on some measures by participants who received both feedback and coaching.

Another example is Chaffin and colleagues (Chaffin, Hecht, Bard, Silovsky, & Beasley, 2012) who conducted a rigorous 2 × 2 study (ESI vs. service as usual × coaching vs. uncoached implementation support) targeted at parents identified for child maltreatment (N = 2,175). Relevant to this chapter, the researchers looked at the effect of coaching on practitioners' use of an intervention on intervention outcomes. They compared Child Protection Services recidivism outcomes between an ESI home visiting model for child neglect known as SafeCare and a comparable home-based service across two types of implementation support strategies: one in which practitioners where coached to improve their implementation and one in which practitioners delivered services without coaching support. Significant effects, in favor of the SafeCare model, were found across both coached and uncoached implementation support models. The results, though, showed that larger effects were seen among participants that best matched the inclusion criteria for SafeCare and, importantly, parents were more likely to show gains from the combination of coaching and SafeCare than SafeCare alone if they fell outside the regular inclusion criteria for the intervention. The researchers concluded that coaching as an implementation support strategy for the SafeCare model may not be necessary for all practitioners in all cases. However, they hypothesized that the provision of coaching may be important when working with a more heterogeneous group that falls outside the standard inclusion criteria.

Several meta-analyses and reviews of training effectiveness support variations of the approaches mentioned above including training that focuses on both cognitive and interpersonal skills and tasks (Wandersman et al., 2008); training that presents information, provides demonstrations, and allows opportunities for behavioral rehearsal (Fixsen et al., 2005); training that includes modeling, role-playing, and performance feedback offered in a supportive emotional atmosphere (Durlak & Dupre, 2008); and training that includes presentation of theory, modeling or demonstration of the skill, practice under simulated conditions, and structured feedback (Joyce & Showers, 1980). In their model for skills-based classroom training, Berdie, Leake, and Parry (2010) draw on adult learning models to propose six steps in an effective training approach: (1) explain and discuss; (2) demonstrate/model and discuss; (3) practice; (4) feedback; (5) discussion of transfer of learning implications; (6) embedded evaluation to determine the degree to which trainees are learning the skills taught in the training. Using foundational approaches such as follow-up coaching, technical assistance, and feedback is bound to be more fruitful.

Finally, in a very useful summary of the training research area, Lyon and colleagues (2011) conducted an interdisciplinary literature review to identify useful training and support approaches with the aim of identifying strategies that facilitate the successful training of mental health practitioners in ESIs. Again, they found that single-exposure training models and simple provision of information were reinforced as ineffective training methods. Rather, continued consultation and support following training workshops, congruence between training content and practitioner experience, and a focus on provider motivation were found to be important. Six empirically supported training approaches were described (academic detailing, interprofessional education, problem-based learning, coaching, reminders, and self-regulated learning) along with training techniques associated with each approach and the associated research on their effectiveness. Nine techniques (interactive didactics, goal identification, small group discussion, critical thinking, self-reflection, peer collaboration, independent access to information, direct feedback, and follow-up) were shared by at least two of the selected training approaches. The authors noted that in a classic review of the training literature (Oxman, Thomson, Davis, & Haynes, 1995) the effects of training approaches increase when they are used in combination rather than alone, a finding similar to more recent evidence that a combination of training and supportive technical assistance enhances learning outcomes (Miller et al., 2004). Importantly, the researchers concluded that, even with mounting evidence to support the use of various training approaches, the challenge becomes knowing which approaches should be considered when developing a training and workforce development plan. They note that the lack of comparisons between approaches limits conclusions that can be drawn as to the most effective model and that future research should focus on systematically comparing different approaches.

FIDELITY AND STAFF EVALUATION

This section briefly handles two important, but connected, critical components identified in all implementation frameworks discussed or mentioned above. First, intervention fidelity—although there is a degree of variation in the child welfare and related fields as to the definition of fidelity, in general fidelity refers to the assessment of practitioner adherence and competence when delivering ESIs or ESPs (Schoenwald et al, 2010). Adherence refers to the extent to which the programs and practices implemented both within a single session (e.g., planned content delivered using the specified techniques to deliver it) and within the service as a whole (e.g., number of sessions delivered, frequency of sessions, and method of supervision) match the intentions of the program developers (Aarons et al., 2012). Competence refers to the practitioner's skills used to deliver the program or practices (Aarons et al., 2012). Staff evaluation refers to the degree to which practitioners, supervisors, and the organization are prepared to and actually deliver the ESIs or ESPs (Fixsen et al., 2005). Both concepts are interlinked. That is, fidelity data can be used as one way to monitor and provide feedback on staff performance.

Importantly, the way in which fidelity monitoring and staff evaluation activities are conducted may also be important. For example, Aarons, Sommerfeld, Hecht, et al. (2009) conducted a randomized control trial testing the impact on worker retention of supervisory fidelity monitoring of practitioners providing SafeCare. Workers were less likely to leave their job if they received consultative supervision during the fidelity monitoring process rather than no supervisory monitoring or administrative monitoring that focused more on corrective action. This finding of increased retention is likely related to an observed reduction in the level of exhaustion found among staff employing an ESP as opposed to treatment as usual (Aarons, Sommerfeld, Hecht, et al. 2009).

Model developers and researchers tend to focus on model fidelity. In order to truly evaluate whether a service or program works when delivered, model fidelity must be high. Fixsen and colleagues (2005) connect staff evaluation with fidelity and discuss the measures of both as they pertain to factors that must be in place for a program or practice to operate (context), the extent to which providers use core intervention components in their practice (compliance), and level of provider skills in delivering the ESI (competence). Fidelity measures are usually derived from the overall mission, goals, and implementation plans of the ESI or ESP. In their implementation research synthesis, Fixsen et al. (2005) give examples of different types of fidelity measures across several programs for each of these three factors (context, compliance, and competence). Using the example of the teaching-family model, they describe practitioner-family ratios and practitioner training and coaching as measures of context; the completion of treatment plans and all paperwork as measures of compliance; and observations of how well the teaching-family trained practitioners engage family members in the process of the program and provide specific and useful feedback as measures of competence.

Staff evaluation measures not only examine the degree to which providers are prepared to and actually deliver effective ESIs but some also measure the impact of the practitioner's delivery of the intervention on recipients of the ESI. The multisystemic therapy (MST) program, for example, evaluates provider adherence to MST via monthly telephone calls with parents who rate the practitioner on 27 items (Schoenwald et al., 2000). Henggeler, Melton, Brondino, Scherer, and Hanley (1997) found that parent ratings indicating high practitioner fidelity to the program model during treatment were associated with better delinquency outcomes for youth. This finding (that ESIs delivered with higher fidelity produce better outcomes for consumers) resonates across many programs (Fixsen et al., 2005).

Numerous primary studies and reviews of research use information on fidelity as both a measure of implementation and as a predictor of intervention outcomes. These studies show that ESIs implemented with high fidelity produce better outcomes for the children and families who receive them compared with those who receive ESIs implemented with low fidelity (e.g., Durlak and DuPre, 2008; Felner et al., 2001; Forthman, Wooster, Hill, Homa-Lowry, & DesHarnais, 2003; Henggeler et al., 1997; Henggeler, Pickrel, & Brondino, 1999; Kirigin, Braukmann, Atwater, & Wolf, 1982; Kutash, Duchnowski, Sumi, Rudo, & Harris, 2002). Studies have also documented how early monitoring of implementation through the measurement of fidelity can identify practitioners who are having difficulties implementing the program as planned, and that subsequent retraining and assistance can lead to dramatic improvements in implementation (Durlak & DuPre, 2008; Fixsen et al., 2005; Greenwood et al., 2003).

SUMMARY

While some research support exists in varying degrees for each of the steps outlined in the implementation frameworks discussed here, the strength of the evidence for each is variable and, so far, the strongest empirical support appears to be related to training and ongoing technical assistance. These, and to a lesser known extent, some of the activities commonly named in implementation frameworks as critical components in achieving high-quality implementation are likely essential for changing the behavior of practitioners and other personnel who are key providers of ESIs and ESPs within organizations (Fixsen et al., 2009). However, these components do not exist in isolation. They are contained within and supported by systems within organizations. Another component, while less studied, may also be crucial. Referred to by Fixsen et al. (2005) as facilitative administration and clearly stressed by others (e.g., Aarons et al., 2011), putting in place or changing processes and procedures needed to facilitate the introduction and continued use of the other implementation components (e.g., ensuring that human resource policies allow for appropriate staff selection and promote retention) and ensuring that systems outside an organization support successful implementation (e.g., necessary funding is available; relationships with other stakeholders, particularly those on the referral pathway, are developed and maintained) are necessary if implementation is to be successful. These represent the inner and outer systems—those procedures and processes that can help or hinder effective planning and installation of strategies that are more likely to lead to effective staff selection, training, coaching, and evaluation of the performance of practitioners and other key staff members; ensure that program evaluation functions are used to guide decision-making; and intervene in external systems to assure the flow of ongoing resources and support for practice change within organizations.

Conclusion

Although considerable effort and progress have been made in promoting the dissemination and adoption of ESIs and ESPs in recent times, what is known about what it takes to fully implement these at sufficiently high quality has been limited. To maximize the benefits of ESIs and ESPs for the children and families being supported by the child welfare system, the ESIs and ESPs themselves need to be effectively and fully implemented. To achieve this we need to pay attention not only to the "what" (programs and practice), but also to the "how" (the implementation frameworks and essential components being applied). Supportive organizational systems and structures are as likely to be critical for achieving outcomes as the empirical evidence of the effectiveness of the programs and practices themselves. An organization decides to proceed with implementation, selects and hires/reassigns practitioners and supervisors with the aim of improving the fit between the knowledge and skills required to deliver the ESIs or ESPs and those held by staff; determines the optimum training and coaching/consultation model to build staff skills to implement the ESI or ESPs; institutes ongoing fidelity and staff evaluation measures that serve as ongoing appraisals of implementation progress; realigns facilitative administrative procedures and policies to support implementation of the ESI or ESPs; and works with external systems to assure adequate financing and support. The thoughtful and diligent application of the key implementation components highlighted here can, ultimately, be the difference between improved outcomes for vulnerable children and families and the provision of services with little effect.

The Question Drives the Method

DIFFERENT TYPES OF EVIDENCE AND THEIR USE

6

POVERTY AND THE BLACK/WHITE PLACEMENT GAP

Using Context to Understand the Role of Evidence-Based Interventions

Fred Wulczyn, Bridgette Lery, and Lonnie Snowden

Introduction

Although the emphasis on evidence-based interventions represents a major step toward improving child protection systems, there are other equally important decisions to be made if we expect to use evidence-based child welfare services as a way to reduce the exposure to and consequences of child maltreatment. Among those questions, where and when to invest in services are especially important, context-sensitive questions. Although reform-minded policymakers often see problems in systemic, one size fits all, in reality the next dollar spent on system improvements may yield substantially different benefits, depending on what is true in any given jurisdiction relative to other jurisdictions.

In this chapter, we illustrate how paying closer attention to context could shape decisions about where and when to implement evidence-based interventions. As an example, we consider the Black/White placement gap and ask whether information about where the gap is the greatest should influence how the field thinks about investing in efforts to reduce the gap. Underlying the question is an assumption that context-related variation in service use offers clues about where and when to invest in services.

The Black/White placement gap refers to the fact that when the rate of placement into foster care for Black children is compared to the rate for White children living in the same area, the Black placement rate is almost always higher than the rate for Whites. Evidence suggests that the gap is quite large, with Black children entering placement at an average rate that is 2.7 times greater than the average rate for Whites (Wulczyn & Lery, 2007). Reducing the placement gap, all else being equal, will lower the overrepresentation of Blacks in the foster care system.

Explanations as to why Black children use more foster care tend to focus on differing needs, racial bias, and policy effects (Fluke et al., 2010; Hines, Lee, Osterling, & Drabble, 2007; Osterling, D'Andrade, & Austin, 2008), a framework that mimics how the Institute of Medicine differentiates the sources of health disparities (Smedley et al., 2003). On nearly all measures of risk—poverty, family structure, unemployment, and adult education levels—Blacks face significantly higher risks. Maltreatment is the main entry point into the child welfare system, and there is a significant body of research pointing to higher rates of maltreatment among Blacks (Drake & Jonson-Reid, 2010; Drake, Lee, & Jonson-Reid, 2008; Sedlak, McPherson, & Das, 2010). Research also suggests that, along the various decision points that determine whether a child will be placed (i.e., investigation, disposition, and service choice), Blacks have a greater likelihood of moving forward in the system than either Hispanics or Whites (Needell, Brookhart, & Lee, 2003; Rivaux et al., 2008), perhaps because they are less likely to be offered in-home services (GAO, 2007; Marts, Lee, McRoy, & McCroskey, 2008).

Despite the substantial body of research that has already been done, there has been very little research focused on whether the gap varies from place to place and whether places with large gaps share other attributes in common. From an investment in equity perspective, the failure to recognize how much and why the gap varies probably reduces the likelihood that anyone intervention will be properly targeted. To address this shortcoming in the literature, we examine the magnitude of placement gap with respect to poverty and then consider whether the evidence offers any clues as to where investments designed to reduce placement disparity offer the greatest potential return.

Present Study

In the simplest possible terms, we are interested in understanding whether places—in this case, counties—with above average poverty rates have an above average Black/White placement gap. In the context of dissemination and implementation, we are interested in whether the results say anything about where one might focus efforts to reduce disparity. Underlying the analysis is an assumption that investments (i.e., policies and practices tied to evidence-based interventions) designed to reduce disparity should treat places differently depending on the magnitude of the problem.

We frame our question and subsequent analysis around three dependent variables: Black child placements per 1,000 Black children, White child placements per 1,000 White children, and the Black/White placement gap, which is defined as the ratio of the White placement rate to the Black placement rate. The Black/White placement gap so defined is also known as the disparity ratio or disparity rate (Braveman, 2006).[1] Formally, the three dependent variables are:

(1) Black placement rate = Number of Black children placed/
(Number of Black children/1,000)

(2) White placement rate = Number of White children placed/
(Number of White children/1,000)

(3) Black/White gap = Black placement rate/White placement rate

INDEPENDENT VARIABLE: CHILD POVERTY

Our principal independent variable is poverty, which is measured at the macrostructural or ecological level. We operationalize poverty as the proportion of children living in families with incomes below the poverty line. We elected to use child poverty rates because they come closest to describing the circumstances in which children find themselves. That is, some families in poverty do not have children and children live in families with diverse structures regardless of income level.

Per Wilson (1987), Sampson and Wilson (1995), and Ousey (1999), poverty is disaggregated by race to account for the differential variability in race-specific levels of poverty. Specifically, poverty rates measured at the areal unit level (e.g., census tract, zip code, county, or state) are higher for Blacks than for Whites, and Black poverty rates exhibit much greater variability overall. Disaggregating both the independent and dependent variables by race allows for a more nuanced understanding of how race, poverty, and placement into out-of-home care interact.

STATISTICAL METHODS

We use a multilevel, random effects Poisson event count model to study the Black/White gap (Gibbons, Hur, Bhaumik, & Bell, 2007; Osgood, 2000; Raudenbush & Bryk, 2002). The basic count model is of the following form. If Y_j is the number of placements in county j and m_j is the number of children living in the county (i.e., exposure), then the expected number of placements is:

$$E(Y_j \mid \lambda_j) = m_j \lambda_j.$$

---

[1] We use the terms *Black/White placement gap* and *placement disparity* interchangeably.

The log link $\eta_j = \log(\lambda_j)$ provides a fixed effect model for estimating the county placement rate:

$$\eta_j = \beta_{oj}.$$

The unconditional level-two model, with a random effect, is:

$$\beta_{oj} = \gamma_{oo} + \mu_{oj}.$$

The mixed model is:

$$\eta_{ij} = \gamma_{oo} + \mu_{oj}.$$

The random effect model adjusts for the fact that small counties and/or counties with small event counts provide less reliable estimates of the true placement rate (Osgood, 2000).

Without the random effect, the expected number of events is simply:

$$\eta_{ij} = \gamma_{oo}.$$

With respect to the counts of placements, we show empirically that an unconditional fixed effect estimate of η_{ij} is equivalent to the weighted placement rate.

SAMPLE COUNTIES

The sample used for the study consists of all 822 counties from a diverse group of 16 states. Data include a count of all children placed for the first time, by county. Children are included in the count if they were below the age of 18 at the time of their first ever admission. The count of children includes children admitted for reasons of abuse, neglect, or dependency; juvenile delinquents, to the extent they are counted as part of a state's foster care population, were excluded. To preserve the relevance of the census data, only children admitted in 2000 were counted. Using the 2000 census files, we selected the number of children under the age of 18, the percent of children living in families with incomes below the 1999 poverty line, and data corresponding to the four measures described above.

RESEARCH QUESTIONS

In our study, the Black/White placement gap is treated as the *dependent* variable. Among the counties in our sample, the Black/White placement gap ranges from less than 1 (i.e., Whites are more likely to enter care) to better than 20 to 1. We want to understand whether the gap is correlated with poverty rates.

Because the Black/White placement gap is a function of the Black admission rate relative to the comparable White rate, we start the analysis by considering the Black placement rate, the White placement rate, and the relationship between the two race-specific rates of placement and race-specific poverty rates. In summary form, the questions (and the corresponding Table/Model number) are:

1. What is the Black child placement rate (Table 6.2, Model 2)?
   a. How is White child poverty related to the Black child placement rate? (Table 6.4, Model 9)?
   b. How is Black child poverty related to the Black child placement rate (Table 6.4, Model 10)?
2. What is the White child placement rate (Table 6.2, Model 3)?
   a. How is White child poverty related to the White child placement rate (Table 6.4, Model 11)?
   b. How is Black child poverty related to the White child placement rate (Table 6.4, Model 12)?

We then take up the question of whether the Black/White placement gap is correlated with poverty. The answer to this question is built around a simple model: whether the Black/White gap in county (j) is a function of its poverty rate. With this model, described in greater detail in the results section, we answer three additional questions:

3. What is the Black/White placement gap? (Table 6.2, Model 5)
   a. How is poverty related to the gap (Table 6.5, Model 13)?
   b. How is White child poverty related to the gap (Table 6.5, Model 14)?
   c. How is Black child poverty related to the gap (Table 6.5, Model 15)?

Results

The results are presented in two sections. We start with univariate and bivariate descriptions of the counties. We do this to pinpoint the Black and White child placement rates and the placement gap. We show both weighted and unweighted measures. In the subsequent section, we connect these rates to the Poisson model. Then, in the second section, we examine the core research question: In what way is poverty related to the Black/White placement gap?

PLACEMENT RATES AND COUNTY SOCIAL DEMOGRAPHICS

Table 6.1 presents the basic county data used in the analysis. In the sampled counties, there were slightly more than 21.3 million resident children in 2000. Of those, 4.6 million were Black (21%). There were 45,617 total admissions and 20,959 Black admissions to foster care. The average county placement was 5.98 per 1,000 children; the rate for Black children and White children was 10.04 and 1.92 respectively. The unweighted disparity ratio was 5.24. The weighted rates sum the counts without regard to county (i.e., the total number of Black children and the total number of Black children placed). The weighted

TABLE 6.1

NUMBER OF CHILDREN, NUMBER OF PLACEMENTS, AND DISPARITY RATIOS BY
URBAN/RURAL: 2000

Feature	Number	Feature	Number
Children	21,328,016	Ave. of county placement rates	5.98
Black	4,600,106	Black	10.04
White	16,727,910	White	1.92
		Disparity Ratio	5.24
Children placed	45,617		
Black	20,959	County placement rate (weighted)	2.14
White	24,658	Black	4.56
		White	1.47
Total counties	822	Disparity ratio	3.09

	Mean	S.D.	Min.	Max
Child Poverty	17.2%	8.4%	2.3%	56.8%
Black	32.5%	19.7%	0.0%	100.0%
White	11.9%	5.7%	1.8%	40.7%

rates remove the influence of the small number of counties with relatively few Black children but large placement rates. Overall, there were 4.56 placements per 1,000 Black children and 1.47 placements per 1,000 White children. The ratio of the two rates yields a Black/White placement gap of 3.09 for this sample of counties.

Predictably, counties also differ with respect to poverty rates. For example, one-third of Black children were living in families with incomes below the poverty line. The comparable figure for White children was 11.9%. The standard deviation for Black poverty is 19.7%, but only 5.7% for Whites.

BLACK CHILD AND WHITE CHILD PLACEMENT RATES

We start with three basic models, each of which illustrates how the fixed effect Poisson count model reproduces the weighted placement rates in Table 6.1. The first model shows the expected number of placements is equal to the event rate times the exposure, which is denominated per 1,000 children. The second and third models show the same results for Blacks and for Whites. The key results in Table 6.2 (and the other tables) are found in the shaded column labeled event rate ratio, which is the exponentiated coefficient from the column to the left of the shaded column.

Model 1 says that the expected event rate (ratio) is equal to the weighted average event rate (or grand mean placement rate). In Table 6.1, the weighted average placement rate was 2.14; the corresponding event rate in Table 6.3 is 2.139, which is identical but for the fact that the data in Table 6.1 were rounded. The Black and White placement rates are

TABLE 6.2

PARAMETER ESTIMATES FOR THE OVERALL PLACEMENT RATE, THE BLACK
PLACEMENT RATE, AND THE WHITE PLACEMENT RATE

Model No./Model Specification	Parameter	Coeff.	Event Rate Ratio	Confidence Interval	St. error	t-ratio	p-value
1 $\eta_{ij} = \gamma_{00}$ Placement rate	γ_{00}	0.760	2.139	(2.119, 2.159)	0.052	14.59	<0.001
2 $\eta_{ij} = \gamma_{10}{}^*BL_{ij}$ Black rate	γ_{10}	1.516	4.556	(4.495, 4.618)	0.072	20.95	<0.001
3 $\eta_{ij} = \gamma_{10}{}^*WH_{ij}$ White rate	γ_{10}	0.388	1.474	(1.456, 1.493)	0.049	7.98	<0.001
4 $\eta_{ij} = \gamma_{10}{}^*BL_{ij} +$ $\gamma_{20}{}^*WH_{ij}$ Bl. rate	γ_{10}	1.516	4.556	(4.495, 4.618)	0.024	26.35	<0.001
White rate	γ_{20}	0.388	1.474	(1.456, 1.493)	0.361	3.77	<0.001
5 $\eta_{ij} = \gamma_{00} + \gamma_{10}{}^*BL_{ij}$ White. rate	γ_{00}	0.388	1.474	(1.456, 1.493)	0.057	33.51	<0.001
Black/White gap	γ_{10}	1.128	3.091	(3.034, 3.148)	0.009	120.11	<0.001

also found in Table 6.3. Model 2 reports the Black placement rate in 2000 was 4.556 per 1,000 and the White placement rate was 1.474 per 1,000 White children. Both figures match those in Table 6.1, with rounding.

Model 4 incorporates parameter estimates for both the Black and White placement rates, which is accomplished by dropping the intercept (γ_{00}) from the model specification.

TABLE 6.3

PARAMETER ESTIMATES FOR THE OVERALL PLACEMENT RATE AND THE EFFECT
OF POVERTY, WHITE POVERTY, AND BLACK POVERTY ON PLACEMENT RATES

Model No./Model Specification	Parameter	Coeff.	Event Rate Ratio	Confidence Interval	St. error	t-ratio	p-value
6 $\eta_{ij} = \gamma_{00} + \gamma_{10}{}^*CP_j + \mu_{oj}$							
Placement rate	γ_{00}	0.635	1.887	(1.800, 1.978)	0.05	10.27	<0.001
Poverty	γ_{10}	1.364	3.911	(1.924, 7.952)	0.29	4.92	<0.001
7 $\eta_{ij} = \gamma_{00} + \gamma_{10}{}^*CPW_j + \mu_{oj}$							
Placement rate	γ_{00}	0.642	1.900	(1.816, 1.988)	0.02	27.86	<0.001
White poverty	γ_{10}	3.539	34.435	(14.468, 81.960)	0.44	8.01	<0.001
8 $\eta_{ij} = \gamma_{00} + \gamma_{10}{}^*CPB_j + \mu_{oj}$							
Placement rate	γ_{00}	0.627	1.872	(1.785, 1.963)	0.02	25.81	<0.001
Black poverty	γ_{10}	0.413	1.512	(1.166, 1.960)	0.13	3.13	0.002

The results are identical to Models 2 and 3, which report the Black and White rates separately. Note as well that the event rate ratio for Blacks (4.556) divided by the event rate for Whites (1.474) is 3.09, which is the overall placement gap reported in Table 6.1. Finally, note that in Model 5, the parameterization includes the White placement rate (γ_{00}) and a direct measure of the Black/White gap (γ_{10}), which is 3.09 and identical to the weighted gap reported in Table 6.1. In subsequent models, our interest is in how the level-one fixed effects— γ_{00} and γ_{10}—change with the addition of random effects at level two of the multilevel model.

POVERTY AND PLACEMENT RATES

The results in Table 6.3 show the relationship between poverty and the overall placement rate. In Model 6, γ_{00} is the placement rate for counties with an average poverty rate and γ_{01} is the effect associated with poverty.[2] The data show that counties with higher poverty rates have much higher placement rates, as expected. The coefficient (γ_{01}) in Models 7 and 8 suggests that the impact of poverty found in model 6 is largely a function of the relationship between White child poverty and placement as opposed to Black child poverty and placement. Specifically, the slope describing the relationship between Black child poverty and the overall placement rate (1.51208), while positive, is not as steep as the slope for White child poverty (34.435).

The association between race-specific poverty rates and race-specific placement rates are displayed in Table 6.4. In these models, γ_{10} refers to the Black placement rate (Models 9 and 10) or the White placement rate (Models 11 and 12), whereas γ_{11} refers to the effect of White poverty on the placement rate (Models 9 and 11) and the effect of Black child poverty on the placement rate (Models 10 and 12).

These data generally indicate that higher child poverty rates are associated with *lower* Black child placement rates. For example, at the county level, Black child placement rates decline as White child poverty rates rise. The opposite is true for Whites: higher White child poverty rates and higher Black child poverty rates are both associated with higher White child placement rates. The effect of White child poverty is more pronounced, in part because the wide variation in White child placement rates is set against the relatively narrow range of White child poverty rates.

POVERTY AND THE BLACK/WHITE PLACEMENT GAP

Data showing the relationship between the Black/White placement gap and poverty are found in Table 6.5. The interpretation of the parameters in these models is as follows. The intercept γ_{00} is the White placement rate; the term γ_{10} is the Black/White placement gap, net of any other factors in the model. γ_{01} and γ_{11} show the effect of poverty on the intercept (the White rate) and the placement gap, respectively.

---

[2] In this and all other models, the level-two predictors have been grand-mean centered.

TABLE 6.4

PARAMETER ESTIMATES FOR RACE-SPECIFIC PLACEMENT RATES AND
RACE-SPECIFIC POVERTY RATES

Model No. /Model Specification	Parameter	Coeff.	Event Rate Ratio	Confidence Interval	St. error	t-ratio	p-value
9 $\eta_{ij} = \gamma_{10}{}^*BL_{ij} + \gamma_{11}{}^*CPW_j{}^*BL_{ij} + \mu_{ij}$							
Black placement rate	γ_{10}	1.437	4.206	(3.840, 4.607)	0.046	30.942	<0.001
White poverty	γ_{11}	−1.564	0.209	(0.036, 1.200)	0.890	−1.758	0.079
10 $\eta_{ij} = \gamma_{10}{}^*BL_{ij} + \gamma_{11}{}^*CPB_j{}^*BL_{ij} + \mu_{ij}$							
Black placement rate	γ_{10}	1.459	4.301	(3.938, 4.698)	0.045	32.431	<0.001
Black poverty	γ_{11}	−0.677	0.508	(0.248, 1.041)	0.365	−1.852	0.064
11 $\eta_{ij} = \gamma_{10}{}^*WH_{ij} + \gamma_{11}{}^*CPW_j{}^*WH_{ij} + \mu_{ij}$							
White placement rate	γ_{10}	0.458	1.581	(1.504, 1.661)	0.025	18.201	<0.001
White poverty	γ_{11}	5.284	197.152	(75.729, 513.258)	0.487	10.841	<0.001
12 $\eta_{ij} = \gamma_{10}{}^*WH_{ij} + \gamma_{11}{}^*CPB_j{}^*WH_{ij} + \mu_{ij}$							
White placement rate	γ_{10}	0.434	1.544	(1.462, 1.630)	0.028	15.650	<0.001
Black poverty	γ_{11}	0.431	1.539	(1.157, 2.046)	0.145	2.966	0.003

Model 13 tests the effect of poverty on the placement gap and shows that in counties with higher poverty rates the gap tends to be smaller. The effects of White child and Black child poverty are found in Models 14 and 15. Again, these models show that, with race-specific measures, poverty is associated with a smaller placement gap.

Conclusions

Although the Black/White placement gap has attracted considerable interest in recent years, there have been few studies that explicitly examine the magnitude of the gap and its variability. Fewer still have accounted for the gap with reference to variation in poverty, despite the fact that poverty is often used to explain why Blacks are so much more likely to enter foster care than Whites. There are, seemingly, two reasons for this lack of attention. First, the research done to date has focused on establishing whether the gap exists. Second, it has been largely assumed that where the gap does exist, the presence of the gap is due, in no small part, to differential exposure to individual- or family-level poverty based on race. Simply put, placement rates are bound to be higher for Black children because they are more likely to be touched by poverty.

TABLE 6.5

PARAMETER ESTIMATES FOR BLACK/WHITE PLACEMENT GAP, CONTROLLING FOR RACE SPECIFIC RATES OF POVERTY

Model No./Model Parameter Specification		Coeff.	Event Rate Ratio	Confidence Interval	St. error	t-ratio	p-value
13 $\eta_{ij} = \gamma_{00} + \gamma_{10}{}^{*}CP_j + \gamma_{10}{}^{*}BL_{ij} + \gamma_{11}{}^{*}CP_j{}^{*}BL_{ij} + \mu_{oj} + \mu_{ij}{}^{*}BL_{ij}$							
White placement rate	γ_{00}	0.435	1.545	(1.463, 1.631)	0.028	15.720	<0.001
Poverty	γ_{10}	1.432	4.188	(1.927, 9.101)	0.395	3.622	<0.001
Black/White placement gap	γ_{10}	1.092	2.980	(2.773, 3.203)	0.037	29.694	<0.001
Poverty	γ_{11}	−5.194	0.006	(0.002, 0.014)	0.470	−11.044	<0.001
14 $\eta_{ij} = \gamma_{00} + \gamma_{10}{}^{*}CPW_j + \gamma_{10}{}^{*}BL_{ij} + \gamma_{11}{}^{*}CPW_j{}^{*}BL_{ij} + \mu_{oj} + \mu_{ij}{}^{*}BL_{ij}$							
White placement rate	γ_{00}	0.443	1.558	(1.482, 1.637)	0.025	17.562	<0.001
White poverty	γ_{10}	5.357	212.155	(82.149, 547.906)	0.483	11.084	<0.001
Black/White placement gap	γ_{10}	1.022	2.780	(2.568, 3.009)	0.040	25.344	<0.001
White poverty	γ_{11}	−7.454	0.001	(0.000, 0.003)	0.810	−9.202	<0.001
15 $\eta_{ij} = \gamma_{00} + \gamma_{10}{}^{*}CPB_j + \gamma_{10}{}^{*}BL_{ij} + \gamma_{11}{}^{*}CPB_j{}^{*}BL_{ij} + \mu_{oj} + \mu_{ij}{}^{*}BL_{ij}$							
White placement rate	γ_{00}	0.419	1.520	(1.439, 1.606)	0.028	14.988	<0.001
Black poverty	γ_{10}	0.412	1.510	(1.135, 2.009)	0.145	2.832	0.005
Black/White placement gap	γ_{10}	1.112	3.041	(2.813, 3.287)	0.040	28.025	<0.001
Black poverty	γ_{11}	−1.308	0.270	(0.149, 0.491)	0.304	−4.305	<0.001

Our aim in this study was twofold. On the one hand, we set out to test whether poverty does indeed explain the Black/White placement gap, as the conventional wisdom would suggest. On the other, we were interested in using the findings to raise questions about how one thinks about the implementation and dissemination of evidence-based practices. In particular, we want to raise the importance of understanding context as a factor that has to be considered when trying to improve outcomes through service investments.

To answer the first question, one needs to know whether Black placement rates exceed those of Whites, which is indeed the case. For the second, one needs to understand how the gap changes as a function of poverty and its relationship to Black placement rates and White placement rates, separately. If, on the one hand, the relationship between poverty and placement is the same for Whites and Blacks, then the rate ratio across levels of poverty will be a constant (i.e., no difference in the gap that is attributable to poverty). In this case poverty has no explanatory power vis-à-vis the Black/White placement gap. On the other hand, if the poverty/placement rate relationship differs by race, then the gap will—by definition—grow larger or smaller depending on the nature of that relationship.

Our findings suggest that there is a persistent residual Black/White placement gap even after taking into account poverty. However, the gap is smaller in counties with high White poverty rates; Black poverty rates do not explain the magnitude of the gap, for the most part. The reason for the disparate finding has to do with the fact that Black child poverty rates are not strongly correlated with Black child placement rates in the selection of counties we studied.

That poverty is correlated with placement rates for Whites but less so for Blacks opens a new, compelling line of inquiry in the long-standing discussion about the role of race and the child welfare system in the United States. Where that discussion will take the field is unclear, but one does now have to ask why Black placements are, on average, higher than those for Whites but less elastic with respect to the level of Black social disadvantage measured at the county level.

With respect to using evidence-based interventions to reduce placement disparity, the conventional wisdom would have led one to focus on Black placement rates in high poverty counties. Our findings suggest, however, a more nuanced approach is necessary. Although far from conclusive, the data suggest that the Black/White gap is actually largest in counties with high White poverty rates. Poverty is clearly part of the story, but the specific mechanisms that relate context to the differential rates of contact with the child welfare system are still ambiguous. Unless and until we understand those mechanisms, it will be difficult to derive the full benefit of investments in evidence-based interventions. As a consequence, progress toward greater equity in the child welfare system will remain elusive.

Limitations and Implications for Future Research

The primary goal of our study was to probe the relationship between poverty and the Black/White placement gap and assess whether the findings offer guidance with respect to where one might deploy evidence-based interventions in order to reduce disparity. Although the results are in one sense provocative, the study has important limitations that should be kept in mind. First, we acknowledge that the data we have used are at the ecological level. Ideally, individual-level data would be nested within geographically defined areas so that the likelihood of placement at the individual level could be examined while simultaneously controlling for characteristics of the child and the geographic area using a full mixed effects model. Studies with that scope are rare, although Putnam-Hornstein (2011) has moved in that direction with California birth cohort data. Whether counties are a suitable unit of spatial scale is somewhat up in the air (Lery,

2009). The courts that adjudicate placements are often organized at the county level and are therefore analogous to hospital referral regions used to examine health services disparity (Baicker, Skinner, & Chandra, 2005). However, counties are of more limited utility when theoretical attention turns to the ecological character of neighborhoods and its impact on child well-being.

We also acknowledge that counties differ in ways that are not captured with indicators of social disadvantage. For example, our study does not include any measure of system capacity (e.g., number of CPS workers or service slots), system context (e.g., overall expenditures on social welfare as an indicator of public investment in population well-being), or policy context. Moreover, our study does not include county-specific measures of maltreatment or substantiation rates, two important points of access into the child welfare system where differential treatment of Blacks is thought to occur (Needell, Brookhart, & Lee, 2003; Rivaux et al., 2008). When these attributes of place are added to the model, we may find that poverty's relationship to the Black/White placement gap is mediated (or moderated) through policy and institutional mechanisms.

In addition, our study is limited to a single time point (2000). To the extent the placement gap and social context change over time, our model does not capture those changes. We also assume that the placement gap is constant across age groups within the population of children placed. It may be that the placement gap is differentially connected to social disadvantage based on age-specific risk groups.

These are real limitations, though they say as much, if not more, about the limitations of the knowledge base in the field as it pertains to issues of race and equity. We asked two simple questions: given that there is a Black/White placement gap, do counties with above average poverty rates have above average placement gaps? Second, how should the results be used to target investments designed to address the gap. Considering how the results stack up relative to conventional thinking and the study's limitations, we have a much better feel for why it is important to study context when investing in evidence-based interventions.

Acknowledgments

This chapter is based on an earlier publication appearing in Children and Youth Services Review: Wulczyn, F., Gibbons, R., Snowden, L., & Lery, B. (2013). Poverty, social disadvantage, and the black/white placement gap. *Children and Youth Services Review, 35*(1), 65–74. doi:10.1016/j.childyouth.2012.10.005.

The research presented here would not have been possible without the generous support of the state child welfare directors who sponsor the Center for State Foster Care and Adoption Data. The research itself was supported by a grant from the Annie E. Casey Foundation. We are equally grateful to the Foundation for its support.

7

CHALLENGES TO LEARNING FROM EXPERIMENTS

Lessons from Evaluating Independent Living Services

Mark E. Courtney, Michael Pergamit, Maria Woolverton, and Marla McDaniel

Introduction

US law has recognized the need to help prepare foster youth for adult life since Title IV-E of the Social Security Act, which provides federal funding for foster care, was amended in 1986 to create the Independent Living Program. States received funds specifically intended to provide their foster youth with independent living services. Support for foster youth making the transition to adulthood was enhanced with the passage of the Foster Care Independence Act of 1999, which increased funding to $140 million per year, expanded the age range eligible for services, funded a broader range of activities (e.g., room and board), and granted states the option of extending medical insurance coverage (Medicaid) for youth who age out of foster care until age 21. Amendments to the law added funding for vouchers for postsecondary education and training to the range of federally funded services and supports available to foster youth making the transition to adulthood. More recently, the Fostering Connections to Success and Increasing Adoptions Act of 2008 ("Fostering Connections Act") amended Title IV-E to extend the age of foster care eligibility from 18 to 21 at state option, representing a fundamental shift toward greater federal responsibility for supporting foster youth during the transition to adulthood (Courtney, 2009). Interest in supporting the transition to adulthood for youth exiting state care has also gained considerable attention in policy circles in many other countries in recent years (Stein & Munro, 2008).

In the context of the expenditure of over $2.5 billion on independent living services in the past 25 years in the United States alone, concern has been raised about the effectiveness of independent living services in improving outcomes for foster youth making the transition to adulthood (US General Accounting Office, 1999; Montgomery, Donkoh, & Underhill, 2006). This concern is reflected in the accountability provisions of the Foster Care Independence Act, which required the US Department of Health and Human Services (DHHS) to develop a set of outcome measures to assess state performance in managing independent living programs and directed the secretary of DHHS to commission evaluations of promising independent living programs:

> The Secretary shall conduct evaluations of such State programs funded under this section as the Secretary deems to be innovative or of potential national significance. The evaluation of any such program shall include information on the effects of the program on education, employment, and personal development. To the maximum extent practicable, the evaluations shall be based on rigorous scientific standards including random assignment to treatment and control groups. The Secretary is encouraged to work directly with State and local governments to design methods for conducting the evaluations, directly or by grant, contract, or cooperative agreement (Title IV-E, Section 477 [42 U.S.C. 677], g, 1).

The project commissioned in response to this legislation is called the Multi-Site Evaluation of Foster Youth Programs ("Multi-Site Evaluation"). DHHS contracted with the Urban Institute and its partners—Chapin Hall and the National Opinion Research Center at the University of Chicago—to conduct the Multi-Site Evaluation, which assessed the impact of selected programs funded through the Foster Care Independence Act using experimental methods.[1] The goal of the evaluation was to determine the effects of independent living programs in achieving improvement in key outcomes for participating youth including educational attainment, employment, interpersonal and relationship skills, nonmarital pregnancy and births, delinquency, and crime. The Multi-Site Evaluation includes the first experimental evaluations of independent living programs targeting improvement in the transition to adulthood for foster youth. This chapter provides a description of the Multi-Site Evaluation and briefly describes program impacts before turning to lessons learned from the Multi-Site Evaluation regarding some of the challenges of using experimental evaluation to build evidence in complex areas of human services delivery, such as child welfare services. Challenges identified include: changes in policy context that lead to changes in the

---

[1] The authors of this chapter were involved in conducting the Multi-Site Evaluation. The opinions expressed in this chapter are solely those of the authors and do not reflect the views of the organizations for which they work.

intervention or the counterfactual condition; limited external validity reflecting the unique characteristics of service delivery systems; distinguishing between the impact of "programs" and "practice"; and, limitations of experimental designs for assessing the impact of policy change.

The Multi-Site Evaluation

The key research question for the Multi-Site Evaluation was: What impact does access to the identified intervention have for youths, compared with similar youths who have access to "services as usual," on key outcomes? A secondary set of research questions addressed program implementation and external validity of evaluation findings. These questions were:

- Did implementation follow the program's logic model?
- What types of youths were served?
- Did target populations receive intended services?
- What were barriers to implementation?
- If successful, to what extent might the program be adapted to other locales?

The research team identified promising programs and conducted an evaluability assessment of selected programs between October 2001 and January 2003. The evaluability assessment assessed programs' readiness for rigorous evaluation, the ability to evaluate the program using experimental methods, and the potential contribution an evaluation of the program would make to the field (Trevisan, 2007). A number of program characteristics were used during the evaluability assessment for identifying potential sites for the evaluation:

- Adequacy of potential sample size;
- Excess demand for services;
- Stability in program structure and staffing;
- Service intensity;
- Clarity of program logic model;
- Consistency of implementation;
- Availability of program data needed to understand the flow of clients;
- Willingness of key stakeholders to support experimental evaluation; and
- Willingness to make minor changes needed to accommodate the research.

Based on a review of the literature on independent living services and discussions with thought leaders in the field, the research team developed a typology of such services (Courtney & Terao, 2002), including the following program domains: life skills training;

mentoring programs; housing; health and behavioral health services; educational services; and employment services. The review also indicated that case management was a common element of many approaches to imparting life skills and connecting youth with services and supports to help them make the transition to adulthood successfully. Ultimately four programs were selected, representing a range of program types that fall into several of the domains described in the typology: life skills training; tutoring (education services); case management; and employment-focused services.

EVALUATION DESIGN

The Multi-Site Evaluation utilized a random assignment design whereby some youths were assigned to a treatment group (i.e., they were offered the program of interest, though not required to participate) or a control group that was prohibited from receiving the focal services, but permitted to receive other services available to youth in the area. In each of the four sites, youth were selected for the study and then randomized to a treatment group that was offered the program of interest or a control group that continued to receive the other services available to youth in the area.[2] These experiments followed an "intent-to-treat" procedure whereby service participation was voluntary and impacts are measured on all youth in the groups not just those who received services. Not all youth who were offered the service elected to engage in it. An intent-to-treat experiment is considered helpful for policymakers because it gives them an idea of program impacts if all youth in a jurisdiction were offered the service.

During the evaluability assessment phase of the project, concerns were raised in some potential sites about the ethics of using an experimental design to assess program impacts. Specifically, some program managers had concerns about denying services to youth assigned to a control group. The study team's approach to such concerns was straightforward. First, we reminded those concerned that provision of services to vulnerable populations in the absence of rigorously obtained evidence of positive program impacts raises it own ethical questions. Is it ethical to use scarce resources for interventions that may be of no benefit to the population served? Might an intervention that has not yet been rigorously evaluated actually have negative impacts that have not been identified? Second, since our evaluability assessment only sought programs that had excess demand for services, in other words, youth deemed eligible for services were already being denied services, we pointed out that random assignment was arguably a more ethical approach to assigning youth to services than the idiosyncratic procedures programs were then using to ration the services they had available.

The main source of data for identifying program impacts came from in-person interviews with foster youths. Each respondent was asked to participate in three interviews—an initial interview prior to service receipt and two follow-up interviews (one 12 months

[2] In one site, youths were referred in pairs to the program and then randomized, with one youth gaining access to the program. In the other three sites, youth were randomized from a list or referrals or upon individual referral. In all cases, a 50-50 randomization was used.

after baseline and the second 24 months after baseline). The youth questionnaire offered information about youths' backgrounds and experiences, the interventions and services they had received, demographic information, family relationships, and community characteristics. Key areas covered in the follow-up questionnaires included: educational attainment, employment, physical health, fertility, economic hardship, mental health, incarceration, and victimization. In addition to the impact study, the evaluation included a process or implementation study, which sought to describe and analyze the programs by addressing the current and changing context and the implementation of the services.

THE PROGRAMS

The evaluation included four programs in three sites. Two of these—Life Skills Training (LST) and Early Start to Emancipation Preparation-Tutoring (ESTEP)—were in Los Angeles County, California, and were operated by The Community College Foundation (TCCF; Courtney et al., 2008a, 2008b). A third program—Independent Living Employment Services (IL-ES)—operated in Kern County, California (Courtney, Zinn, Koralek, & Bess, 2011), while a fourth program—Adolescent Outreach (Outreach)— was in operation throughout the Commonwealth of Massachusetts (Courtney, Zinn, Johnson, & Malm, 2011). Table 7.1 briefly outlines key aspects of each program and the size of each study sample.

PROGRAM TAKE-UP AND DOSAGE

Program take-up is defined differently across the four evaluated programs, reflecting differences in program design and referral processes. For example, for the LST and ESTEP programs, take-up is defined by attendance at one or more classes or sessions. In contrast, take-up for the IL-ES and Outreach programs are defined, respectively, by receipt of an IL-ES newsletter and assignment of an Outreach caseworker. Because take-up requires little or no effort on the part of youth referred to the IL-ES and Outreach programs, the rates of take-up in those programs (IL-ES: 97.8%; Outreach: 100.0%) are much higher than they are for the LST (70.1%) and ESTEP (61.8%) programs.

The dosage, or intensity of program participation, also varies considerably across programs. For example, a large majority (92.7%) of LST youth who attended one or more classes graduated from the program. Similarly, on average, ESTEP youth who attended at least one tutoring session received 18 hours of math instruction, and 17 hours of reading instruction. In contrast, only about two-thirds (66.2%) of IL-ES youth received any assistance beyond the receipt of a newsletter, and less than a fifth (18.4%) received any of the most intensive services.[3] Program data were not available for youth served by the

---

[3] Job assistance, shopping for interview clothes, or attending an employment workshop.

TABLE 7.1
PROGRAMS INCLUDED IN THE MULTI-SITE EVALUATION OF FOSTER YOUTH PROGRAMS

Site	Program	Type of Service	Service Provision Structure	Age of Focus	Length of Service Provision	Key Outcomes of Interest
California, Los Angeles County (n = 482)	Community College Life Skills Training (LST) Program	Classroom-based and experiential life skills training, teen support group, and exposure to community college opportunities	Publicly administered, contracted services provided by trainers at 19 community colleges	17	5 weeks (10 workshops)	education, employment, housing stability, avoidance of risk behaviors
California, Los Angeles County (n = 465)	Early Start to Emancipation Preparation (ESTEP)	Structured tutoring and mentoring curriculum for youth 1–3 years behind grade level in reading and math skills	Publicly administered, contracted services provided by 12 community colleges	14–15	6 months of tutoring on average, mentoring continues less intensively after tutoring ends for 3 months on average	education, employment, interpersonal and relationship skills
California, Kern County (n = 254)	Independent Living—Employment Services (IL-ES)	Employment skills training, job referral, and employment support provided through county TANF agency	Publicly administered through partnership between county child welfare and TANF agencies	16	ongoing through age 21	employment and economic self-sufficiency
Massachusetts (n = 194)	Adolescent Outreach Program (Outreach)	Individualized, one-on-one work with youth to prepare them for adulthood; focus on education	Publicly administered statewide	17–18	22 months on average; includes about 16 months of services followed by 6 months of tracking	education, employment, housing stability and economic self-sufficiency

Outreach program, but the design of the program makes it likely that program youth had extensive one-on-one contact with their Outreach worker.

Impact Findings

Below is a brief summary of findings from the impact evaluation. The evaluation was intended to assess the impact of programs on outcomes referenced in the Foster Care Independence Act, including: employment and income; education; physical and mental health; fertility and family formation; economic hardship; homelessness; and victimization. For two of the programs, LST and Outreach, we looked for impacts on all of the potential outcomes of interest, whereas for ESTEP and IL-ES we focused on outcomes that were specifically targeted by those programs (i.e., education outcomes in the case of ESTEP and employment outcomes in the case of IL-ES).

In order to better understand impact findings we also examined whether the programs appeared to have an influence on the kinds of services and help that youth received in preparing for independent living. If a program had little or no impact on the help youth received it would not be expected to have much impact on the outcomes we assessed. The surveys included questions about specific types of help the youth might have received in the areas of education, employment, money management, finding housing, and health and hygiene. For some programs we found little evidence that the program had increased the likelihood that youth would receive the help we asked about. For example, at the second follow-up interview we found that LST program youth differed from control group youth only in being more likely to report having attended any classes or group sessions that were intended to help them get ready for being on their own—not surprising given the nature of the intervention—and in receiving help finding an apartment (Courtney et al., 2008a). For the IL-ES program, we found that a larger proportion of control group youths than program youth reported receiving assistance finding an apartment, or training related to health and hygiene, whereas a larger proportion of program group youths reported receiving help using a budget than did control group youths (Courtney, Zinn, Koralek, et al., 2011). Importantly, there were no statistically significant differences in the proportions of youths receiving employment-related services, though that was the focus of the program. ESTEP had no effect on the likelihood that youth would receive help in the areas we asked about, except that program youth were more likely than control group youth to have received in-home tutoring and less likely to have received school-based tutoring (Courtney et al., 2008b). The Massachusetts Adolescent Outreach Program clearly had the greatest influence increasing youths' likelihood of receiving help, with program youth being significantly more likely to report receiving help in the areas of education, employment, money management, and housing (Courtney, Zinn, Johnson, et al., 2011).

There were no statistically significant impacts on targeted outcomes in the three California programs evaluated. However, in the Massachusetts site several differences emerged that favored the treatment group, which experienced extremely high rates of program take-up (only one youth in the treatment group did not receive Outreach services; Courtney, Zinn, Johnson,, et al., 2011). First, the youth in the treatment group were more likely to get drivers' licenses. While this may not seem to be a significant outcome, getting a driver's license can have several important implications. Beyond having identification (a key focus for many preparation programs), a driver's license enables youth to drive (regardless of whether they have access to a car), which could help them get to services, school, or employment more easily, particularly in those parts of Massachusetts that lack public transportation.

More importantly, findings from the evaluation show that youth who participated in Outreach were more likely to enroll in postsecondary education and to stay involved with the foster care system beyond their 18th birthday. Interviews with program staff suggested that these two outcomes were areas of focus for Outreach workers. They strongly encouraged youth to think about postsecondary education and often engaged in activities with them that would support their enrollment, such as working through financial aid materials or applications with youth. Outreach workers also encouraged eligible youths to sign voluntary placement agreements with the public child welfare agency after they had exited care at age 18 so that they could continue to receive services until age 23. In Massachusetts, a youth must be enrolled in school or vocational training to remain in care past age 18. Further analyses of these last two findings suggest that the higher rate of college attendance among Outreach youths is strongly associated with the fact that Outreach youths are more likely to remain involved with the child welfare system.[4] This finding is consistent with other research suggesting that allowing youth to remain in care past age 18 leads to increased college enrollment (Courtney, Dworsky, & Pollack, 2007).

Lessons Learned from the Multi-Site Evaluation

The Multi-Site Evaluation of Foster Youth Programs was the first experimental evaluation of independent living programs. As such, it is a landmark in efforts to identify "evidence-based" interventions in this field to the extent that validation of program effects through experimental evaluation is considered the gold standard by which to judge whether an intervention should be called evidence-based. Despite the fact that the findings showed few positive impacts of the four tested programs on outcomes of interest, there is still much to be learned from this study.

SOME GOOD NEWS

For those interested in developing experimental evidence for the effectiveness of child welfare services there is much good news to celebrate. The Multi-Site Evaluation provides

---

[4] To explore the possibility that the higher rate of college attendance among Outreach youths is a function of the fact that Outreach youths are more likely to remain involved with the child welfare system, we examined whether the relationships between college outcomes and Outreach program participation were mediated by system involvement.

important evidence that rigorous evaluation can be implemented in child welfare settings serving adolescents:

- Random assignment is feasible. Conducting an experiment may involve minor changes in the flow of clients to services, though it generally need not affect the nature, duration, or intensity of the intervention. Further, it does not take up significant time of workers, supervisors, and managers.
- High response rates can be achieved interviewing youth in foster care and tracking them for follow-up over multiple years. The study team interviewed over 95% of in-scope youth in each site at the baseline and follow-up response rates approached or exceeded 90% in all four sites.
- Administrative data can enhance survey data. The Multi-Site Evaluation collected various types of administrative data and linked them to the survey data to enhance analyses, including: (1) data on service take-up and dosage; (2) child welfare program data (e.g., placement histories, reasons for removal, etc.); and (3) data on selected outcomes (e.g., Unemployment Insurance wage records and data on college enrollment from the National Student Clearinghouse).

Put simply, the often-heard objections from the field that experimental evaluation of child welfare programs is not feasible should be put to rest. To be sure, there are multiple logistical problems to address. Moreover, not all interventions are appropriate for experimental evaluation. In particular, policy changes or interventions that result in comprehensive change to the overall service delivery context cannot be tested by randomly assigning *individuals* to an intervention and control group. For example, the policy of extending foster care past 18 to age 21 cannot easily be evaluated by simply allowing some youth to remain in care while denying that option to others. Extending care is intended to create fundamental changes in an array of services (e.g., employment and training, postsecondary education supports, parenting supports, placement settings) and the behavior of a variety of key institutional players (e.g., foster care providers and court personnel), the potential impacts of which are impossible to restrict to a treatment group in a given child welfare jurisdiction. Nevertheless, these kinds of organization- or system-level interventions are in many cases amenable to experimental evaluation based on site-based assignment to intervention and control conditions (Bloom, 2004; Raudenbusch, Martinex, & Spybrook, 2007). Going forward, objections to experimental evaluation of child welfare programs should be based on substantive grounds and not the vague notion that "it cannot be done."

CHALLENGES TO LEARNING FROM EXPERIMENTAL EVALUATION

While the Multi-Site Evaluation experienced numerous successes, the evaluation also encountered challenges that are important to consider for future foster youth programming and evaluation. While some of these challenges have to do with mounting experimental evaluations per se, the focus here is on issues that influence the ability of policymakers and practitioners to *learn* from the evidence obtained from experimental evaluations. Challenges encountered in drawing implications for the field from the findings of the Multi-Site Evaluation include: changes in policy context that lead to changes in the intervention or the counterfactual condition; limited external validity reflecting the unique characteristics of service delivery systems; distinguishing between the impact of "programs" and "practice"; and, limitations of experimental designs for assessing the impact of policy change.

Changes in the Policy Context

Like many areas of human services delivery, services intended to improve the transition to adulthood for foster youth operate in the context of not only child welfare policy, but also policy in a wide range of areas, including economic support, employment, education, mental and behavioral health, and housing, to name a few. The Multi-Site Evaluation provides evidence of the challenge posed by changes in these policy domains on the expected impact of an intervention and the interpretation of evaluation findings. For example, the implementation of federal No Child Left Behind Act (NCLB) during the study period arguably contributed to the fact that youth in the control group in the evaluation of ESTEP were as likely to have reported receiving some form of tutoring as youth in the experimental group. Through various provisions of the law, NCLB significantly increased school districts' provision of tutoring to students performing behind grade level and to schools labeled as underperforming under the act, provisions that almost certainly increased the likelihood that foster children received tutoring. Thus, it is important to keep in mind that the ESTEP evaluation cannot be used to assess the potential benefits of tutoring for foster youth in the United States, since a change in US education policy fundamentally changed the context of providing tutoring to foster youth. This challenge to interpreting the results of experimental evaluations is certainly not unique to evaluation of child welfare programs. However, that the outcomes of child welfare programs often depend heavily on the availability of inputs from these other systems means that evaluation of child welfare programs is particularly prone to the challenges posed by changing policy context. This means that assessments of the evaluability of child welfare services should carefully map the policy and service system context of an intervention prior to deciding whether an evaluation is warranted. Those contexts should also be monitored during the course of an evaluation in order to maximize the likelihood that observed effects of interventions—or the lack thereof—can be better understood.

Limits to External Validity

There is no national child welfare system in the United States. Rather, there are 50 state systems, some of which have devolved administration of child welfare services to counties, and distinct systems in the US territories and the District of Columbia. Some interventions in child welfare service settings that are amenable to experimental evaluation can be implemented in ways that are relatively immune to the service delivery context in which they are being implemented. However, many if not most interventions are likely to be very sensitive to organizational context, both in terms of ease of implementation and the likelihood of a program impact. A variety of characteristics of the service delivery system could potentially influence the external validity of evaluation findings; here we describe three that are apparent in the Multi-Site Evaluation.

Geographic Concentration of the Target Population

Many interventions targeting foster youth can only be implemented in places where there is a large concentration of foster youth in relatively close proximity to each other. This can limit the relevance of evaluation findings obtained in urban areas to rural or even suburban areas. The Multi-Site Evaluation provides examples of this. The ability of the LST program to elicit a take-up rate of nearly three-quarters of youth in the experimental group in community-college-based life skills training may be largely a function of the concentration of foster youth in Los Angeles County in close proximity to community colleges. This created economies of scale for the program provider and the community colleges and made offering transportation of youth to LST classes—outreach staff for LST could pick up youth and transport them to the community colleges—cost-effective. Even if LST had shown an impact on targeted outcomes it is questionable whether the program as designed could be implemented outside of major urban areas. In Kern County, even though the program was operated directly by Kern County and not by a contract provider, the IL-ES program only operated in the city of Bakersfield and its immediate vicinity. IL-ES services were not available for foster youth living in most of Kern County, a vast rural area.

Organization of the Service Delivery System

How service delivery is organized in a jurisdiction where an intervention is evaluated can also limit the external validity of evaluation findings. Two elements of the organization of service delivery are particularly important. First, the division of labor between the public and private sector in delivering services can play a role in whether a given intervention can be implemented easily, or at all, in a given jurisdiction. This potentially limits the external validity of evaluation findings obtained in a particular context. For example, in Massachusetts, Outreach program services were delivered by state employees. The case management services these public employees provided were in addition to specialized casework provided by employees of a variety of private not-for-profit intensive foster care providers who supervised the foster homes in which the Outreach youth lived. To what extent the impact of the provision of Outreach services on youth outcomes was moderated or mediated by the "extra" services provided by the private agencies could not be determined using the experimental design employed in the Multi-Site Evaluation. Moreover, an argument is sometimes made that public employees can access more easily than employees of private agencies a variety of public benefits for their clients. If true, that would raise questions about how well evaluation findings obtained in a setting where public employees provide a service apply in settings where contract employees provide a service, and vice versa.

Second, in the United States, whether an intervention is provided in a state-administered as opposed to a county-administered human services system can have implications for the external validity of evaluation findings. Most states directly administer child welfare services in the United States, operating services with varying levels of administrative decentralization. However, states are also allowed by the federal government to operate child welfare systems wherein the state is responsible for supervising service provision, but services are directly administered by counties or other local governments. In state-run systems, services are generally organized around administrative regions that include multiple counties and courts (juvenile and family courts are generally organized at the county level in the United States). Both the possibility of economies of scale in provision of services and relations between child welfare agencies and other institutions (particularly the courts)—factors that can influence intervention impacts—are arguably affected by whether services are administered at the state versus the county level.

Broader Policy Context

The policy context of service delivery can also limit the external validity of evaluation findings. For example, the impact of the Massachusetts Outreach program on college enrollment and persistence appears to be strongly dependent on its impact on increasing the likelihood that youth remain in foster care past age 18. But few states currently allow youth to remain in care past age 18, and Massachusetts only allows this for youth who are enrolled in school. Thus, while the evaluation of Outreach finds a positive impact of the intervention, the evaluation cannot provide clear guidance regarding whether the same program would have an impact in jurisdictions whose policy concerning remaining in care past 18 differs from that of Massachusetts.

"Programs" versus "Practice"

Learning from experimental evaluation of child welfare services can be seriously complicated by failure to carefully distinguish between practice (i.e., what child welfare workers and foster care providers do, or at least might do, on a regular basis) and programs (i.e., specialized interventions provided in addition to standard practice). Two issues emerge in this regard. First, failure to understand in advance the nature of practice in a given jurisdiction can lead to faulty assumptions regarding the likely impact of a program. The evaluation of the LST program provides an example of this. While LST demonstrated an impressive rate of engagement of foster youth in life skills training and the program did have a significant affect on youth's likelihood of participating in life skills training classes, there were no impacts on self-reported receipt of help acquiring a wide variety of life skills. The youths' responses to questions about where they obtained this help suggest that much of it came from their caseworkers and foster care providers. In this case, failure to understand in advance the level of life skills training provided through standard child welfare practice in Los Angeles County resulted in the design, implementation, and evaluation of a program that sought to provide help that was in many cases already being provided. In other words, "treatment as usual" often looked very much like the intervention in some important respects.

Second, since discrete programs are generally easier than practices to evaluate using experimental methods, programs may end up being evaluated when changes in practice may ultimately be more important in achieving positive outcomes for youth. For example, the evaluability assessment leading up to the Multi-Site Evaluation identified training programs for foster parents intended to encourage them to provide foster youth with life skills as a potentially important factor influencing youths' outcomes, but the logistics of trying to evaluate these strategies for changing basic practice rendered random assignment evaluation unworkable. Nevertheless, a strong argument can be made that life skills training should ideally be provided by youths' day-to-day caregivers rather than through life skills programs.

Experimental Designs and Systems Change

While experimental designs may be somewhat limited in evaluating changes in practice, they are often of no utility in evaluating major changes in policy. However, policy changes can have huge impacts on practice and programs, thereby changing outcomes for youth. One of the most obvious examples of the impact of policy on foster youth transitions to adulthood is law and regulation regarding the age at which the state stops providing foster care. Nonexperimental policy research has shown that youths' ability to remain in care into early adulthood is associated with positive outcomes in a number of areas (Courtney et al., 2007; Peters et al., 2009). However, as noted above, while it might initially sound appealing to try to assess the impact of extending care by randomly assigning youth to be discharged at a certain date or have the option of remaining in care for an additional period of time, this evaluation design would not likely provide an accurate estimate of the impact of changing policy to extend care. It is interesting to note that on several occasions during the course of the Multi-Site Evaluation advocates suggested that the research team try to evaluate policy initiatives such as extensions of foster care or medical insurance coverage past age 18, believing that these policies held out great promise for improving foster youth transitions to adulthood. Since the Multi-Site Evaluation was restricted to using experimental designs, it was not possible to evaluate the impact of such policy initiatives.

Implications

The challenges described above have implications for evaluators, policymakers, and practitioners alike. While these lessons learned emerge from a project involving experimental evaluation of child welfare services, we believe that they apply even in cases where other evaluation approaches will be used. For evaluators, more scrutiny of program context prior to launching an evaluation and during implementation, so that changes in context can be identified, is in order. In all of the evaluation sites, the context in which the intervention was offered had substantial implications for the ability of the intervention to show an impact on targeted outcomes, but in every case it was only after the evaluation was well underway that these implications became clear. Future evaluation of child welfare services should be conducted in a manner that allows for thorough consideration of the following contextual factors before the decision is made to move forward with an evaluation:

- Existing availability of services that approximate those provided by an intervention targeted for evaluation.
- Likelihood of policy change that fundamentally alters the comparison of the treatment condition to the comparison condition. While it is certainly difficult to anticipate policy changes that can influence the likely impact of an intervention, every effort should be made to do so during evaluability assessment (Trevisan, 2007).
- Likelihood of program continuity throughout the evaluation period. Given the frequently evolving policy, funding, and leadership context in state and local human service agencies, it is almost impossible to predict with certainty whether a human services program, particularly one that may be relatively new or innovative, will be provided in a consistent manner over an extended period of time. Nevertheless, future evaluation research on child welfare services should include evaluability assessments that involve thorough examinations of the factors likely to influence program longevity and consistency over time.

Better consideration of program context prior to launching an evaluation by avoiding programs that provide little more than "treatment as usual," and by minimizing the likelihood that changes in the fiscal, organizational, or policy context will cripple an intervention or render it superfluous, should significantly improve the prospects for evaluating interventions that have a strong a probability of showing a positive impact on targeted outcomes.

As consumers of evaluation research, policymakers, and practitioners would be wise to carefully consider the context in which an intervention was evaluated before accepting a program as evidence-based in their own context. Questions to pose in this regard include:

- *Are we in a red state or a blue state?* Does the policy context where the intervention was evaluated differ from the policy context in my jurisdiction in potentially significant ways?

- *What is the least common denominator?* How similar were services as usual in the evaluation site to those in my jurisdiction?
- *Don't we already do that here?* To what extent are important elements of a "program" that has been evaluated and deemed evidence-based already a part of "practice" in my jurisdiction?

Lastly, although arguably many if not most child welfare services are best evaluated using randomized experiments, evaluators, policymakers, and practitioners alike should be careful not to ignore potentially important changes in policy and practice simply because they are not amenable to experimental evaluation. Although they suffer from significant methodological limitations in comparison to experimental designs, nonexperimental designs that make use of such methods as regression discontinuity analysis (Bloom, 2009), propensity score matching methods (Guo & Fraser, 2010; Michalopoulos et al., 2004), and instrumental variables (Moffitt, 1991) can be used in some cases to estimate the effects of interventions.

Since these methods often rely on the availability of accurate large-sample data on program populations, services, and outcomes, access to reliable administrative data from government institutions and service providers will be important to their successful use in evaluation of child welfare services. Indeed, efforts by government and voluntary sector service providers to improve the range and reliability of the data they collect on client characteristics, service provision, and outcomes can only improve the prospects for program evaluation. One element of good news from the Multi-site Evaluation was the success of the project in using administrative data to study service delivery and program outcomes. Planning for both experimental and nonexperimental evaluations of the impacts of policies on outcomes for children and families should include attention to accessing relevant administrative data and, when possible, ensuring that survey data collected from human subjects can be linked to administrative data. This requires that researchers ensure that the consent procedures used in survey research allow for such data linking and that access to administrative data is sought early in the research planning process.

Conclusion

The Multi-Site Evaluation of Foster Youth Programs is an important milestone in the development of evidence regarding the effectiveness of programs intended to provide independent living skills to foster youth making the transitions to adulthood. The Multi-Site Evaluation demonstrated that experimental methods can be used to rigorously evaluate a wide range of child welfare services. At the same time, the project provided examples of some of the challenges the field will encounter in trying to learn how to improve policy and practice through program evaluations. Evaluators, program developers, and policymakers would do well to pay attention to these challenges as they continue to attempt to improve the evidence base for child welfare services.

Acknowledgments

The authors thank other members of the Multi-Site Evaluation of Foster Youth Programs project team, without whose work this chapter would not have been possible, including: Roseanna Bess, Robert Geen, Karin Malm, Cassandra Simmel, Matthew Stagner, Erica Zielewski, and Andrew Zinn.

8

THE CASE FOR A NEEDS-BASED MODEL IN CHILD WELFARE

A Concept to Address Child Well-Being

Katherine L. Casillas and John D. Fluke

CHILD WELL-BEING IS one of three primary goals for US child welfare services and has been a strong focus since the passage of the Adoption and Safe Families Act of 1997 (ASFA; Wulczyn, Barth, Yuan, Harden, & Landsverk, 2005). This issue is also important internationally, because similar challenges exist across most child welfare systems in high-income countries (Gilbert, Parton, & Skivenes, 2011). The US Child and Family Services Reviews identify three indicators of well-being that are used to track how well agencies are doing in meeting this goal: (1) Families have enhanced capacity to provide for their children's needs; (2) Children receive appropriate services to meet their educational needs; (3) Children receive adequate services to meet their physical and mental health needs (US Department of Health and Human Services [USDHHS], 2006). Yet the field still awaits an effective way to define and measure child well-being, as well as effective ways for families and professionals to work toward enhancing it. Child welfare service reviews (CFSR) across years 2007–2010 found that states were generally underperforming on indicators (1) and (3), with mean state performance across the outcomes at 42% and 75%, respectively (USDHHS, 2011). Common challenges identified in meeting well-being indicators included the inadequate provision of assessments, lack of concerted efforts to involve children and parents in case planning, caseworker inability or failure to focus on pertinent issues during visits, and insufficient availability of services (USDHHS, 2011).

In order to proceed, there must be a common understanding that integrates well-being and needs. Understanding the interaction between well-being and needs is critical for several reasons. In principal, addressing problems should go beyond reducing needs to turning those issues into strengths and well-being. Practically speaking, promoting the well-being of the family is of utmost necessity for the family to have the capacity to care for their children's needs. Even more concretely, a common understanding of both well-being and needs will lead to a greater understanding about the necessary forms of assessment and monitoring, services most likely to help those in need, and strategies for engaging families in effective services.

In order to move the field forward in defining, measuring, and addressing well-being, we believe that we must expand our focus and activities toward a *needs-based model* that can contribute to resolving each of these challenges—from assessment to family engagement to the scale-up of evidence-based practices. This chapter draws heavily from published reports of the National Survey of Child and Adolescent Well-Being (NSCAW), the best source of information in the United States and possibly internationally for a nationally representative sample of children and families investigated for maltreatment. The NSCAW data includes comprehensive and longitudinal assessments of child and family needs, and as such will be used to develop a picture of the needs present in this population, as well as a proposed solution to addressing those needs based on their inherent complexity and the multiple systems they touch.

Addressing Complex needs in the Context of Improving Well-Being

INTENSITY AND MULTIDIMENSIONALITY OF NEEDS

Needs among children in the child welfare system can be defined as cognitive and socioemotional conditions relating to emotional/behavioral disturbances, speech/language impairments, and learning/developmental delays. These problems are particularly important as they occur at a much higher rate compared with children in the general population (USDHHS, Administration for Children and Families [USDHHS-ACF], 2007a). Child welfare studies estimate that 23% to 80% of children exhibit mental health problems, while chronic health problems range from 35% to 80%, and educational difficulties range between 31% and 67% (Chernoff, Combs-Orme, Risley-Curtiss, & Heisler, 1994; Clausen, Landsverk, Ganger, Chadwick, & Litrownik, 1998; Pilowsky, 1995; Schor, 1982; Simms, 1989; Stein, Evans, Mazumdar, & Rae-Grant, 1996; Szilagyi, 1998). Using a representative US sample, NSCAW showed that within 3 years of a child welfare investigation, 22% of children have been identified as having a learning disability (vs. 8% of US children), 15% with an emotional disturbance (vs. 6%), and 13% with a speech impairment (vs. 5%–9%; USDHHS-ACF, 2007a). Similar numbers have been found in Australia, Sweden, and Canada (Bromfield, Lamont, Parker, & Horsfall, 2010; Hessle & Vinnerljung, 1999; Trocmé et al., 2010). Compounding these problems, it appears to be the norm that children with a special need tend to have multiple needs. In fact, 42% of children in this US National Survey of Child and Adolescent Well-Being (NSCAW) who were identified as having a special need actually had two identified needs, and another 31% had three or more needs (USDHHS-ACF, 2007a).

Likewise, caregivers exhibit a number of service needs, including substance abuse, mental health problems, and cognitive impairments. Some of these needs are especially pervasive. For example, in one study of families involved in a child welfare investigation Burns and colleagues found that 40% of mothers suffered from depression (Burns et al., 2009). The mental health needs of caregivers of young children (ages 1 to 4 years) in the NSCAW seem to be similar, with 46% of caregivers experiencing major depression at some point across the 5- to 6-year Wave 5 follow-up (USDHHS-ACF, 2009). Furthermore, 40% of caregivers of young children had major depression at more than one point in time. Likewise, caseworkers' reports on families with an infant or adolescent show that caregivers abuse alcohol (7%–14%) and drugs (8%–30%), and have serious mental health problems (18%–23%), cognitive impairments (7%–11%), poor parenting skills (41%–43%), and unrealistic expectations of their child (15%–22%; USDHHS-ACF, 2008a, 2008b). As with children followed in the same study, these problems tend to co-occur (USDHHS-ACF, 2009). Other co-occurring needs include basic living assistance (33%; e.g., transportation, food, housing), child care assistance (30%), individual services (19%; e.g., job-related, support groups, legal aid), and home assistance services (12%; e.g., home management training; USDHHS-ACF, 2008a). While these issues come from US child welfare data, similar challenges are also of concern in other nations such as Australia (Bromfield, Lamont, Parker, & Horsfall, 2010), Canada (Burnside, 2012), England (Cleaver, Nicholson, Tarr, & Cleaver, 2007), and Scotland (Rosengard, Laing, Ridley, & Hunter, 2007).

UNDERSERVICING OF NEEDS

Unfortunately, it appears that both child and family needs are being underserviced. While there is substantial need for specialized services that address the complex and multidimensional issues facing children and families in the child welfare system, these special needs are not being adequately met. With respect to children, findings from the NSCAW indicate that children investigated for child maltreatment in the United States have a much greater risk of cognitive and socioemotional problems when compared with normed national samples (USDHHS-ACF, 2005). However, they are not receiving needed services. Depending on the time of assessment, between 35% and 42% of children assessed at baseline when they were 3 years of age or younger had a developmental delay or an established medical condition, or will have developed one within the next 5 to 6 years. Yet only 10%–26% of those in need received necessary developmental or medical services, with percentages worsening the longer children were involved with the child welfare system (USDHHS-ACF, 2007b). Similarly, although 31% of preschoolers had cognitive deficits and 27% had behavior problems, only 13% and 12% respectively of those in need received special educational services to address them (USDHHS-ACF, 2005). The situation is similar for school age children investigated for maltreatment in the United States. Depending on the measure, 5%–12% of school age children exhibited cognitive development or academic achievement risks (intelligence; reading; math), and another 10%–45% exhibited developmental risk on one or more socioemotional measures (problem behavior; social skills; living skills; depression). Yet, only 54% of those school age children who exhibited risk on at least one of the measures were receiving special education services for cognitive/academic difficulties and 25% for socioemotional functioning (USDHHS-ACF, 2005).

With respect to caregivers, although 27% had a mental health need, a minimum of 26% of those in need received a mental health service (USDHHS-ACF, 2008a). Most often the mental health service received was psychotropic medication, with few actually ever seeing a mental health practitioner. Similarly, almost no caregivers of infants received substance abuse services (though 30% were in need). The services more often provided were basic living assistance (33%; e.g., transportation, food, housing), child care assistance (30%), individual services (19%; e.g., job-related, support groups, legal aid), and home assistance services (12%; e.g., home management training; USDHHS-ACF, 2008a).

Although far fewer children and caregivers receive services than those in need, involvement with child welfare has been shown to increase service receipt. That is, similar children and families who are not involved with the child welfare system are even less likely to receive needed services. For instance, across child age groups there is an increase in receipt of school-based or specialty mental health services for child welfare cases (Leslie et al., 2005). Thus, despite high levels of unmet need, the ability of the child welfare system to connect families to services is promising.

However, factors other than type of services needed appear to influence which services are received. For example, for children 3 years and under, the percentage of those with developmental or medical risks receiving services does not differ from the percentage of those without such risk receiving services. Furthermore, although children in substantiated and unsubstantiated cases have similar special needs (Drake, 1996; USDHHS-ACF, 2007c), service receipt is instead best predicted by substantiation and poverty, irrespective of current developmental status (at least between baseline and 12-month follow-up for children 3 years and under; USDHHS-ACF, 2007b). This is important because services are being implemented similarly across clients regardless of their actual need, resulting in wasted service provision for some, and a lack of service provision for others that actually need it. Such inadvertent care translates into financial waste or potential deterioration in functioning depending on which group is in question. The child welfare field must better understand these complex needs that touch multiple systems, and better integrate across systems to get those needs addressed.

Integrating Systems that Serve the Child Welfare Population
ABSENCE OF INTEGRATIVE TREATMENT PROTOCOLS

There is an absence of integrated assessment protocols. On one hand, a variety of organizations have issued guidelines and screening tools for the assessment and treatment of children, including the array of issues faced by children and caregivers involved in the child welfare system (American Academy of Child and Adolescent Psychiatry, 1997a, 1997b, 2007; Spivak, Sege, Flanigan, & Licenziato, American Academy of Pediatrics, 2006; Scottish Executive, 2005). The set of tools as a whole cover just about every issue possibly faced by any family. Yet concrete guidance is missing on how and when to use this information, and this disconnect is crucial given the high degree of complexity in both the lives of children and families and the service system of which they are a part. In order to proceed effectively, guidance is needed with respect to organizing multiple assessments across different problem domains, coordination of care across multiple needs, and selection and timing of specific empirically supported treatments or interventions (Johnson et al., 2006; Lou, Anthony, Stone, Vu, & Austin, 2006).

We face a similar problem in treatment planning and service integration. To date, most of the intervention and treatment research has relied on variable-centered approaches, which assume all individuals come from the same population. Perhaps as a product of this, as well as our focus on internal over external validity, most evidence-based treatments are designed for single conditions, or groups of closely related conditions (e.g., a cluster of anxiety disorders with partially overlapping symptoms). However, the high degree of comorbidity of conditions calls this approach into question. Recent studies of treatment effectiveness have found decreases in effectiveness as impairment increases, if co-occurring conditions are present, or if multiple concrete needs are observed (Curry et al., 2006; Hinshaw, 2007; Jensen et al., 2007; Owens& Chard, 2003). These findings seem to indicate that children and families with multiple needs should be identified and provided with applicable services, perhaps using collaborative, cross-systems approaches. However, we would argue that treatment-as-usual is not enough, nor is mere coordination (Bickman, 1996). Rather than just determining which cross-systems approaches are needed, so too must we determine how to prioritize, order, and integrate multiple services.

THE ROLE OF CHILD WELFARE IN SCREENING AND PRIORITIZING NEEDS

Child welfare can be viewed as a surveillance and referral system that is dealing with a complex array of needs for both children and their caregivers. In and across systems beyond child welfare, there are certain barriers to effective care for the social, educational, and health care needs of children and families. These systems rarely interact in the United States, and when they do the inherent structure within each does not promote the sharing of information or the integration of services. Yet, as the gatekeepers to many needed supports and services, some barriers are contained or controlled by the child welfare system. Obstacles that could hinder a caseworker from helping children and families receive effective care include: skill deficits in assessment, engagement, and referral (Burns et al., 2009). Without effectively knowing how to best screen for and prioritize needs, appropriate referrals are all but impossible.

Figuring out needs is no simple task. Assessments must be comprehensive enough to identify an array of needs while maintaining speed, accuracy, and client engagement. Once needs are ascertained, those posing the greatest risk are prioritized and balanced with the stated desires of the clients. If needs are multiple and complex, the process may need to include consultation with mental health or other systems representatives. Again, the desires and input of the client are critical along every step to obtain needs that are meaningful and to promote client engagement (Gibbs, 2003; Gibbs & Gambrill, 2002). Like a medical screening test, screening for multiple and complex needs should come first, followed by substantial assessment by the requisite professional. Despite the existence of statements regarding the importance of screening, there is little guidance let alone research concerning what to use, when, or what professionals should conduct these processes.

THE ROLE OF CHILD WELFARE IN SERVICE ENGAGEMENT
AND TRACKING OUTCOMES

Child welfare caseworkers also have a key role in getting children and families to the *right* supports and services. In part, some knowledge is needed about which evidence-based practices are best for which problems. Additionally, knowledge of the family's support network and the community service base is necessary, including which services are at least evidence-informed or evidence-based. Finally, referral skills are needed to be able to describe and share the nature of the problem, as well as engage and build a relationship with supports and services. Client input and engagement is again critical.

In order to address well-being, child welfare also needs to be able to monitor well-being outcomes. Completing services does not just mean showing up. While service fields surely expect more, we also must assure that improvement is based on decreasing those risk factors and improving strengths in the caregivers that in turn result in improvements in children's well-being. This approach is likely to have the best outcomes if it is comprehensive and addresses multiple targeted risk and protective factors using community-level approaches (Hawkins et al., 2008). Hawkins et al.'s Communities That Care program is a public health approach to substance abuse prevention that targets multiple problematic youth behaviors (e.g., delinquency, school drop-out, substance abuse). The relevancy here is that multiple community stakeholders are engaged to share knowledge and the tracking of outcomes across the multiple systems that affect these youth (e.g., public health, education, criminology).

Studies in the psychotherapy literature have found that improved client outcomes can be achieved simply by providing ongoing feedback (Lambert, Hansen, & Finch, 2001), and this common factor should be considered when setting up case plans. Goals should be achievable, some in the short term, and client feedback on progress should be regularly provided. However, there may be insufficient outcome monitoring supports and structures in child welfare settings (Burns et al., 2009), hindering the delivery of effective services. Monitoring outcomes must be a part of services from the beginning stages of engagement in order to reinforce positive changes and be alerted to movement in the other direction. Practitioners of course have the flexibility to adjust the intervention to tailor it to individual client needs, yet need to keep a consistent measure of change that can be shared with the child welfare system. It almost goes without saying, especially in populations with multiple needs, that transitioning back and forth between implementing an intervention and evaluating ongoing change is particularly necessary in cases where the intervention was modified to fit a client's needs (Mildon, Dickerson, & Shlonsky, Chapter 5, this book).

The Importance of a Needs-Based Model for the Scale-Up of Evidence-Based Practices in Child Welfare: A Systems Agenda

We have argued based on the research regarding co-occurring conditions among child welfare populations (Fluke, Shusterman, Hollinshead, & Yuan, 2008) that one missing aspect of information hindering the implementation of effective programs and practices is a better understanding of these conditions and how often they occur. For example, NSCAW has provided us an extensive national review of the special needs among children in the child welfare system (i.e., developmental, behavioral, and emotional; USDHHS-ACF, 2007a), but we still do not have any comprehensive national-level estimates of the need for various services *which focus on more than a few critical needs at one time*. Missing to date for child welfare is a valid starting point for identifying treatment subgroups early on that, in turn, can guide integrated assessment, treatment planning, and service delivery. As opposed to variable-centered process, a person-oriented approach asserts that human development must be understood by examining multiple factors in relation to one another (Magnusson, 1995). According to this theory, development is a product of the pattern of relevant factors, and the related research requires identifying configurations of factors that distinguish different subgroups (Bergman & Magnusson, 1997; Magnusson, 1998). Thus far with some exception attention has been paid to isolating and enumerating single conditions that could be the focus of empirically supported programs and practices. For example, such conditions could be caregivers with substance abuse issues, children who experience types of maltreatment, children who experience trauma, and family poverty. Taken together these individual enumerations constitute an overall profile of the needs of children and families (Samuels, 2012; USDHHS-ACF, 2007a).

Combined interventions have proven advantages and improved robustness when addressing more severe individual needs or multiple conditions (Curry et al., 2006; Hinshaw, 2007; Jensen et al., 2007; Owens and Chard, 2003). We would argue that it is important, also, to know how to prioritize needs in order to guide a superior matched combination and ordering of effective programs and practices, including evidenced-based practices. From a child welfare service delivery system perspective, this concept leads to other implications. For one, the information could be used for planning purposes to determine how many families would benefit from specific interventions. For another, it would be crucial in identifying gaps in the fabric of the existing array of evidence-based treatments and services. In addition, some combinations of treatment type, dose, and timing may work better than others. Further, families are typically already overwhelmed when they come to the attention of child welfare. They cannot do everything at once and some decisions need to be made with respect to what should be addressed first. No doubt, the client should have some say. But so, too, should the evidence.

This goal is not easy to achieve, but if successful, could result in a practical model that can successfully account for the complexity of these conditions, one that both systematically organizes the cases for intervention planning and evaluation, but retains the complexities of the underlying conditions. To that end we propose utilizing more sophisticated multivariate procedures that can identify the most commonly co-occurring conditions.

Figure 8.1 schematically depicts a multidimensional matrix of patterns of co-occuring conditions. The number of patterns that could be identified is potentially infinite, but it is much more likely that a finite set of patterns would emerge, and it is also likely that a relatively small number of patterns would account for most of the cases in the child welfare system.

Each pattern contains a set of cases. Figure 8.2 shows some examples of the underlying conditions and characteristics of children and families that could be associated with the

FIGURE 8.1. Needs-based framework: multiple co-occurrence patterns.

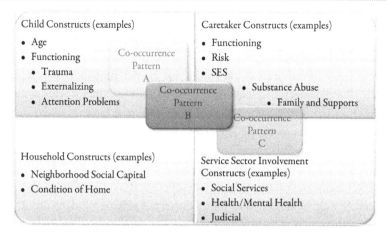

FIGURE 8.2. Needs-based framework single pattern—co-occurrence (A).

patterns. While each pattern would be independent in principle, it is clear that characteristics would overlap to some extent and that case members in the pattern would share distributions. Nevertheless a specific set of cases would be classified within each pattern, referred to as a class.

Among the requirements for such a system is representative samples of child welfare cases (this could be within an administrative jurisdiction, a state, or even nationally) that includes a comprehensive set of assessment data. Once identified, these classes can be deconstructed in turn for content and evaluated relative to possibilities of improving conditions through the application of empirically supported interventions. Alternatively, it may be that given the underlying conditions, no intervention would likely be effective for the class, and this represents an intervention gap.

Based on this information several possibilities emerge:

- For classes where empirically supported interventions may be effective, further tests of these interventions could be performed with cases in the class to determine the level of expected efficacy for the class. This could also be "staged," as it seems clear that multiple simultaneous interventions may not be effective (Chaffin, Bard, Hecht, & Silovsky, 2011). However, sequencing these services in minimally overlapping ways over a proscribed period of time may be more effective than a simultaneous or haphazard delivery of multiple services.
- The size of the class and its distribution with respect to population concentration, length of service delivery, and its estimated effect size could be used to estimate the type, scope, and dose (as in concentration across area) of specific empirically supported interventions or treatments that would be needed to achieve predetermined goals. This would have implications for determining effectiveness as well as for workforce development, workload, and costing.

- Some classes may not benefit or only minimally benefit from the existing array of empirically supported interventions. Thus the existence of certain patterns may highlight the gaps in the available array of effective services and practices. Identification of such gaps would also be tied to a determination of the size of the class allowing for an informed evaluation of the utility of prioritizing research and evaluation efforts that could address these gaps.
- Outcomes could be monitored relative to the class of which the family is a member. This would also serve as a form of risk adjustment such that outcome expectations could be formulated relative to expected efficacy for the class.
- Finally, because class membership could shift over time, a longitudinal approach could be employed to "tune" the service array as the dynamics of the family shift.

These prospects at the system level hold a great deal of promise with respect to implementing empirically supported interventions, and may be vital if the expectations regarding such interventions are to be realized.

Summary

As Fixsen and colleagues have stated, it is not only critical to identify what the core components of effective programs are, but it is also critical to implement them with fidelity (Fixsen, Blase, Naoom, & Wallace, 2009). Similarly, it is important to identify the most prevalent needs of the population that we serve, and how the potential evidence supported array of services can be made optimally available. In order to move the field forward in defining, measuring, and targeting well-being, we believe that we must expand our conceptualization and implementation to that of a *needs* assessment that maps on to other empirically derived indicators across established fields. This means being able to connect children and families in the child welfare system to the supports and services that are best able to meet the most critical of those needs—especially over the course of time. Concomitantly, the well-being of the child is dependent on that of their primary caregivers and family. Any definition of child well-being is deficient without also including caregiver and family well-being. Similarly, if we want our agency partners in child welfare to broadly implement effective practices and programs, the onus is on researchers to provide them with the necessary tools. In sum, we argue for a focus on children's needs, as well as those of their network of caregivers, if we are to ever truly address child well-being, and do so while handing back the protective role to the family.

The Delivery of Services within an Agency Context

9

HUMAN SERVICE ORGANIZATIONS AND THEIR USE

OF EVIDENCE

Hillel Schmid

Background

In recent decades, there has been increasing theoretical and empirical research interest in evidence-based practice in human service organizations (Gambrill, 2003, 2006; Johnson & Austin, 2006; McCracken & Marsh, 2007; Proctor, 2007). The development of evidence-based practice in human service organizations (HSOs) follows efforts to implement the evidence-based approach in medicine and in the health system. The evidence-based approach encourages professionals to use factual information and empirical research findings in the process of decision-making and in clinical judgments (Arndt & Bigelow, 1999, 2009; Kovner, 2003; Kovner & Rundall, 2006; Mendelson & Carino, 2005; Sackett, Rosenberg, Gray, Haynes, & Richardson, 1996; Sackett, Straus, Richardson, Rosenberg, & Haynes, 2000; Walshe & Rundall, 2001).

In a similar vein, there has also been growing interest in evidence-based management. However, studies on the topic have dealt mainly with management of commercial for-profit organizations (Pfeffer & Sutton, 2006a, 2006b; Rousseau, 2006a, 2006b, 2007; Rousseau & McCarthy, 2007). These studies have focused on conceptualizing the term *evidence*, while scholars have relied mainly on previous theoretical and conceptual developments in the health system. Beyond attempts to gain a better understanding of the concept of evidence-based management and its uses, researchers have proposed strategies for assimilating factual information and research evidence in the routine work of organizations in order to improve the processes of policymaking, decision-making, and problem solving. In this context, the theoretical assumptions of management science and organizational theories are: (1) Decisions based on evidence will yield anticipated results (Kovner, Elton, & Billings, 2000; Kovner & Rundall, 2006). (2) These results are generalizable across organizations (Damore, 2006; Rousseau, 2006b); and (3) evidence is objective and context free (Arndt & Bigelow, 2009; Fine, 2006).

According to management science, in the complex reality of organizations that operate in rapidly changing environments, decisions must be based not only on the intuition of executives, their past experience, and internal organizational information, but also on a systematic set of solid facts and empirical evidence that can help reduce uncertainty in the organization. In the context of nonprofit human service organizations (NPHSOs), there has been growing pressure in recent decades to exhibit higher levels of performance, to define measurable outcomes, and to become more transparent and accountable to their constituencies and stakeholders (Collins-Camargo, McBeath, & Ensign, 2011; McBeath, Briggs, & Aisenberg, 2009; Meezan & McBeath, 2011; Miller, Bogotova, & Caraghan, 2012). Nonetheless, there is a lack of theoretical and empirical literature on the use of evidence in NPHSOs, even though the topic has become increasingly relevant to them (Briggs & McBeath, 2009; Walker, Briggs, Koroloff, & Friesen, 2007).

Against this backdrop, the present chapter will deal with the use of evidence in NPHSOs in light of the unique characteristics and attributes that distinguish them from other organizations, and examine how differences can play out across contexts. In the following sections, I will present the concept of evidence-based management (EBMgt), and discuss the barriers and restraining forces that prevent implementation of this approach in NPHSOs due to the distinctive nature of these organizations. In addition, I will discuss the conditions that might facilitate its assimilation, as well as dilemmas related to that process. Finally, I will delineate the steps that need to be taken in order to increase the use of evidence in NPHSOs.

Definition of Evidence-Based Management and its Goals

The use of evidence in management in general and in management of NPHSOs in particular is still in its early stages. However, attempts to implement this approach have been made in the fields of medicine, nursing, education, and law enforcement, as well as in the business sector. To better understand the essence of evidence-based management, I will present different definitions that are relevant to the issues discussed in this chapter. Rousseau (2006a) proposed the following definition:

> Evidence-Based Management means translating principles based on evidence into organizational practices. Through evidence-based management, practicing managers develop into experts who make organizational decisions informed by social science and organizational research—part of the *zeitgeist* moving professional

decisions away from personal preference and unsystematic experience toward those based on the best available evidence (p. 256).

This definition highlights the importance of using empirical knowledge and evidence in the daily administrative practices of organizations. In this way, executives become experts who use basic, scientific, systematic, and rational organizational research as a basis for their decisions instead of relying on their intuition and their personal and organizational experience. Specifically, the use of knowledge and empirical evidence serves as a basis for formulating strategies of action in the organization (Rousseau & McCarthy, 2007).

Another definition refers to "systematic application of the best available evidence to the evaluation of managerial strategies" (Kovner & Rundall, 2006, p. 6), in which executives "routinely review the findings of relevant research studies and research syntheses before making decisions" (Walshe & Rundall, 2001, p. 449). This definition adds the use of empirical evidence in ongoing evaluation of organizational activities and performance, and not only at the stage of decision-making. These evaluations cannot be based on superficial considerations. Rather, they need to be based on accepted theoretical and methodological approaches for evaluation of effectiveness, as well as on systematic empirical knowledge which documents processes and outcomes using quantitative and qualitative methods. The empirical evidence helps executives and organizations learn lessons and plan future activities, to identify deviations from the original plans, and to reevaluate and adapt themselves to the changing environments. Thus, evidence-based management combines conscientious, judicious use of the best evidence with individual expertise and ethics as well as with valid, reliable business and organizational facts. In so doing, the impact of this evidence on stakeholders is also taken into consideration.

In summary, evidence-based management aims to achieve several goals:

1. To increase the effectiveness of organizational leadership while also catalyzing new research that addresses practical, relevant, and important questions.
2. To offer executives a set of methods for clarifying how they use information to make strategic decisions. This includes available information within the organization, which relates to the specific decision at hand, as well as relevant information deriving from the findings of research on topics that are relevant to those decisions. Through these methods, executives can improve the quality of decision-making and problem solving.
3. To exhibit accountability, transparency, and organizational performance. In light of the pressures and expectations of the organization's constituencies and interest groups, it is also expected that through the use of evidence-based management, the organizations will be perceived as more accountable and more transparent. This, in turn, will make possible higher levels of organizational performance and effectiveness.

4. To minimize or prevent overuse, underuse, and misuse of management practices and eliminate a presumed gap between research and practice (Fine, 2006; Walshe & Rundall, 2001), or between best and common practice (Kovner, 2003).

5. To prevent executives from relying on casual benchmarking, from doing what seems to have worked in the past, and from following deeply held, unexamined ideologies.

6. To encourage and support critical thinking and decision-making according to specified criteria.

All of these goals are intended to replace past practices that tended to rely on intuitive judgment with an approach that bases decision-making on solid research evidence. The evidence-based approach equips executives with advanced scientific methods for managing their organizations, while supporting their decisions with rational processes and increasing the transparency and accountability of their actions. Nonetheless, not all organizations and executives attribute the same degree of importance to this approach. In fact, difficulties have been encountered in the attempt to implement EBMgt in organizations in general and in NPHSOs in particular.

Barriers and Restraining Forces that Prevent the Implementation of Evidence-Based Management in Human Service Organizations

As in any attempt to introduce change, various interest groups in the organization resist the implementation of EBMgt on the grounds that it would undermine existing practices by introducing new, systematic, and scientific ways of thinking into the conservative organizational reality. As such, the implementation of EBMgt is not perceived as a first-order change, which is incremental in nature and involves modifications that do not deviate substantially from the organization's identity and core activity (Bartunek & Moch, 1987). Rather, the introduction of EBMgt is a second-order change that involves the conscious modification of present schemata in a particular direction, and entails major changes in existing organizational strategies, structure, and administrative processes (Bartunek & Moch, 1994).

From this point of view, EBMgt has the potential to fundamentally alter the behavior of organizations and the management styles of their executives. Against this background, EBMgt can encounter resistance as a result of difficulties deriving from three sources: (1) the organizational and structural complexity of nonprofit human service organizations; (2) the administrative behavior of the executives; (3) the relationship between research and practice, and conceptual gaps between researchers and practitioners.

DIFFICULTIES DERIVING FROM THE UNIQUE NATURE OF NONPROFIT HUMAN
SERVICE ORGANIZATIONS

NPHSOs have unique characteristics that distinguish them from governmental, industrial, and business organizations (Hasenfeld, 1988, 1992, 2010; Hasenfeld & Schmid,

1989). These organizations usually lack their own capital, and are highly dependent on resources controlled by other agents such as the government and the private sector (e.g., private philanthropists and philanthropic foundations). In recent decades, a division of labor has been established between these organizations and the government in most European and North American countries. According to this division of labor, the government has been responsible for setting the policies that govern social services as well as for financing those services, establishing service programs, setting standards of quality, and overseeing and controlling program implementation. NPHSOs are responsible for the provision of services that are contracted out by the government. These relationships have several implications for the organizational behavior and management of NPHSOs, which are relevant to this chapter. In order to ensure the continuation of the contracts, the organizations need to adopt advanced patterns of management that are consistent with the nature of their clientele and with the competitive environment in which they operate. As a result, NPHSOs need to exhibit higher levels of effectiveness, efficiency, and performance in order to ensure a steady flow of resources from the funding sources as well as to ensure their clients' loyalty. Toward that end, they also need to be more transparent and accountable to their clients and constituencies, who have an interest in the organization's activities and programs (Shoham, Rubio, & Vigoda, 2006).

The context in which these organizations operate is considered to be highly politicized. Different interest groups operating inside and outside of the organizations compete for the scarce resources, and strive to control a large share of those resources. In that way, these groups seek to make others dependent on them, while imposing goals and policies that they are interested in promoting. Moreover, external environments control the resources and legitimacy that the organizations need, and generate dependence of the organizations on the external agencies. In light of the tension between the organization and the environment, administrators in NPHSOs tend to adopt a more politically oriented approach aimed at management of the external environment, and focus less on the internal organizational system. This style of management emphasizes negotiation and bargaining with environmental agencies in an attempt to reduce the organization's dependence and ensure its autonomy. The political orientation and pattern of management adopted by executives in modern organizations require different skills than those of professionals, who base their decisions on formal knowledge and empirical evidence. Oftentimes, the political orientation leads to goal displacement, where the means adopted by the organization become ends in themselves. In these cases, the use of empirical evidence is limited.

The service technologies adopted by NPHSOs are considered to be indeterminate and difficult to evaluate in terms of their contribution to the well-being of their clients. Notably, the client populations of these organizations may differ in terms of age, ethnic origin, socioeconomic status, and religious affiliation. As such, NPHSOs employ numerous service technologies that are translated into a wide range of programs. However, the implementation of such diverse technologies, each calling for different sets of skills and expertise as well as for different structural arrangements, poses major challenges and dilemmas for executives. This prevents the organizations from systematically accumulating relevant expertise that is adequate for the variety of service technologies employed by professional workers. All of this indicates that the processes of professionalization, formalization, bureaucratization, and adoption of advanced patterns of management run counter to the organic, informal, and nonbureaucratic processes that organizations have adopted to survive in the service arena.

The prior adoption of these informal characteristics highlights a critical tension faced by NPHSOs. In order to respond to a changing environment, they need to show operative flexibility and remove formal barriers that obstruct the vertical and horizontal flow of information. In this context, it is necessary to allow for open communication and exchange of knowledge and experience among staff members. Concurrently, there is a need to flatten the organizational structure in a way that will enable rapid, flexible adaptation to changing environments while creating effective responses to the needs of clients. This kind of structure which, by nature, facilitates the use of available knowledge and information, does not necessarily encourage the members of the organization to seek formal empirical evidence that may not be "user friendly." The use of formal evidence-based knowledge, which is presented in guidelines for management practices and obtained through rational, systematic, and advanced scientific methods, is not always welcome in organic organizational systems, where knowledge flows from the bottom up and top down. In these contexts, knowledge is diffuse—unlike formal knowledge, which is based on empirical academic research, and is somewhat detached from organizational complexities.

Finally, organizational activity and management based on evidence, which is available at various levels of the organization, can undermine the director's formal authority. In these cases, the knowledge is not exclusively available to the director, because it is disseminated at various levels of the organization. This results in a major change in the balance of power, which is known as the "power revolution" (Schmid, 2013). That is, when organizational activity is based on empirical evidence, the power that was controlled by the director is transferred to various levels of the organization. Therefore, some executives may resist the dissemination and implementation of empirical knowledge because it has the potential to undermine their status, power, and authority. The implementation of EBMgt probably requires a charismatic, dynamic leader who is not afraid of criticism and self-reflection, has an aptitude for shared decision-making, and can bring the organization together around the idea of using evidence to inform practice.

DIFFICULTIES DERIVING FROM THE ADMINISTRATIVE BEHAVIOR OF EXECUTIVES

Most of the studies that have investigated the administrative behavior of executives in different organizational settings, including NPHSOs, have found that their plans are short-term and ad hoc rather than long-range and strategic (Schmid, Bargal, & Hasenfeld, 1991). As such, they concentrate more on providing solutions for the "here and now," and spend more time on organizational maintenance than on planning, innovation, and representation (Schmid, 2010).

The work of executives generally consists of numerous episodes in which information and issues requiring extensive consideration and decision-making are crowded into very short periods of time, and the amount of time devoted to management activity is minimal. As Kotter (1982) suggested, executives operate very efficiently, and even seemingly inefficient behavior can be characterized by a certain efficiency, which Mintzberg (1973) defined as "proficient superficiality."

Most studies have also found verbal communication to be the prevalent form of communication used by executives, although this mix has almost certainly changed with the dawning of the information age. Executives prefer unmediated contacts, and receive most of their information from conversations with their own staff or with people outside of the organization than from long, complicated reports and position papers (Schmid, Bargal, & Hasenfeld, 1991).

As for contact with clients, some studies have found that executives devote relatively little time to their clientele, and focus more on managing internal organizational affairs such as finance management, human resources, and general administration and maintenance (Schmid et al., 1991). In addition, executives spend relatively little time managing the external environment, whereas more efforts should be invested in managing the external environment in order to ensure a stream of resources as well as formal and informal legitimacy (Aldrich & Reuf, 2006; Schmid, 2009). Studies have also found that a considerable proportion of organizational activities are initiated by executives (Schmid et al., 1991).

Although these trends may have changed, the reality is that the fast-paced nature of the job as well as the immediate challenges resulting from uncertain funding and the changing mix of populations and services may cause executives to use a more reactive than a proactive approach. They may prefer short-term projects, because long-range goals are considered vague and indeterminate. Moreover, they are accountable to constituencies and interest groups, and therefore strive to attain visible, immediate outcomes that provide them with legitimacy and ensure the flow of resources to the organization. If executives concentrate on internal problems and on maintenance of the organization without planning for the future, they will have no choice but to adopt a style of management geared toward crisis management, as reflected in solving immediate problems and removing obstacles as they arise.

Research has also indicated that executives may tend toward centralization. If so, they will concentrate decision-making authority in their own hands, and prevent employees from functioning autonomously or reaching decisions in their domains of responsibility. This trend has been attributed to a wealth of objective and subjective factors within and outside of the organization, such as lack of management know-how and skills, inability to motivate employees, reluctance to take risks, intolerance of ambiguity, and preference for a "one-man show." It is also possible that centralization evolves out of the executive's lack of self-confidence and professionalism. In such instances, the concentration of information and decision-making authority is aimed at making others dependent on them. Conversely, centralization can be ascribed to the executives' lack of confidence in the ability of their staff to operate independently (Schmid, 1990). All of this causes them to enforce tight control over subordinates rather than to exercise control in accordance with results (Stern, Schmid, & Nirel, 1994). In that situation, centralization may not be conducive to the implementation of EBMgt.

Furthermore, executives do not always base their decisions on sound ideas, established theories, or solid evidence. Rather, their actions are often based on emulating what appears to be successful to others, and on repeating what seems to have worked in the past (Rousseau, 2006b). Executives may also follow the latest fads that are written up in the business press and published by management consultants (Blanchard & Johnson, 1983), and these may or may not be based on solid evidence. Moreover, it has been found that in some cases, only a small percentage of executives read the professional literature. In a study of human resource managers, Rynes, Colbert, and Brown (2002) reported that only 1% of the participants had been exposed to academic literature and read that literature regularly. This raises the question: What are their decisions based on? A study conducted in a large Quebec Youth Protection Centre among about 450 clinicians and executives revealed that only 22% of the executives and 18% of the clinicians often use research-based evidence to guide their practices (Chagnon, Pouliot, Malo, Gervais, & Pigeon, 2010).

All of this poses a major difficulty for implementation of evidence-based management. The administrative behavior of some executives in human service organizations focuses on crisis management, and aims to provide rapid solutions to a large number of problems without comprehensive exploration of solutions and reliance on empirical research findings in decision-making. The desire to show visibility to various constituencies in order to attain legitimacy and ensure a flow of resources to the organization may force executives to adopt a task-oriented style of management. In so doing, they seek to achieve short-term results without basing their organizational systems and patterns of management on systematic, planned, and evidence-based work that requires time, attention, and intellectual curiosity.

DIFFICULTIES DERIVING FROM THE RELATIONSHIP BETWEEN RESEARCH AND PRACTICE, AND CONCEPTUAL GAPS BETWEEN RESEARCHERS AND PRACTITIONERS IN THE FIELD

Many of the difficulties in implementation of EBMgt derive from the relationship between research and practice and from conceptual gaps between researchers and practitioners. Researchers and practitioners may adhere to different ideologies and professional values, and may have fundamentally different approaches. Management researchers are primarily interested in questions deriving from a deep-rooted theoretical understanding of organizational and administrative processes. Although this knowledge provides theoretical insights, its practical contribution is somewhat limited. In contrast, practitioners seek concrete, immediate responses to urgent issues and daily crises for which theoretical knowledge does not provide practical solutions. There are also clear gaps between the definition of research questions by researchers on the one hand, and "real questions" encountered by executives, which demand practical rather than ambiguous theoretical solutions. Findings have indicated that unlike researchers, executives show some resistance to theoretical pluralism (Arndt & Bigelow, 2009). Whereas researchers are interested in exploring various theoretical perspectives that can explain human behavior as well as social, economic, and political processes and current trends, practitioners seek one best practical solution to an existing problem, and they become confused when they are confronted with too many theoretical approaches.

Furthermore, academic researchers and executives differ with regard to their pace of life and the amount of time that they devote to research questions. Researchers operate under conditions of uncertainty, and need to have a high level of tolerance for ambiguity. They formulate research questions which are examined in a slow, gradual process of collection and analysis of data. Therefore, they do not offer responses or conclusions until they are certain that they have attained a high level of understanding of the processes from a long-range perspective. As indicated, although practitioners also work under conditions of uncertainty, they need to provide immediate solutions to numerous problems and crises. Hence, they operate in brief, limited time intervals, and may not have the flexibility to postpone their decisions until they obtain conclusive empirical evidence.

Additionally, research findings are usually presented in academic and statistical language, which can be unclear and unfriendly, and can discourage practitioners from using the evidence. By nature, researchers are obligated to follow academic rules and norms for publication of evidence. However, practitioners may lack appropriate education and training for critical review of scientific articles or empirical research. Thus, practitioners may disregard research findings, failing to use evidence in their routine work because their understanding of the information is limited and because they do not have time for comprehensive examination of the evidence (Johnson & Austin, 2006). Such disconnection may create communication barriers between researchers and practitioners, preventing the proper implementation of EBMgt. The tension between researchers and practitioners is a conflict between the formal processes of research evidence and the chaotic reality in which practitioners function. This reality is largely shaped by the dynamics and pace of change in the external environment and by the activities of interest groups, as well as by ideologies, beliefs, public opinion, expectations, and the changing needs of clients (Williams, 2006; Wuenschel, 2006).

Facilitating the Implementation of Evidence-Based Management in Nonprofit Human Service Organizations

The implementation of EBMgt in NPHSOs is contingent on several preconditions. The most important precondition for introducing EBMgt in NPHSOs is the creation of a supportive organizational culture that encourages the use of evidence and its assimilation in the organization. Such an organizational culture is based on an ongoing process of examining organizational events and processes, which facilitates openness to changing environments while maintaining organizational boundaries that are permeable to external influences. In this culture, the organization absorbs stimuli from the external environment and translates them into innovative, creative responses as reflected in social programs.

An organization that supports the implementation of EBMgt needs to be able to learn lessons and draw conclusions based on decisions and programs that have been implemented, as well as on the organization's successes and failures. This organizational culture emphasizes skepticism, intellectual curiosity, and critical thinking. This kind of organizational culture encourages key figures at various levels of the organization to base their activities and decisions on empirical data and reliable information that supplements their experience and intuition (Learmonth & Harding, 2006). An organizational culture that facilitates the assimilation of EBMgt is one that promotes the use of research literature to support decisions. This is done by organizing forums for the presentation of relevant ideas, research findings, and empirical evidence from other organizational systems that have succeeded in implementing changes, learning lessons, and drawing appropriate conclusions on the basis of empirical evidence (Schmid, 2010). This culture also supports the establishment of databases for organizational activity that are accessible and available to key figures at various levels of the organization (Fixen et al., 2005).

In this supportive culture, the executives serve as role models, and show that they are willing to use empirical evidence themselves in the process of making decisions. In addition, they need to define the use of evidence as a goal for the entire organization—particularly in contracts with service providers. In accordance with these contracts, the provider organization needs to establish clear criteria for measuring the attainment of those goals using advanced, evidence-based methods of evaluation (Briggs & McBeath, 2009).

Without a doubt, NPHSOs have begun to implement modern methods of management, as indicated at the beginning of this chapter. These methods relate to processes of strategic planning as well as to the introduction of standards and measures of service quality, with emphasis on performance and measurable outcomes. In many countries, these processes are still in the initial stages of assimilation. Notably, social welfare agencies in the United States and Canada have made more intensive efforts to implement evidence-based programs, and have created an appropriate organizational culture that enhances and supports the use of evidence in administrative processes and decisions (Fixen et al., 2005; Trocmé, Milne, Esposito, Laurendeau, & Gervais, Chapter 11, this book). This organizational culture encourages cooperation with academic institutions in order to reduce the inherent tension and alienation between the two systems and improve clinical as well as administrative decisions. Cooperation with academic institutions can be implemented through joint projects and professional teams, which aim to promote learning centers at the community and agency level for the benefit of children, especially children at risk (Aarons, Hurlburt, & Horwitz, 2011; Schmid & Blit-Cohen, 2009; Trocmé et al., Chapter 11, this book).

This organizational culture also needs to encourage client participation in processes of policymaking. Clients have extensive knowledge about their needs, and can offer new ideas that deviate from the routine of the organizations, stimulating alternative ways of thinking. Moreover, the information possessed by clients can contribute to creating an organizational culture that considers the clients' information and knowledge to be an important basis for making decisions.

In addition to the impact of organizational culture, the style of management in these organizations might also play an important role in facilitating the assimilation of EBMgt. Notably, it has been found that when executives involve their staff members in processes of decision-making and problem solving, and encourage the use of knowledge and information, the introduction of EBMgt can be facilitated and implemented in the organization (Pfeffer & Sutton, 2006b). This contradicts the classic approaches that still prevail in many organizations, which are based on a hierarchical structure in which the executive is the central authority who leads the organization toward achieving its goals in the shortest, most efficient way. However, in dynamic, uncertain, and unstable environments, hierarchical structures that rely on formal authority rather than on empirical knowledge and information possessed by key figures are inappropriate, inefficient, ineffective, and fail to achieve their goals. In fact, this kind of hierarchical structure can undermine the organization's stability and endanger its survival.

As for the executives, the functioning and styles of management that they need have a strong impact on the implementation of EBMgt. In that context, they need to base their activities on empirical research findings rather than simply relying on their own past experience, on the experience of colleagues and competitors, or on intuition and partial impressions and perceptions of the situation. As such, they also need to utilize scientific literature rather than rely on popular books that present passing fads in management.

An important condition for implementing EBMgt is a change in the style of proficient superficiality. Instead of adopting an approach that focuses on crises, emphasis should be placed on preventing the crises from happening altogether. One way of preventing crises is to provide an outlet for executives to release the daily tensions they face, and to change their perception that routine work takes precedence over creativity and planning.

An approach that focuses on crisis management deters executives from using empirical evidence because they seek short-term, ad hoc solutions to remove obstacles as they arise. In contrast, they should understand that in order to implement evidence-based management, it is essential to develop an approach that encourages decentralization and delegation of power and authority at various levels of the organization. This approach should be based on comprehensive processes of thought, long-range planning, and tolerance for ambiguity rather than on short-term programs that reflect the visibility of the executive's activity. In this process, executives need to take risks and must be able to deal with potential failure. Beyond that, they need to overcome anticipated resistance from colleagues and workers who prefer to rely on personal experience and available information rather than engage in a comprehensive, systematic review of research findings that can improve the quality of their work or collaborate with others who can, such as academics or purveyors of effective services.

Another important condition for implementing EBMgt is commitment to this approach on the part of directors as well as other members of the organization. Furthermore, executives need to understand that the use of evidence can not only contribute substantially to improving the quality of the organization's administration, functioning, and performance, but can also make a symbolic contribution to establishing the organization's status and positioning the organization in its task environment. Organizations that implement advanced approaches based on use of empirical evidence and collaboration with academic researchers gain more prestige and recognition from various constituencies. The improvement in their status is accompanied by an improvement in the level of legitimacy that they receive from the government and interest groups as well as from their clients, who prefer to receive services from organizations that implement cutting-edge EBMgt and practice. The use of empirical evidence clearly contributes to establishing the organization's professional identity, which distinguishes it from its competitors (Trocmé et al., Chapter 11, this book).

Structural Dilemmas in Implementation of Evidence-Based Management in Nonprofit Human Service Organizations

Notwithstanding the importance of using evidence in administrative processes, many organizations—including NPHSOs—are still far from establishing the conditions and culture that enable this approach to be implemented. Although it is difficult to oppose the use of evidence and empirical knowledge, there is still a gap between theoretical and empirical research findings on the one hand, and the reality in which these organizations operate on the other. In some cases, it appears that the empirical knowledge produced by academic institutions is not relevant to the reality of these organizations and to the work of their executives. This is the situation, even though the government and private donors have high expectations that universities will provide relevant evidence and empirical findings that might contribute to the public, which has to benefit from the knowledge produced by researchers and academic scholars. In this organizational reality, and in light of the pressure exerted on the executives, there are issues and dilemmas that the organizations need to deal with, and which are rooted in the distinctive characteristics of the organizations as well as in the distinctive characteristics of EBMgt.

One major dilemma relates to the relative weight and importance of values and facts in decision-making by top executives. Undoubtedly, both values and facts are important considerations in decision-making. However, it appears that for top executives, the relative weight of values in the decision-making process may be greater than that of facts

(Simon, 1991). Values reflect the social, economic, political, religious, and ethical ideologies of executives, as well as their attitudes toward risk-taking, their openness and willingness to implement changes, and their tolerance for ambiguity in situations of uncertainty. Values tend to be based on personal attributes and educational background (Weick, 1995), which are not necessarily based on evidence but play an important role in the processes of management and decision-making, and which are crucial for the organization's development. In these cases, empirical evidence based solely on research findings can be less important than personal values, because it can confuse the executive, especially when the findings conflict with considerations and values that the executive has chosen in the decision-making process. This structural tension between the contribution of empirical evidence based on research and personal values is an aspect of organizational life that needs to be addressed in the attempt to implement EBMgt.

The second dilemma also relates to the decision-making process in the organization. In this process, values and facts are not the only important components. Rather, both rational and irrational variables play a major role. Although decision-making should ostensibly be based on rational judgment and problem solving should be based on empirical findings and facts, it is also important to be aware of the irrational considerations and behavior that affect this process. Irrational considerations can derive from the value system of the executives, as well as from alternative perceptions of reality, including opportunities, risks, and challenges faced by the organization. In this case, as well, there is structural tension between rationalism, which is represented by research-based evidence in our case, and irrationalism, which is based on the executives' perceptions, attitudes, and behavior and might be considered as essential information for decision-making.

The third dilemma relates to the conflict between use of empirical evidence in order to encourage systematic work based on formal practice guidelines, and the executive's ability for creative and innovative improvisation. EBMgt largely represents formal, organized, systematic, and rational dogmatism, which characterizes academic research. The aim is to implement EBMgt in the work and decision-making processes of executives and professionals in human service organizations. As mentioned, this approach is appropriate for mechanistic and formal organizational systems. However, it is not necessarily appropriate for organizations operating in dynamic, rapidly changing, and uncertain environments, which require unconventional and spontaneous solutions based on creative improvisation and thinking "outside of the box." Consequently, there are tensions in integrating formal, mechanistic components with flexible, organic structures. In that situation, directors and executives in NPHSOs need to find a balance between those properties before the EBMgt approach can be implemented (see also Burns & Stalker, 1961; Schmid, 2009; Woodward, 1965).

Finally, the fourth dilemma relates to the use of evidence and empirical knowledge in tactical and operative decisions versus long-range strategic decisions. From our description of the nature of NPHSOs and the administrative behavior of their executives, it appears almost impossible to apply an evidence-based approach to making tactical and operative decisions. Because executives in NPHSOs have to respond to numerous crises, they adopt a pattern of management that focuses on short-term solutions, although the tendency to implement strategic planning is increasing. However, strategic thought and planning require time and careful consideration. These processes include creating an organizational vision and setting goals, collection and analysis of information, choosing modes of operation, and mobilization of material and human resources. In these processes, it is often necessary to integrate the use of relevant research findings with learning from the experience of others and to collaborate with management consultants and academic scholars who specialize in the organization's areas of interest and can guide the organization in its future development based on a systematic way of thinking and planning. Thus, NPHSOs would do well to open themselves up to the use of research-based evidence and information-based systems, which can make a valuable contribution to improving administrative and strategic processes.

Summary and Future Directions

EBMgt is a relatively new approach that has only been partially applied in organizations in general and NPHSOs in particular. Like earlier evidence-based approaches such as evidence-based medicine and evidence-based practice, EBMgt attempts to base the activities and management of organizations on systematic empirical evidence produced at universities as well as at other institutions. Specifically, the aim is to base decision-making processes on empirical data that is available to directors and staff members in the organization. Whereas the directors of NPHSOs have tended to rely on their experience and on interactions with colleagues rather than on comprehensive reading of research findings and relevant literature, the EBMgt approach seeks to equip them with formal, systematic knowledge that can enhance the organization's performance, transparency, and accountability. Notably, there is very little comparative research on the performance of organizations that have implemented EBMgt versus the performance of organizations that have not implemented this approach (Briggs & McBeath, 2009).

In order to encourage directors of NPHSOs to adopt the EBMgt approach, there is a need to invest more efforts and resources in conducting research that will shed light on the contribution of EBMgt to improving organizational performance and executive decision-making processes. In particular, NPHSOs and their directors need to invest time and other resources in changing their administrative behavior and adopting a new approach which creates an organizational culture that supports the use of evidence. The organizations also need to be confident that the efforts invested in implementing this approach and that the changes in at least some of the existing organizational patterns and processes will have measurable, visible, and effective results. Without conducting research on the relationships between the resources invested and administrative processes that aim to overcome resistance to these changes, it will be difficult to implement EBMgt and persuade executives that this approach has added value.

Against this background, an ambivalent attitude toward EBMgt in NPHSOs is under-
standable. On the one hand, EBMgt is encouraged and viewed as normative executive
behavior in these settings (Johnson & Austin, 2006). On the other hand, it has been
argued that such behavior might cause frustration and impede the organization's performance due to the lack of fit between research findings and the organization's reality
(Walshe & Rundall, 2001). To overcome this ambivalence and promote the implementation of EBMgt in NPHSOs, both parties, that is, the organizations and academic scholars, need to take several essential steps aimed at bridging the gap between theory and
practice by transforming practice into evidence-based information. Researchers in academic institutions are primarily interested in conducting studies that promote their areas
of interest. However, the knowledge produced in this process is not necessarily relevant
to the work of practitioners in the field or to the work of the organization's executives.
If academic researchers believe that it is essential to use empirical evidence, they need to
invest at least some resources in examining issues that concern the organizations. Toward
that end, they need to cooperate with the organizations in formulating the research questions to be examined, and in presenting empirical data that is friendly to the executives
and staff members in those organizations.

However, academic scholars are not solely responsible for bridging the gap between
research and practice. The staff members and directors of NPHSOs, who largely perpetuate the avoidance of using essential empirical information, also need to show that
they are willing to change their style of leadership and work, and invest some of their
time in reviewing recent professional literature and applying it toward dealing with the
issues and dilemmas that the organization faces. They need to change their administrative
behavior, which focuses on crisis management, and integrate the use of evidence in their
work programs as well as in decision-making and evaluation processes.

This change is not easy to implement in the organizational and administrative reality described in this chapter, which encourages the introduction and implementation of
EBMgt. It would be easier to implement EBMgt if academic scholars and practitioners
were to cooperate more closely with each other, and if the practitioners received appropriate guidance in the use of research evidence at an early stage of their professional career
or even beforehand, while they are still enrolled in academic training programs. If they are
not trained to read, review, and use research to promote and support their professional
work—whether their roles are clinical or administrative—it is difficult to expect that
EBMgt will be introduced in these organizations. This applies particularly to directors of
NPHSOs, most of whom were trained as clinicians and promoted to executive positions.
Many of these directors have not been exposed to empirical and theoretical professional
literature, and are not familiar with research in the field. In the best case, they apply their
practical on-the-job training and skills, as well as their personal experience and the experience of their predecessors. In that way, they perpetuate existing organizational practices
and often rely on oral tradition rather than on empirical evidence that can provide them
with new knowledge and enable them to improve their work. To remedy this situation,

NPHSOs need to change their attitude toward the use of evidence-based information and establish bases of knowledge and information that are simple, comprehensible, succinct, accessible, and available (Rousseau & McCarthy, 2007).

As mentioned, the implementation of EBMgt depends not only on changing the attitudes and behavior of the directors, staff members of the organization, and researchers, but also on creating an organizational culture that encourages and supports evidence-based work processes. In this way, it will be possible to promote the use of evidence in organizational and administrative processes in order to improve the functioning of these organizations. Furthermore, creative thinking, critical evaluation, and improvisation should be integrated with strict planning, and brainstorming should be integrated with rational, structured, systematic processes. This combination of approaches will enable NPHSOs to adapt better to the dynamic, rapidly changing reality where some of these organizations have already begun to implement advanced management methods and techniques that rely on evidence-based information and knowledge.

TRAINING SOCIAL WORKERS TO UNDERSTAND

AND USE EVIDENCE

Anat Zeira

THE USE OF research-based knowledge in social work direct practice has been a challenge since the early days of the profession (Dorfman, 1988; Thyer, 2008). This challenge had recently been intensified with the advancement of evidence-based practice (EBP) in social work (Cnaan & Dichter, 2008). Despite the potential contribution of EBP to the effectiveness, efficiency, and accountability of social work (Yunog & Fengzhi, 2009) the profession has encountered several difficulties in bringing EBP to front-line workers (Proctor & Rosen, 2008; Vaughn, Howard, & Thyer, 2009). Consequently, it appears that the effort to implement EBP is yet another round in the research-practice debate (Rubin & Parish, 2010). The purpose of this chapter is to explore some of these difficulties and to suggest strategies for helping social workers understand and systematically use research-generated knowledge in their everyday practice.

More specifically, I claim that advancement of research use in social work direct practice requires a cognitive shift that must be accompanied by a change in the organizational culture and climate of the profession. I suggest that incorporating evaluation processes as part of routine practice could serve as a first step toward enhancing social workers' understanding and use of evidence. Routine evaluation of practice, conducted by practitioners, provides the link between general research knowledge about broader populations and the more specific characteristics of individual clients (Grady, 2010). The result of this incorporation may be an increased use of evidence in their practice decisions, as suggested by EBP models (Howard, McMillen, & Pollio, 2003).

The chapter first briefly reviews the need to train social workers to use evidence in their daily practice and describes types of knowledge that could be useful in the field. It then identifies a number of factors that promote and hinder the use of evidence in practice and suggests possible strategies to incorporate evaluation process as part of their routine practice. Finally, it discusses the need to create an organizational climate that will introduce and maintain the core principles of EBP, stressing the need for ongoing and consistent feedback and supervision that will facilitate its implementation.

Use of Evidence in Social Work Direct Practice—Past and Present

The use of evidence in direct practice has been a central debate in social work since its inception nearly 100 years ago, when Abraham Flexner (1915, as cited in 2001) charged that social work lacked the necessary scientific knowledge to be defined as a profession. In the context of defining social work as a profession, Flexner also discussed Goethe's quote: "To do is easy; to think is hard." In this discussion he emphasized the interrelationships between professional acts (i.e., what professionals are doing) and the rationale behind the act (i.e., why they do it) that at the time lacked any empirical support. Despite the tremendous progress the profession has achieved since Flexner's constitutive speech, the discussion over the scientific base for social work is as relevant as ever.

EBP is the integration of clients' clinical state and circumstances, clients' values and preferences, and research evidence, and optimally combining these three pieces of information into the decision-making process would be considered clinical expertise (see Sackett, Straus, Richardson, Rosenberg, & Haynes, 2000, for the original model; Gibbs, 2003, for the adaptation of the model to social work; and Haynes, Devereaux, & Guyatt, 2002, for the leap to clinical expertise). Looking at the underpinning of these three interrelated components it seems that, at least in social work, using the best research evidence appears to be the weakest link because of a traditional reluctance to refer to the research literature (Mullen & Bacon, 2006) and a perceived lack of a high quality, readily accessible body of evidence to support practice (Gibbs & Gambrill, 2002). Early adaptations of this model for social work describe a "systematic process that blends current best evidence, client preferences (where possible), and clinical expertise, resulting in services that are both individualized and empirically sound" (Shlonsky & Gibbs, 2004, p. 137). When looking at the components of this definition, it seems that "clinical expertise" has long been recognized as a primary source of information for practice decisions (Rosen, 1994; Rosen, Proctor, Morrow-Howell, & Staudt, 1995). The second component, addressing clients' values and expectations is considered a core element of social work education and is usually controlled for by using various supervision mechanisms (Bogo, 2005). However, when it comes to the third component, integrating evidence into practice and providing service that is both individualized and empirically sound, it seems that the challenge has not yet been met (Mullen, Shlonsky, Bledsoe, & Bellamy, 2005).

Good practice decision-making requires explicating thinking about the "how to" prior to performing the professional acts (Morris & Barnes, 2008). Moreover, explicating social workers' thinking about their professional acts may be, in fact, a call for accountability (Rosen, 2003). Yet honestly describing one's thinking processes, and then sharing them with another (i.e., in supervision) are not trivial tasks. There may be serious resistance among social workers due to a fear of criticism and, perhaps, to a general lack of critical thinking skills. In the context of social work EBP, critical appraisals of thinking are paramount, and their absence may impede the use of evidence in social work direct practice.

Encouraging workers to explicate their thinking about their professional choices requires preparing them for two separate yet related tasks. One is to spell out their decision process and the other is to overcome organizational and individual obstacles that are involved in the explication process. Moreover, implementing EBP requires and assumes that professionals will systematically acquaint themselves with the extant literature related to a client or similar groups of clients (Soydan, 2007). In other words, what are the interventions that have valid empirical data on effectiveness for specific outcomes within specific populations? Unfortunately, there is consistent indication that social workers do not see research as a primary source of information for their practice decisions (Rosen, 1994; Rosen et al., 1995; Mullen & Bacon, 2006).

The discussion over the use of research in direct practice takes us back to the 1970s (Long & Wodarski, 2010) and has taken many forms over the years (Parrish & Rubin, 2011). Some of it was dedicated to the development of reliable and valid methods of assessing the interventions employed and their attained outcomes (c.f. Corcoran & Fischer, 2000; Hudson, 1982). Such focus on causal results of social interventions was promulgated by a movement in the field to focus on outcomes, and this enhanced the development and promotion of single-system designs (Odom & Strain, 2002). Later these activities, also known as the social work empirical movement (Reid, 2002), sparked the debate over the differential merit of quantitative and qualitative methods in assessing the attained outcomes (Shaw, 2005). Additionally, it should be noted that despite the recognition that qualitative methods had gained traction in the field, these are sometimes treated as less rigorous evidence (Thyer, 2008). Despite the tremendous changes over the years and hundreds of scholarly articles and books exhorting implementation of research-generated knowledge in the daily practice of social work, an easy path to its incorporation into practice has yet to be found.

What Knowledge Could be Useful for Practitioners?

The types of knowledge typically suggested to support decision-making about the effectiveness of interventions have been rank-ordered based on the internal validity of their methods (Petr & Walter, 2009). Generally, results of randomized controlled trials reside at the top of the hierarchy, followed by quasi-experiments, correlations studies, qualitative studies, and case studies (Epstein, 2009, p. 225). It has been suggested that most of these forms of knowledge on effective interventions lack guidelines that are required for their actual application to daily professional practice decisions (Proctor & Rosen, 2008). Moreover, social workers usually become involved when problems and living situations are more complex, thus practice decisions cannot be "bureaucratic," based on rules or manuals only; they sometimes have to be based exclusively on discretion (Zeira et al., 2008). The judgments underpinning this exercise of discretion must result from weighing the evidence about what is likely to work in the majority of cases, and then considering their likely impact in a particular case. For this reason, the literature reflects a drift from the rigorous definition of EBP to the use of terms such as *knowledge-based practice* (Pawson, Boaz, Grayson, Long, & Barnes, 2003) and *evidence-informed practice* (Chalmers, 2005). The differences in the terminology reflect the idea that the evidence and knowledge used to inform practice should incorporate a wide range of sources (Nevo & Slonim-Nevo, 2011) including the expertise and cumulative experience of practitioners.

Moreover, Thyer (2004) argues that "EBP also mandates that we systematically evaluate our own service outcomes" (p. 175). In other words, monitoring and constant evaluation of practice as part of the routine work is necessary to find what best fits the client's current situation (Zeira et al., 2008), and is also a vehicle for linking knowledge from research and practice (Cheetham, 1997). In the next section I will present my understanding of monitoring and evaluation as part of the routine work, and how these activities are related to and contribute to use of evidence by social workers.

Systematic Evaluation and Systematic Planned Practice

Systematic planned practice (SPP; Rosen, 1994) is an important part of evaluation for guiding individual practitioners in their daily work, providing specific steps that facilitate critical thinking at key decision points (Zeira, 2002). SPP was first developed as a framework for planning the entire intervention process (see Rosen & Proctor, 1978, for the general conceptualization; Rosen, 1993, for the model; and Zeira, 2010, for a specific child welfare example) and then became the basis for the conceptual development of practice guidelines (Rosen & Proctor, 2003). While practice guidelines cannot substitute for the process of evidence-informed practice (Gambrill, 2006), the steps of SPP can be applied as part of a broader approach to evaluating individual practice. This conceptual framework is especially useful with regard to developing treatment goals and has been used in past research to explicate social workers' practice wisdom (Zeira, 2010; Zeira & Rosen, 2000).

SPP is based on the notion that professional intervention should involve conscious and rational decisions (Rosen, Proctor, & Livne, 1985). It concerns future activities (i.e., planning the treatment) that reflect the intentions of the worker without the compromises made due to daily concerns, such as caseload or lack of time. Furthermore, it is "content free" and thus can be applied to all theoretical approaches, client units, and administrative procedure. Figure 10.1 is a simplified version of this model that

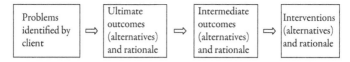

FIGURE 10.1. Core components of systematic planned practice.

demonstrates the logical sequence between its core components. A treatment plan that is undertaken in phases comprises three basic components: the client problems, the desired outcomes, and the intervention strategies. Such a treatment plan resembles a cognitive map (Bitonti, 1993) or other models of cognitive schemata. It starts with the client's presented problem/s that lead the worker to identifying all relevant alternatives for ultimate outcomes (i.e., possible solutions to the problem) and the necessary intermediate outcomes and their alternatives (i.e., steps on the way to the ultimate outcome/s). Finally, the worker identifies the interventions (and their alternatives) that best fit to attain each of the intermediate outcomes. To each of these steps the worker is asked to provide a rationale that ideally should be based on current best knowledge and client's preferences and values. Eliciting the worker's reasoning for each step manifests the clinical expertise notion of EBP. Moreover, treatment plans are client-specific, which means that workers think about the specific sequence of their professional acts and as a result select interventions that are likely to attain the specific desired outcomes for each of the different clients in their caseload.

SPP is a practical device because it is a self-administered tool that practitioners can use as part of documenting the daily activities without any investment in technological devices such as expensive computerized programs. Incorporating the SPP model in the routine work of human services creates situations that force practitioners to think prior to acting, to search for evidence and focus attention on their decision-making process. Further, SPPs are one of the fundamental building blocks of learning at an agency or institutional level. They are a virtual gold mine of clinical data on the actual practice decisions of social workers and, in aggregate, tell the story of services and can be used for evaluative purposes (Epstein, 2010). Treatment plans are "ready sources of information that may be utilized by managers for service improvements and strategic planning" (Foster, Harris, Jackson, & Glendinning, 2008, p. 547). The linkage between outcomes and interventions enforced by SPP and the requirement to provide a client-specific rationale for these choices makes this model particularly appealing to enhance evidence use by social workers (Rosen & Proctor, 2003).

Evaluation as Part of Routine Social Work Direct Practice

Professional intervention aims generally to preserve or improve the well-being of clients. Since each professional intervention is intentional and is directed toward a goal, every professional action should have a desired outcome (Rosen, 1994). Yet, social workers experience difficulties in articulating the rationales that guide them through the process of identifying an outcome related to a client's presenting problem, let alone measuring the attainment of that outcome. Instead, they frequently report only that they feel they are doing well with their clients (Shaw & Shaw, 1997). As nice as this feeling may be, it is not a substitute for a systematic evaluation of what is done to what effect.

Evaluation of direct social work practice thus should primarily reflect the extent to which interventions are implemented as planned and the degree to which the desired outcomes have been attained (Grinnell & Unrau, 2008). In other words, we ask if the problematic situation for which the intervention was implemented (hopefully, as intended) has been resolved. If there is still a problem, what is its extent? Is there a need for further intervention? Moreover, the evaluation should focus not only on the extent to which the outcome is attained, but also should look at the causal relationships between the interventions and outcomes. Hence, practice evaluation should be a process that includes systematic, ongoing monitoring of the interventions implemented and the various outcomes they yield (Levin-Rozalis, 2003).

Systematic evaluation of the intervention process should be based on a reasoned presentation of its components indicating a logical connection between them. That is, it should provide a description of the portion of the change in the client's condition that can be attributed to the intervention employed. Therefore, the intervention process should be documented to facilitate the tracking of its operation. The concept of treatment fidelity pertains to the extent of congruence between what was actually done and what was suggested by the intervention model, and its measurement is critical to systematic evaluation of program effectiveness (Royse, Thyer, & Padgett, 2006). A stronger congruence reflects increased internal validity (i.e., measuring what we say we are measuring) resulting in greater certainty that the intervention prompted the outcome. However, the reality of providing services in less controlled situations (i.e., not as part of a study) often results in deviation from the planned intervention. Therefore, it is necessary to keep a record of the changes made to the model that was actually implemented. Well-documented treatment plans followed by documentation of the process of service provision may provide opportunity to address issues of treatment fidelity.

The process of systematic evaluation is largely parallel to the four-phase problem-solving process (Rosen, 1993) that can run in tandem with the process of evidence-informed practice. The first phase is to identify the problem/s for treatment. In other words, make a decision on the foci of the intervention. This could be a problem(s) faced by a single client or a problem faced by a group of clients. In the second phase, based on the problems identified, the worker lays out the various interventions or alternatives for action. Evidence-informed processes of searching for and appraising current best evidence are well situated in this phase. In the third phase the worker chooses interventions that, if employed, are most likely to attain the desired outcomes. This is a combination of quality appraisal and considering whether the intervention is likely to work for a specific client or group of clients. Finally, in the fourth phase, the worker assesses the extent to which outcomes were attained. Workers need this information in order to decide whether to continue, change, or terminate an intervention with a specific client (Ivanoff, Blythe, & Tripodi, 1994).

While the articulation of the client's problem is performed as part of the intake process and during the initial interview, making decisions about the desired outcomes is a complex planning activity. It requires that the worker know not only the Clients' problems but also their strengths, resources, and values. At the same time the worker should be familiar with a diverse range of alternative outcomes to these problems. Decisions about the desired outcomes will determine the variety of interventions that are available for this case. Carrying out these planning activities requires extensive knowledge about effective interventions (Long & Wodarski, 2010). Hence, training social workers to plan their professional activities and to carry them out with high fidelity should increase the proper use of evidence.

Implementation of Systematic Evaluation: Barriers and Facilitators

The successful implementation of systematic evaluation at an individual practitioner-client level requires personal skills and commitment, as well as a setting that is conducive to such an approach. Below is a review of factors that promote and hinder such implementation, and suggestions to overcome the barriers.

PERSONAL—EMOTIONAL FACTORS

Professional help is a process that must be explicitly reasoned and based on best available knowledge and efficient use of resources (Rosen, 1994), and we must find ways through which it will be possible to trace professional actions. Transparency of professional workers' decision-making process is the cornerstone of accountability both in terms of what is provided to clients and how well practitioners are performing. However, systematic observation of worker action and performance can create substantial unease and resistance (Reid & Smith, 1989). Observing the process of providing help—whether it is done by the external researchers or internal procedures—exposes workers to possible criticism. The fear of criticism may result in a lack of cooperation, hindering the implementation of systematic evaluation as part of routine work.

Exposure to possible criticism raises many concerns—implicit and explicit—among workers. Expressions of implicit concern may come in the form of avoiding participation in evaluation activities, possibly resulting in dismissive attitudes toward evaluation that can be reflected in contemptuous statements (e.g., evaluation is unnecessary and will not advance the clients; we are already doing these activities but with different tools; I know my clients better than these tools) and poor data collection efforts (Reid & Smith, 1989).

Dismissive attitudes are sometimes also an expression of a lack of confidence or even professional distress. Social workers who struggle to reveal the reasoning behind their decisions may be masking a lack of confidence or even competence, and this may translate to poor quality services for clients (Proctor & Rosen, 2008). Such expressions should be treated as learning opportunities, making it important to detect workers who show such concerns, particularly those that utilize passive resistance, and to normalize their discomfort and provide appropriate support, training, and supervision.

PERSONAL—COGNITIVE FACTORS

The second group of personal factors that hinders the implementation of systematic evaluation as part of routine work is related to the misconception that practice and evaluation activities are separate. Just like physicians who are expected to treat their patients according to reasoned protocols, social workers should be expected to provide reasoning about their processes of assessment and intervention. However, workers may perceive the requirement to provide such systematic accounts of the intervention and its aftermath as a "research" activity that is not relevant to their practice work with clients (Zeira, 2002). Additionally, field workers are too often busy with their workload and may find it difficult to see the bigger picture. Therefore, if they do not see an immediate benefit of incorporating systematic procedures of evaluation, they may dismiss them as irrelevant. For example, in an effort to save time, workers may write occasional notes instead of using standardized forms to record information. Such notes are sometimes destroyed to maintain the confidentiality of clients, they do not include the date or the larger context of the situation, they tend to be sporadically written, and they lack structure. Taken together, it is difficult to see how such information gathering is useful for exploration of decision-making either at the moment or at a later date.

Thus, it may be that negative perceptions and misconceptions of systematic evaluation and its procedures impede their use, and efforts to counter such thinking should be included in any process of change. One strategy to overcome this difficulty is to reach an agreement between the workers and the organization about the necessity and usefulness of systematic evaluation and its components, including SPP. This requires a cognitive shift about the inherent benefits of this approach to both the individual client and all clients treated by a single worker as well as the entire organization. Systematic information that is common and relevant to many clients and is available to everyone in the organization will have positive effects on the design of the interventions (Greenhalgh, Robert, MacFarlane, Bate, & Kyriakidou, 2004). In fact, several instruments are designed for use in practice, directly with clients, to improve the quality of service (Hudson, 1982; Mullen, Bledsoe, & Bellamy, 2008), making them far more than tools for researchers. Workers who understand and accept this idea are more likely to adopt procedures included in systematic evaluation.

ORGANIZATION-LEVEL FACTORS

Too often, organizational factors (e.g., lack of time, large caseload, and insufficient technology) have been identified as barriers to the use of research in practice (Bellamy,

Bledsoe, Mullen, Fang, & Manuel, 2008; Edmond, Megivern, Williams, Rochman, & Howard, 2006; Greenhalgh et al., 2004; Proctor et al., 2007). To overcome this obstacle it may be necessary to alter certain organizational culture and/or allocation of resources. For example, allowing workers sufficient time to complete structured forms (e.g., SPP). Many social workers perceive such tasks as administrative duties rather than an important part of practice and thus give them inadequate attention (Zeira, 2002). Lack of time may also be used as an argument to avoid proper documentation (Zeira & Wolfsfeld, 2003). However, the lack of systematic documentation processes may actually harm the work of the organization and result in a waste of resources. For example, resources that are needed to reconstruct missing information in files (e.g., past interventions and outcomes) exceed those that are necessary for proper documentation in the first place. Additionally, such reconstructed information would probably be biased and inadequately reflect past interventions (Benbenishty, 1996). Therefore, giving social workers additional time to systematically document their activities, as they occur, may actually be time-saving in the long run and can increase the effectiveness of service. At an organizational level, the completion of measures should be formally included in workload calculations, thus matching organizational expectations with organizational behavior and giving workers the time they need to reliably complete their tasks. Though this may cost money in the short term, the investment will pay off with higher quality services as the information is used to guide decisions and evaluate practice.

Another organizational factor pertains to introducing organizational change. In this case, implementing systematic evaluation as part of the routine work may be a major change in the way a social service organization operates. To successfully implement such wholesale change, the participation and coordination of all the professional and administrative staff in the organization is necessary (Fernandez & Rainey, 2006), and a serious attempt to follow a well-constructed implementation protocol (Mildon, Dickinson, & Shlonsky, Chapter 5, this book) is advisable.

One innovative way to adjust organizational culture and behavior is to partner with a university that is interested in facilitating the application of evidence-informed practice in real-world settings. Partnerships between university researchers and social workers aimed at promoting evaluation procedures are especially useful, as researchers bring research expertise (Begun, Berger, Otto-Salaj, & Rose, 2010; Mullen, 1998) and help workers decide what to measure and how and then help them analyze the data. For example, in the UK there is a national university-based collaborative research dissemination initiative "Making Research Count" that works in partnership with local authorities (http://www.york.ac.uk/spsw/research/mrc). Another example from Canada is detailed elsewhere (Trocmé, Milne, Esposito, Laurendeau, & Gervais, Chapter 11, this book).

Such initiatives aim to disseminate research from academics, practitioners, and users, to improve local services by encouraging knowledge sharing and networking among professionals and to support social workers in undertaking research and evaluation. They could evoke mechanisms embedded in the agencies resulting in management information systems that can make comparisons at the regional or national level. By doing so, the university and the local agency develop a much needed critical perspective about practice-relevant knowledge.

Concluding Thoughts

Since the early 2000's we have witnessed the growth of a body of knowledge about effective interventions in various forms. Treatment manuals, findings of intervention research, meta-analyses of studies, and systematic reviews in specific areas are now easily accessible thanks to advances in technology. Still, the problem of idiographic application of empirical generalizations remains. The result is that social workers may not be using the best evidence in their practice decisions, leaving the research-practice gap intact. Moreover, increasingly sophisticated statistics about effects of interventions can be inaccessible to the field workers, making it far less likely that they will use this information in practice.

To enhance the use of evidence in direct practice, social workers need constant support of many kinds and on many levels. On the personal level, supervision is essential for unraveling complex cases and identifying and defining treatment goals. Training practitioners to carry out systematic evaluations of their work as part of their daily routine is considered of major importance to the delivery of effective services (Long & Wodarski, 2010). Thus, supporting practitioners to develop these skills is vital.

At the same time, closer partnerships with researchers are needed to make research-generated knowledge more applicable. Such partnerships are also vital for the research agenda contributing to EBP (Epstein, 2010). On the organizational level, understanding what practitioners need (e.g., resources such as time and infrastructure) in order to become more systematic is essential for promoting the use of research evidence in the decision-making process.

Last, systematic evaluation is a way to test whether what is done in practice results in positive outcomes (Weiss, 1997). Engaging practitioners in systematic evaluation procedures involving their own practice increases their need for evidence to better inform their professional decisions. If research evidence is provided in an easily accessible format and its use is accommodated by a strong organizational culture, the likelihood that evidence will actually be used in practice will increase, resulting in higher quality services and, ultimately, improved outcomes for clients.

11

SUPPORTING EVIDENCE-BASED MANAGEMENT IN CHILD PROTECTION

A Canadian University-Agency Collaboration

Nico Trocmé, Lise Milne, Tonino Esposito, Claude Laurendeau,

and Mathieu-Joel Gervais

Introduction

Child protection services make up one of the fastest growing social service delivery sectors in Canada. The number of maltreatment investigations conducted by child protection authorities has doubled since 1998, with over 235,000 children per year being investigated due to suspected child maltreatment (Trocmé et al., 2010). Canada spends three to four billion dollars per year on direct child protection services, and the annual indirect costs are estimated to be over 15 billion dollars (Bowlus, McKenna, Day, & Wright, 2003). Despite this rapid expansion, surprisingly little is known about the children and families receiving these services, and even less is known about the efficacy of the services (Flynn & Bouchard, 2005). Information provided by the provinces and territories responsible for delivering these services is generally limited to annual service volume counts, while most jurisdictions do not report on key indicators such as rates of investigation substantiation, length of service, stability of placement, and rates of recurrence. While in some jurisdictions the failure to report on these key indicators can be attributed to limitations in information systems, in others it appears that the full potential of existing clinical information systems has not been used. Experience from sectors that have invested more heavily in research shows that the challenge is not simply to do more research and collect more data, but that organizations must develop learning cultures where the question of what works becomes a central component of all decision-making (Dash, Gowman, & Traynor, 2003; Davis & Howden-Chapman, 1996; Huberman, 1993; Lomas, 2003). Since 2003 child protection agencies in the province of Québec have had access to one of the most sophisticated computerized client information systems in Canada, and the province has invested more in child protection research than any other jurisdiction in Canada. Nevertheless, Québec child protection agencies have made limited use of these data and research in general. This chapter describes a knowledge mobilization (KMb) initiative in a midsize urban child protection agency in Québec designed to support a management culture shift where the question of such data, research, and overall evidence would become central to decision-making.

The evidence-based management (EBM) in child protection initiative aimed to implement a focused KMb strategy that would bring together managers, researchers, and clinicians to integrate the best available evidence at all levels of policy and service delivery decision-making. The project was initiated following a request from Batshaw Youth and Family Centres (BYFC), Montréal's Anglophone child protection agency, for assistance from McGill's Centre for Research on Children and Families (CRCF) in helping them make better use of evidence-based practices and develop mechanisms to determine the impact of their services. The 4-year EBM pilot project was funded through a Social Sciences and Humanities Research Council (SSHRC) Knowledge Impact in Society grant, with financial and in-kind contributions from McGill University, BYFC, and the Association des Centres Jeunesse du Québec (ACJQ).

Knowledge Mobilization Partnerships

Traditional research dissemination strategies have only limited impact on policies and practices (Bate & Robert, 2002; Waddell et al., 2005). Jonathan Lomas, director of the Canadian Health Services Research Foundation (CHSRF), argues that the most successful examples of health services research affecting practice emerge from organizations that have invested significantly in research and have integrated research at all levels of their organizational structure (Lomas, 2003).

The CHSRF defines knowledge exchange to be the:

collaborative problem-solving between researchers and decision makers that happens through linkage and exchange. Effective knowledge exchange involves interaction between decision makers and researchers and results in mutual learning through the process of planning, producing, disseminating, and applying existing or new research in decision-making. (http://www.chsrf.ca/keys/glossary_e.php)

KMb moves beyond a unidirectional dissemination model by embedding knowledge utilization and knowledge generation within the core structure of organizations (Clark & Kelly, 2005).

RESEARCHER AND USER COLLABORATION STRATEGIES

Collaboration strategies aim to increase the use of research evidence by reinforcing the links between researchers, clinicians, and managers. They rely on continuous exchanges that permit the sharing of knowledge between actors (Landry, Amara, & Lamari, 2001). Collaborative strategies are grounded in constructivist theories of learning. These theories assume that new knowledge is filtered and shaped by a preexisting understanding that individuals constantly construct meaning and explanations based on their experience (Walter, Nutley, & Davies, 2003). Collaboration between researchers, clinicians, and managers can be increased using two strategies: structuring networks of formal and informal exchanges and using a knowledge broker.

NETWORKS OF FORMAL AND INFORMAL EXCHANGES

Formal and informal exchange mechanisms between researchers, clinicians, and managers contribute to bringing producers and users of research evidence closer and thus increasing receptivity toward evidence-based practices (Amara, Ouimet, & Landry, 2004; Landry et al., 2001). Studies show that active participation of users in the research process supports instrumental and conceptual use of evidence (Cousins & Simon, 1996; Huberman, 1993). Similarly, recent research shows that relational capital (i.e., the quality and frequency of exchanges between researchers and users) is crucial in supporting the use of evidence (Amara et al., 2004; Baumbusch et al., 2008; Kothari, Birch, & Charles, 2005). The importance of establishing networks of formal and informal exchanges between researchers, clinicians, and managers in order to increase evidence-based practices is now recognized within the field of child and family services (Tribble et al., 2008; Nutley, Walter, & Davies, 2009).

Structuring networks of formal and informal exchanges also relies on the influence of social actors such as opinion leaders to inform and persuade their colleagues of the usefulness of evidence-based practices. Opinion leaders represent individuals such as colleagues, researchers, and managers who have a strong capacity to influence the beliefs and actions of their peers (Locock, Dopson, Chambers, & Gabbay, 2001). These leaders generally are perceived as qualified in their field of practice, have well-developed social skills, conform to the organizational values and have high social status (Rogers, 2003). They are seen as key actors to facilitate the adoption of new evidence-based practices within an organization (Eccles & Foy, 2009; Nutley & Davies, 2001).

KNOWLEDGE BROKERING

The role of the knowledge broker is primarily to facilitate the process of transfer, sharing, and use of research evidence. The CHSRF defines knowledge brokering as activities that link decision-makers with researchers by facilitating their interactions in order to understand their respective goals and professional cultures, influence their work, create new partnerships, and promote the use of research-informed evidence in decision-making (2003). However, due to its recent adoption in the health and social services fields, the effectiveness of knowledge brokering has not yet been evaluated in a systematic way. Nonetheless, qualitative and nonrandomized studies suggest that knowledge brokering seems to be effective in supporting use of research-informed evidence (Kramer & Cole, 2003; Kramer & Wells, 2005; Sharp, 2005).

ORGANIZATIONAL STRATEGIES

Organizational strategies aim to create the structural and organizational conditions necessary to improve evidence-based decision-making, and can be compared to the organizational excellence model proposed by Walter et al. (2003). In this model the key to developing research-based practice lies not with individual users or policymakers, but with the leadership, management, and organization of social care organizations. The model focuses on adapting and learning from research at the organizational level to reflect local circumstances and priorities. Practitioner knowledge becomes integrated with research knowledge in a much more dynamic and interactive process, through testing out research findings and shaping them to local contexts and experience.

However, creating change at the organizational level is often difficult, expensive, and lengthy. A literature review carried out by Heller and Arozullah (2001) highlights the importance of four key elements to set up effective and efficient organizational strategies: (1) clear and strong leadership on behalf of management teams; (2) well-defined change goals/objectives; (3) a facilitative infrastructure and adequate resources (monetary, material, human); and (4) a formal engagement to integrate change into everyday practices. Several authors stress the importance of the commitment of senior managers (Rogers, 2003; VanDeusan Lukas et al., 2007; Zohar, 2002), the establishment of a common and shared vision of the desired impacts (Greenhalgh, Knight, Hind, Beverley, & Walters, 2005), adequate organizational resources (Grol, 2002), and receptivity to acquiring new knowledge (VanDeusen Lukas et al., 2007) in order to support evidence-based decision-making at the organizational level.

KNOWLEDGE PRODUCTION PARTNERSHIPS

Most KMb initiatives have evolved through attempts to extend the impact of research, initially through greater focus on dissemination and, more recently, through the development of research partnerships designed to better integrate research with the needs of policymakers and service providers (Gollop et al., 2006). Denis and Lomas (as cited in Gollop et al., 2006) describe collaborative research as "an evolving research program based on cumulative discovery" between researchers and decision-makers. They argue that collaboration goes far beyond developing research agreements in order to achieve predetermined objectives. In their experience full collaboration occurs when: (1) the investment of time and other resources required of collaborative research is identified as worthwhile by both researchers and practitioners; (2) trust is predicated on informal interactions that are essential to the success of collaborative research; (3) in combination with the above, the involvement of people may be more important to the success of collaborative research than the processes put in place; and (4) researchers and practitioners are on a mutual journey toward collaborative research that does not have a clear destination This process-intensive collaboration is seen as a necessary condition to developing research that will be trusted and used by decision-makers (Bate & Robert, 2002 ; Lomas, 2000).

Successful research partnerships are built on trust between researchers, decision-makers, and practitioners (CHRSF, 2003.; Hemsley-Brown, 2004). All invested parties benefit when they "learn about each other's working culture and establish personal relationships" (CHSRF, 2003). The development of communication networks between researchers and practitioners/decision-makers and their involvement in the research process has been found to improve research use (Hemsley-Brown, 2004). Trust is developed and nurtured over time and via positive experiences between the partners. Both unstructured and structured interactions and formal and informal interactions are important for building trust in the relationship and for assessing the progress and planning next steps (CHSRF, 2003).

The relationship between researchers, decision-makers, and policymakers is one of the fundamental factors for promoting research utilization within an agency. Consistent contact (e.g., face-to-face, e-mail, phone), formal and informal exchanges, mutual respect and trust, and open dialogues are imperative qualities of the partnership. Researchers, decision-makers, and policymakers have different career trajectories and skills, and are part of different occupational cultures that rarely intersect without a concerted effort. This underscores the difficulties of establishing a collaborative relationship with a mutual understanding and mutual goals (Dash et al., 2003). For these reasons, consistent efforts must be made to link the parties on a regular basis and to clearly identify mutual objectives and goals as well as the processes and resources required. Given the different professional languages spoken in their respective sectors, a dialogue of mutual understanding should be coconstructed (Dash et al., 2003).

RELEVANCE AND TIMELINESS

Studies examining health research in the United Kingdom show that use of such research depends on the extent to which it is seen as relevant to the National Health Services agenda (Hemsley-Brown & Sharp, 2003). Research evidence is less likely to be used if it is not perceived as relevant to the issues that decision-makers are grappling with, and if it is not readily available in a timely manner (Hemsley-Brown, 2004). Topics that are of interest to decision-makers, clear delineation of policy and practice implications of the research findings, and a realistic appraisal of the research findings are critical for addressing this barrier (CHSRF, 2003; Hemsley-Brown, 2004). The relevance and utilization of research depends in part on the extent to which policymakers and service providers participate in setting the research agenda.

EVIDENCE-BASED SERVICES FOR CHILDREN AND FAMILIES

There is an increasing need to improve the quality of the psychosocial services intended for children and families in difficulty (Hoagwood & Johnson, 2003; Walter, Nutley, Percy-Smith, McNeish, & Frost, 2004; Webb, 2002). Recent research also supports the importance of the application of evidence-based practices in regard to treatments in order to improve the services offered within child protection centres (Goyette & Charest, 2007; Trocmé, Esposito, Laurendeau, Thomson, & Milne, 2009; Turcotte, Lamonde, & Beaudoin, 2009).

In order to develop practices in conformity with research evidence in child protection centres, managers must be able to support their strategic choices and management decisions with research-informed evidence. Although desirable, the task of bringing research and practice together within child protection centres must overcome important obstacles that may lead to inadequate use of research-informed evidence (Aarons & Palinkas, 2007; Proctor et al., 2009). Researchers have examined the use of research-informed evidence and have shown that in spite of the investment of effort, a gap persists between the development of empirical knowledge and its use by the clinicians and the managers working within the field of child and family services. A recent investigation carried out in a large urban Québec child protection centre with nearly 450 clinicians and managers concluded that only 22% of the managers and 18% of the clinicians often use research-informed evidence in order to guide their practices (Chagnon, Pouliot, Malo, Gervais, & Pigeon, 2010). These results are similar to those from an Ontario Department of Mental Health for Youth investigation carried out with a similar sample of managers and clinicians which showed that more than half of the participants estimate that their organization does not adequately apply research-informed evidence in order to improve clinical practices (Barwick et al., 2008). These results point to the importance of examining and understanding the conditions that ensure that research-informed evidence is adequately used in practice by child protection centre managers and clinicians.

The use of research to inform policy and practice decisions depends on the extent to which the research is perceived by decision-makers as being relevant and credible. Relevance and credibility, in turn, depend on the extent to which research emerges from a partnership between researchers and decision-makers. Effective partnerships require that researchers be prepared to let service providers and policymakers participate and shape the research agenda, and also make use of a broad range of sources of evidence. KMb requires: (1) making time and resources available to support accessing research; and (2) demonstrating this commitment by integrating research within core management structures. In this context, partnerships between researchers, service providers, and policymakers must move beyond shared research projects to develop mechanisms for universities and related research centres. These mechanisms should make their skills and resources available to service organizations as they move toward evidence-based management, providing the organizational infrastructure and culture to support evidence-based practice.

The Evidence-Based Management Model

The EBM initiative was designed as a child protection. KMb model that places the question of evidence at the forefront of management and service delivery decisions in a child protection agency. As described below, three sets of principles drove the project.

MOBILIZING KNOWLEDGE TO SUPPORT MANAGEMENT-LEVEL DECISIONS

The overall objective of the EBM initiative was to develop and support a management culture where the question of evidence was at the forefront of key management decisions. While this may seem to be a fairly trite objective, in practice decisions about child protection policies and programs have generally not been evidence-based but have relied on legal statutes and regulations, tradition, and opinion based on personal experience. EBM seeks to support managers' capacities to evaluate evidence that a program has been shown to be effective in the past, and, once implemented, to monitor the extent to which the program is in fact meeting its objectives.

The first phase of the project focused on developing a KMb program in a single midsize child protection agency: Batshaw Youth and Family Centres (BYFC). BYFC provides child protection services to Montreal's Anglophone and Jewish communities, serving approximately 5,000 children a year with a staff of 1,100 employees including 100 clinical managers. The decision to focus on a single agency was based on several considerations. First and foremost, the BYFC had approached the university to request help in making better use of research as a management tool. Given the developmental nature of the project, it was important to operate in an environment where different strategies could be explored and evaluated. Furthermore, we anticipated that this type of culture change exercise would require a high level of engagement from the partnering agency, as well as from the university. Experience from similar exercises in the health sector indicated that without full engagement of the management structure this type of initiative could drift into becoming a satellite research project (Lomas, 2003; Sharp, 2005).

Managers rather than clinicians were targeted, given that studies evaluating the effectiveness of KMb initiatives in the health and education sectors show that shifting to an evidence-based organizational culture hinges on the extent to which managers value and use research (Hemsley-Brown & Sharp, 2003). The term *evidence-based management* (EBM) was used rather than *evidence-based practice* (EBP) because the types of decisions and evidence primarily targeted focused on broader policy and service-delivery questions rather than client-specific decisions. This focus on management-level decisions was driven both by our organizational culture-change objective as well as by some of the challenges that had been previously identified in implementing EBP at the clinical level in child protection (Briggs & McBeath, 2009; Fixsen, Naoom, Blase, Friedman, & Wallace, 2005; Pfeffer & Sutton, 2006).

INCLUDING MULTIPLE FORMS OF EVIDENCE

While the principle of basing management decisions on the best available evidence naturally met with strong support, careful thought needed to be given to what types of information should count as "evidence." In order to respond effectively to the types of management decisions that need to be made on a day-to-day basis in a child protection organization, the concept of *evidence* used for this project could not be limited to published research and systematic reviews; rather it was expanded to also include statistics derived from the agency's client and service information systems, as well as clinical and client expertise. This inclusive definition of *evidence* was illustrated in the form of an *Evidence Triangle* that was referred to in presenting the project to agency staff.

RELEVANT, ACCURATE, TIMELY, AND LOCAL

Building on a model developed by the CHSRF (Lomas, 2003; Sharp, 2005) the EBM initiative was based on the assumption that to develop a strong agency culture where research is valued, KMb must be driven by: (1) relevant questions that decision-makers are faced with in their day-to-day activities; (2) accurate responses to these questions; (3) responses to these questions that are provided in a timely fashion (weeks or months, not years); and (4) responses that make as much use as possible of local expertise and information, avoiding wherever possible time-consuming and resource-intensive supplementary data collection procedures. Questions can range from relatively narrow technical issues (e.g., sorting out unit of analysis problems created by a data base that confounded complaints and number of complainants or helping select clinical measures) to questions related to program planning or evaluation (e.g., analyzing service trends, conducting client surveys, or evaluating program outcomes). Along with the *Evidence Triangle* described in the previous paragraph, the *relevant, accurate, timely, and local* (RATL) principles helped shape the activities that were developed to support the EBM project.

EBM Activities

A range of strategies for supporting access to and integrating evidence into management decisions were initiated, eventually leading to five types of activities: (1) using service statistics to track client outcomes; (2) supporting the use of published research through "clinical integration groups"; (3) using survey methods to systematically gather information from clinicians or clients; (4) developing an in-house research publication; and (5) giving managers access to knowledge brokers (KBs).

SERVICE STATISTICS INTEGRATION GROUPS

BYFC has a comprehensive computerized client information system based on a common platform shared by all child protection centres across Québec. While the information system was being used extensively as an individual client clinical information recording system and was used for management purposes to generate a range of reports, primarily in the form of month-end or year-end case-counts, it did not provide managers with the kind of information they needed to understand client service trajectories. Making better use of the clinical information system was in fact one of the primary reasons that BYFC originally approached the CRCF for assistance. The Service Statistics Interpretation Group (SSIG) was designed to bring the CRCF data analysis team together with agency managers in an iterative group process that moves from conceptualizing data requests to interpreting the data to reporting it (Trocmé et al., 2009). Over a period of three years the SSIG met on a regular basis (every 6 to 8 weeks) to select indicators, develop operational definitions, interpret and contextualize results, identify additional avenues for analysis, and guide the development of dissemination materials. Between meetings, the research team and the agency's IT specialist developed definitional and analytic options that were then brought back to the SSIG for discussion. Several senior managers including the agency's executive director participated actively in the SSIG and provided critical support and leadership in supporting the development and deployment of the indicators.

The SSIG operationalized and analyzed seven outcome indicators, including developing an innovative method for tracking service cohorts. Additional indicators have been analyzed for exploratory purposes, and supplementary analyses have been used to identify client profiles requiring closer attention. By its third year, the SSIG was in a position to report on the outcome indicators internally and publicly. Within BYFC, results were shared with the senior management committee, the board of directors, and a range of management and staff groups. Findings regarding the indicators on recurrence of maltreatment, court rates, school delay, placement rate, placement stability, and time in out-of-home care were highlighted in issues of *In-the-Know*, an in-house research publication developed for the project that will be discussed further on. Externally, data have been presented to other Québec child protection agencies, to the Québec Ministry of Health and Social Services, to officials in Ontario, Alberta, France, and Belgium, and at national and international academic conferences. The indicators developed at BYFC are being adopted as a core set of indicators by child protection agencies across Québec, and several First Nations organizations have expressed interest in piloting them in their agencies.

CLINICAL INTEGRATION GROUPS

Keeping up with the literature is a challenge for professionals in any field and especially in areas like child protection, where the urgency of the work always seems to trump reading books and journal articles. Clinical integration groups (CIGs) were developed as a forum that would allow for the integration of the three forms of evidence targeted by EBM, including reviewing agency-generated data, drawing on the experience and knowledge of clinicians, and accessing relevant published research and literature. The group meets approximately every 6 weeks. CIGs are composed of approximately 15 to 20 members, including managers and clinicians representing various points of service in BYFC. Members can also include community experts, facilitating an information-sharing process. The CIGs are led by two agency cochairs and supported by a knowledge brokering team including a university-affiliated researcher who has expertise in the clinical area and a research assistant who provides support for the group's activities. This team model provides an opportunity for the researcher to engage with clinical experts at the agency, and for a paid student research assistant interested in the area to support the researcher and the group by conducting literature searches, obtaining articles, and taking minutes. BYFC Library Services has all material reviewed in the groups available to agency staff. Two CIGs were developed through EBM and continue to operate, one on sexual abuse and one on conjugal violence.

CLINICAL SERVICE SURVEYS

Clinical expertise and client experiences can be difficult to capture in a systematic fashion, yet provide information that is not available from administrative information systems. Although a number of case review procedures are standard practice, there is no mechanism to draw out and aggregate this information at an agency-wide level. Likewise there are a number of mechanisms for addressing client complaints, but these experiences are not necessarily representative of all clients. Surveys can provide a low-cost method to systematically tap into clinical expertise and client experiences to assist managers in monitoring services and developing new programs. With access to CRCF expertise in designing questionnaires and collecting and analyzing data, surveys were seen as a management tool that could feasibly be deployed within the context of the EBM initiative. A first survey was used to consult with agency reviewers who regularly oversee the intervention plans for all cases open for ongoing services. Using an online survey form developed in consultation with the reviewers, information was collected on 348 consecutive cases to examine the comprehensiveness of assessments and the extent to which clients were included in case planning. A second survey was conducted to support the development of an agency-wide neglect program. Focus groups were first held with 40 clinicians to identify service needs specific to situations involving child neglect, and then clinicians completed a survey to systematically track case information regarding 929 children. A third survey examined client satisfaction using telephone-administered questionnaires with 100 parents whose children were involved with the agency. In-kind costs for managing, distributing, and completing the surveys were covered by the agency, while costs for extracting, cleaning, and analyzing data were covered by the research grant.

"IN-THE-KNOW" RESEARCH NEWSLETTER

In-the-Know (ITK, or *Branché* in French) was developed as a BYFC research newsletter supported by CRCF to highlight research activities at BYFC, particularly results from the SSIG analyses of the client outcome indicators. The publication targets BYFC clinical personnel and the agency's partners. The tone and style of the newsletter attempts to strike a balance between establishing a professional look while maintaining an approachable tone that encourages comments from readers. ITK is a quarterly four-page color printed newsletter. In the spirit of recognizing a variety of knowledge and evidence forms, the newsletter includes: (1) analyses of child protection outcome indicators; (2) summaries of student theses and other MSW research papers related to child protection, many of which are completed by BYFC staff returning to study at McGill; (3) summaries of other BYFC research activities; and (4) announcements regarding upcoming research-related activities. Editorial responsibility is shared between BYFC and CRCF.

KNOWLEDGE BROKERS

Developing an efficient process for providing research support is one of the challenges inherent in a university-community partnership like this EBM initiative. Providing evidence in a timely fashion to support management decisions can be particularly challenging in a traditional academic culture where the cost and timelines of thorough and systematic reviews of the literature can be prohibitive (see "Relevant, Local, Accurate, and Timely"). The challenge is to find mechanisms whereby academics can provide technical support without having to provide a fully researched academic opinion. A knowledge broker model provides an interactive approach that tailors research and best practice reviews to the needs and timeframe of the users (Clark & Kelly, 2005; Kramer & Cole, 2003; Kramer & Wells, 2005; Sharp, 2005). Academics with relevant research expertise, usually teamed up with paid graduate students, were recruited as knowledge brokers (KBs) to work in tandem with BYFC managers. Academics agreed to participate because these KB activities provided an opportunity to develop linkages that could serve in developing future research collaborations and helped them keep abreast of current service and policy issues. Furthermore, access to paid research assistants who gathered and organized materials helped to minimize the participation burden for the academics.

The KB teams help formulate research-related questions, access and interpret service statistics from information systems, access and interpret research literature, help design and analyze surveys and evaluations, and link decision-makers to experts who can provide more specialized consultation. While KBs provide technical assistance, the leadership for the projects rests with a BYFC manager. In addition to supporting SSIGs, CIGs, and the three surveys, KBs have supported a number of policy and program activities, such as assisting in extending and monitoring permanency planning policies, analyzing client complaints, and interpreting data on the disproportionate representation of Black children and youth within the agency.

Evaluation

Evaluation of the EBM initiative involved two components: (1) ongoing monitoring and analysis of products and processes by the EBM coordinating team, involving the primary investigator, the director of the Division of Professional Services and the project manager, and (2) participant interviews and questionnaires including a pretest posttest questionnaire (N = 54), focus groups with managers (N = 76) at the beginning of the project, and individual interviews with a selection of managers and researchers at the end of the project (N = 26). An external research team from the University of Québec at Montréal conducted and analyzed the posttest interviews in order to provide an independent perspective.

IMPACT ON PARTICIPANTS

Over 80 BYFC staff and close to 20 students and academics were directly involved in EBM activities over the course of 4 years. At the outset of the project managers had identified a number of barriers to accessing service statistics and research, including difficulties generating consistent aggregated statistics using the agency's client information system, limited access to published research, poor match between research and the management-related questions they need to make decisions about, and lack of protected time to read relevant studies and reports.

An information utilization survey examining the use of agency statistics, integration of research findings, and access to clinical expertise was distributed to BYFC managers during the beginning of the project and 3 years later as the project was coming to an end. Access and use was rated using Likert-type 7-point scales ranging from 1= "not at all" or "strongly disagree" or "easy" to 7 = "completely" or "strongly agree" or "difficult," with 4 = "neutral" or "average." Items were adapted from the General Decision-Making Style Inventory (GDMS; Funk, Champagne, Wiese, & Tornquist, 1991) and the Barriers to Research Utilization Scale (Scott & Bruce, 1995). Items proven to lack clarity were modified or dropped from the posttest version of the questionnaire. The pretest questionnaire was completed in June 2007 at the beginning of a series of needs-assessment focus groups. Seventy-six out of 86 managers responded to the pretest questionnaire. The posttest questionnaire was distributed in July 2010 by internal mail to all managers who had completed the pretest questionnaires and were still on staff. Fifty-four managers completed the posttest questionnaire. As shown in Table 11.1, results from the pretest posttest surveys showed that self-reported use of

TABLE 11.1

USE OF EVIDENCE REPORTED BY BYFC MANAGERS IN 2007 (PRETEST) AND 2010 (POSTTEST) (N = 54)

Mean Scores	2007	2010	Significance
Agency Statistics			
Ease of access to stats in daily work	4.39 (1.54)	3.46 (1.26)	p ≤ 0.01
Stats relevant to decisions made	4.35 (1.56)	4.91 (1.52)	p ≤ 0.02
Stats provide info needed	4.35 (1.27)	4.82 (1.33)	p ≤ 0.02
Easy access for stats interpretation	4.67 (1.40)	5.17 (1.20)	n.s.
Culture highly values agency data	3.65 (1.45)	4.83 (1.02)	p ≤ 0.01
Overall	4.23 (1.06)	4.64 (0.77)	**p ≤ 0.01**
Published Research			
Kept informed of latest research	3.69 (1.26)	4.20 (1.36)	p ≤ 0.02
Easy access to research	3.80 (1.56)	4.56 (1.56)	p ≤ 0.01
Access/interpret research not a barrier	3.61 (1.53)	2.98 (1.44)	p ≤ 0.01
Research used in decision-making	3.54 (1.41)	3.96 (1.41)	n.s.
Overall	3.70 (0.97)	3.86 (0.95)	**p ≤ 0.01**
Clinical Expertise			
Frequent reference to clinical issues	4.49 (1.49)	5.20 (1.10)	p ≤ 0.01
Culture values clinical expertise	4.64 (1.30)	5.12 (1.38)	p ≤ 0.05*
Overall	4.58 (1.22)	5.11 (1.19)	**p ≤ 0.01**

* Paired t-test, level of significance set at p ≤ 0.05

evidence had increased significantly in terms of accessing and using agency statistics, published research, and clinical expertise.

STRENGTHS AND CHALLENGES

The EBM interview participants and the coordinating team who were interviewed at the end of the project identified a range of outcomes that reflected the strengths and challenges of the project.

Strengths included: (1) an increased capacity to engage in research, better coordination of research-related activities, and better access to research products; (2) use of information systems and survey results to support program and policy development; and (3) increased ability to engage in research and policy development activities with other agencies and government departments. Participants appreciated the creation of new structures and opportunities for exchange within the organization and highlighted the importance of the collaborative relationship established between BYFC and the CRCF. Participants also appreciated the value placed on tacit and clinical knowledge in the evidence production process and the inclusion and recognition of agency staff at all levels of the project.

The challenges can be broken down into five major areas. First, the project was very resource intensive in an environment where resources for research-related activities remains scarce. To date, most Canadian social service funders do not require that interventions be evidence-based, and support for applied research in social service organizations remains limited. While the project was most resource intensive during the first 3 years as activities were being developed, participants remained concerned over time that the CRCF and BYFC would not be able to maintain support for KBs, CIGs, and ongoing analyses of clinical data with a SSIG. Unlike the University Institutes housed in the province's two largest child protection centres (Québec and Montréal), BYFC has limited access to funding to support research initiatives and KMb. Limited access to research infrastructure funds has also been found to be a barrier to KMb in the healthcare field, where research and KMb activities can be difficult to justify (Dobrow et al., 2004; Greenhalgh et al., 2005; Rycroft-Malone, 2008). Because KMb is not seen in child protection to be a core clinical activity, funds for its support fall into the nonessential category that can be cut in times of fiscal restraint. In fact, all of Québec child protection centres were asked by the Ministry of Health and Social Services to make significant cuts in 2011 to their "administrative budgets," which included funds that would support KMb.

A second challenge was related to the efforts made by the coordinating team to structure the dissemination of the research and evidence. Some participants mentioned that the dissemination efforts rested too heavily on the shoulders of the managers and clinicians involved in the activities. Some were unsure what their role was in regard to the dissemination process, and there was a lack of tools or guidelines to support the dissemination activities. Given that structuring the dissemination of evidence requires important investments in time and resources (Johnson & Austin, 2006; Orlandi, 1996; Rogers, 2003), increased access to infrastructures and resources may have helped the coordinating team improve the impact of the EBM project and make it more "alive" for all BYFC staff.

Third, some participants found the developmental structure of the EBM initiative to be a challenge, perceiving some activities as lacking sufficient clarity in regard to their goals and mandates. This may have resulted from the overall complexity of the project in terms of the involvement of numerous participants at different levels and from different organizations. According to some study participants, there was at times a feeling of uncertainty regarding the roles and responsibilities that each actor was to take.

A fourth challenge was the difficulty in maintaining adequate project infrastructure that is of particular importance in the psychosocial field and already highlighted as important in other fields (Hemmelgarn, Glisson, & James, 2006; Proctor et al., 2007). First, there was a change in project managers on three occasions over the course of the project due to circumstances that were not related to the EBM initiative, which was particularly challenging given the process-intensive and developmental nature of the initiative. The project manager played a critical role in coordinating and guiding KBs, who were engaging with the agency using a collaborative model that they generally were not familiar with. Second, while relevant, timely, and local evidence was produced throughout the project, having an organizational structure to build the capacity to use this information and an organizational culture that values it, are equally important factors (Sharp, 2005). For example, while the EBM child protection outcome indicators were considered a major success of the project, more time and additional analyses are required before they can be fully integrated as standard management tools in the agency.

Finally, tracking and measuring the impact of the EBM project proved to be a methodological challenge for at least three reasons: (1) the EBM model was not static: some of the planned activities were dropped, others were adapted to better address information needs of managers, and some unplanned activities were added; (2) the full impact of the EBM project is more likely to be detected over a longer period of time than allowed within the present evaluation time frame; and (3) unlike in academia, where research outputs are systematically tracked, measuring KMb in a social service context is far more challenging both with respect to finding indicators of KMb as well as ensuring these are systematically documented: while most participants found EBM-related activities interesting, they had more difficulty describing the impact of these activities. Now that the model has been operationalized, there is a range of potential strategies to track change in the use of evidence over time (see Greenhalgh et al., 2005; Titler, Steelman, Budreau, Buckwalter, & Goode, 2001; and Werr & Stjernberg, 2003).

Conclusions

The BYFC-McGill EBM collaboration has been a successful partnership that has supported the development of a stronger research culture at BYFC, that has helped the McGill

CRCF develop a research support and collaboration model that it is applying to new initiatives with other community agencies, and that has generated a province-wide data sharing and utilization initiative. The EBM initiative has started to generate interest from child protection organizations in other provinces and even from several European organizations. The evaluation has demonstrated the importance of establishing strategies that rely on interactive processes between researchers and users in order to ensure effective KM. Denis and Lomas (2003) argue that such processes should include: (1) the investment of time and other resources identified as worthwhile by both researchers and users; (2) trust predicated on informal interactions; (3) in combination with the above, the involvement of people as more important to the success of collaborative research than the processes put in place; and (4) collaborative research as a mutual journey between researchers and users that does not have a clear destination. The study found that the EBM project succeeded in all four of these areas of collaboration, the end result of which was the development of a sustainable knowledge-sharing relationship between BYFC and the CRCF.

The collaboration required a significant investment of time and resources on the part of the researcher and the agency. Leadership from a "hands on" coordinating team was essential, but required an engaged and motivated group of clinicians and managers who were prepared to commit to the EBM activities and a research team that was able to produce evidence that was "relevant, local, accurate and timely." Numerous staff, students, and researchers were involved in the project, resulting in enriched learning experiences and the opportunity to engage in a mutually beneficial process. These mutual benefits were not always easily achieved in light of the differences in the cultures of the two organizations. The fact that these paths rarely intersect without a concerted effort underscores the difficulties of establishing a collaborative relationship with a mutual understanding and mutual goals (Dash et al., 2003). For these reasons, consistent efforts were made to link the CRCF and BYFC staff on a regular basis and to clearly identify mutual objectives and goals, processes and resources required, and to coconstruct a dialogue of mutual understanding (Dash et al., 2003).

As is often the case with developmental projects, lessons learned from initiatives were as useful as successes in refining the model. The difference in cultures and approaches between an agency with a structured service mandate and a university with a teaching and research mandate proved to be a recurrent challenge that required frequent adjustment and clarification of roles and expectations. While BYFC dedicated significant additional resources to support EBM activities, the agency does not have sufficient access to the kinds of resources that would allow it to optimize some of the opportunities that have emerged from the project. Care had to be taken not to generate expectations for new research and learning initiatives that could not be sustained. Despite strong and sustained senior management support for the EBM initiative, the capacity of the organization to fully realize the potential of some of the tools developed through the project remains limited by the resources available. As with most social service organizations, moving to a results-driven management model continues to be a challenge.

The EBM project has brought to the forefront larger issues of funding and management cultures that go beyond the specific organizations involved in the initiative. There is a weak tradition of integrating research and evidence into social service management in Canada. Unlike the health sector, where there are well-established teaching and research hospitals and public health agencies with health surveillance and research mandates, the social service sector remains needs- and regulation-driven rather than outcomes-driven. Ironically, BYFC's limited access to research and evaluation resources may have concealed equally concerning capacity limitations at the level of McGill's CRCF, and more broadly limited research and evaluation capacity in schools of social work across Canada. Had the agency made additional requests for methodological support, it is unlikely that the CRCF would have had the capacity to respond.

The mutual benefits of the agency-university collaboration initiated by the EBM project appear to have set in motion a process that is generating the needed resources to sustain and even expand the collaboration. With funds from the Royal Bank of Canada (RBC), the CRCF is expanding research and evaluation training opportunities for students to help address the Centre's limited capacity to maximize the research potential in child protection agencies. RBC funds are also allowing the CRCF to continue to provide support to BYFC for producing ITK, the joint BYFC-CRCF research publication, and to staff two ongoing CIGs. Furthermore, on the strength of the EBM demonstration project, a partnership including the CRCF, BYFC, three additional midsize child protection centres, the provincial association of child protection centres, and two First Nations organizations has obtained funding for a 7-year SSHRC funded research partnership grant that will support an expansion of EBM and additional research training programs for graduate students. The next challenge will be to assess the extent to which the projects generated by these initiatives are leading improvements in practices and ultimately better outcomes for the children and families receiving these services.

Epilogue

BRINGING TOGETHER LEADING scholars with different viewpoints and expertise can be both rewarding and somewhat contentious, especially with respect to something as central to the academic endeavor as the generation and use of evidence. In our case, though, we discovered more common ground than difference, and this led to detailed discussions about how to better move evidence into practice while accounting for the complexity that characterizes social services.

To begin with, all of our authors supported an increased reliance on the use of evidence in policy, management, and direct services provision. For far too long, social services have functioned without the benefit of an adequate evidence base. Even when evidence is present it is often not used, and the type, extent, and quality of services are dictated more by politics, tradition, opinion, economics, or some other nonevidentiary driver. Despite the consensus about the better use of evidence, all present acknowledged many of the challenges associated with moving evidence into practice, including how to define terms such as *evidence-based* or *evidence-informed*. Indeed, the inherent difficulty of executing anything approaching *evidence-based practice* on a system-wide scale was clear.

Bringing together scholars from different parts of the world helped sharpen one of the issues most central to using evidence—the interplay between context and evidence. Even when adopting an expansive model of evidence-based practice, one that is in line with the original Sackett, Richardson, Rosenberg, and Haynes (1997) model (i.e., is inclusive of different methods and integrates the client into the decision-making process), it turns out that the model is unable to easily incorporate many of the contextual factors at play. We were able to explore how context affects evidence and the extent to which evidence is generalizable across contexts. Simply put, the broader context counts. That is, the broader contexts at the client and service provider levels (i.e., socioeconomic, political, historical, professional, organizational) can sometimes be more influential with respect to outcomes than the actual service that is delivered. The discussions also revealed the multiple and nested contexts that we need to consider both when generating and when using evidence. Exploring how context impacts practices, programs, services, and policies may be one of the most fruitful areas for future scholarly investigations.

Rather than ignoring complexity, our exchange prompted us to acknowledge that the use of evidence in practice and policy is a process rather than a prescription. This process involves describing the complexities of a given service area; identifying the key features of service provision including major decision points, organizational pressures, and desired outcomes; statistically modeling broader demographic trends within communities and the pathways of service recipients through existing systems; identifying target populations and desired outcomes; and systematically locating and reviewing evidence of effectiveness for programs, practices, or policies that address these outcomes. Furthermore, evidence must be implemented well if we expect to observe positive outcomes. Also crucial is employing an implementation science lens focused on using existing empirically supported programs or, alternatively, developing sets of potentially effective common elements into customized programs. Likewise, these programs and practices should be put into operation using implementation science frameworks that better integrate the intervention and the service context. While presented linearly, this process is likely to take many twists and turns as complexity is grappled with and, ultimately, embraced as part of the service delivery process.

Our discussions also led us to a greater appreciation of the richness and multidimensional nature of evidence. Although a *hierarchy of evidence* may exist for evidence of effectiveness, a better way to look at complex social interventions is to first consider the question. If the question involves finding out what the most effective service might be for a specific population with a specific challenge, then high-quality systematic reviews, such as found in the Campbell and Cochrane Collaborations and that include rigorously conducted randomized controlled trials (RCTs) are essential sources of information where they exist. If, however, the information needed involves such things as identifying organizational barriers to implementation within an agency, or the dispersion of a particular kind of problem in a given geographic area, or the likelihood of entering care within a given child protection system, the effectiveness hierarchy is no longer relevant and other methods are needed. Further, as we move away from the original context in which RCTs were used, their findings should be viewed more cautiously and supplemented by additional evidence to support implementation in a different context.

Whereas much of the literature on evidence-based practice has focused on the use of manualized interventions, the field has begun to develop an alternative framework for delivering potentially effective services through the use of common elements. These are commonly used, discrete practices found within programs that have been found to be effective. Using these elements singly or in combination, agencies and practitioners will have a ready alternative to manualized interventions that are sometimes unavailable, expensive, or difficult to master. Furthermore, the use of common elements might better map on to the different contexts in which services are provided, offering an additional opportunity to deliver innovative, flexible, and potentially effective services.

Yet the promise of effective programs and practices can be undermined by poor implementation. The rapid development of implementation science as its own field is an indication that practitioners, agency providers, and policymakers have begun to understand the importance of implementation and the inherent challenge of moving a program or practice successfully into the field. We suggest that implementation strategies should be considered from the very beginning, as early as program development, and that existing implementation frameworks can be used to guide initial program use and eventual scale-up in the field. This suggestion holds for the use of more traditional manualized programs as well as the newer common elements approach. In a very real sense, implementation can be thought of as an extension of program development. That is, a solid implementation framework and plan can lead to successful adaptation that, in turn, can improve a program and its ability to be adapted across contexts.

In all of these movements toward the use of evidence in practice, the generation, collection, and modeling of data are key. Systematic monitoring, ongoing evaluation, and continuous quality improvement are not separate from evidence-informed practice. They are part and parcel of the process and, if agencies are to make a reasonable attempt at using evidence in practice, systems for implementation and outcomes monitoring are crucial. New technologies are making such systems far more affordable.

Complexity does not have to translate into inaction. But complexity does mean that simplistic approaches are unlikely to work, We have, in this book, outlined suggestions and examples for moving evidence into practice using a wide range of tools and ideas, carefully avoiding prescriptions that do not account for the complexity of social services. Our hope is that evidence, in its various forms, will become more thoughtfully, deliberately, and effectively used to improve outcomes for children and families.

References

INTRODUCTION

Aarons, G. A., Hurlburt, M., & Horwitz, S. M. (2011). Advancing a conceptual model of evidence-based practice implementation in public service sectors. *Administration and Policy in Mental Health and Mental Health Services Research, 38*(1), 4–23.

Duncan, B. L., Miller, S. D., Wampold, B. E., & Hubble, M. A. (2010). *The heart and soul of change: Delivering what works in therapy.* Washington, DC: American Psychological Association.

Gambrill, E. (1999). Evidence-based practice: An alternative to authority-based practice. *Families in Society, 80*, 341–350.

Gibbs, L. E. (2003). *Evidence-based practice for the helping professions: A practical guide with integrated multimedia.* Pacific Grove, CA: Brooks/Cole-Thomson Learning.

Gilbert, N., Parton, N., & Skivenes, M. (2011). *Child protection systems: International trends and orientations.* New York: Oxford University Press.

Gilbert, R., Fluke, J., O'Donnell, M., Gonzalez-Izquierdo, A., Brownell, M., Gulliver, P., . . . Sidebotham, P. (2012). Child maltreatment: Variation in trends and policies in six developed countries. *Lancet, 379*(9817), 758–772.

Kadushin, A., & Martin, J. A. (1988). *Child welfare services* (Vol. 4). New York, NY: Macmillan.

Kamerman, S. B., Phipps, S. A., & Ben-Aryeh, A. (2010). *From child welfare to child well-being: An international perspective on knowledge in the service of policy making.* Dordrecht; New York: Springer.

Sackett, D. L., Richardson, W. S., Rosenberg, W., & Haynes, R. B. (1997). *Evidence-based medicine: How to practice and teach EBM.* New York: Churchill Livingstone.

Weightman, K., & Weightman, A. (1995). "Never right, never wrong": Child welfare and social work in England and Sweden. *International Journal of Social Welfare, 4*(2), 75–84. doi:10.1111/j.1468-2397.1995.tb00083.x

CHAPTER 1

Aarons, G. A., Hurlburt, M., & Horwitz, S. M. (2011). Advancing a conceptual model of evidence-based practice implementation in public service sectors. *Administration and Policy in Mental Health and Mental Health Services Research, 38*(1), 4–23.

Australian Government Department Families, Housing, Community Services and Indigenous Affairs. (2009). *National Framework for Protecting Australia's Children 2009–2020*. Retrieved April 16, 2013, from http://www.fahcsia.gov.au/our-responsibilities/families-and-children/publications-articles/protecting-children-is-everyones-business?HTML

Benbenishty, R. (1989). Combining single-system and group comparison approaches to evaluate treatment effectiveness on the agency level. *Journal of Social Service Research, 12*, 31–48.

Benbenishty, R., & Astor, R. (2005). *School violence in context: Culture, neighborhood, family, school, and gender.* New York: Oxford University Press.

Benbenishty, R., & Astor, R. A. (2007). Monitoring indicators of children's victimization in school: Linking national-, regional-, and site-level indicators. *Social Indicators Research, 84*(3), 333–348. doi:10.1007/s11205-007-9116-4

Benbenishty, R., & Astor, R. A. (2012). Monitoring school violence in Israel, national studies and beyond: Implications for theory, practice, and policy. In S. R. Jimerson, A. B. Nickerson, M. J. Mayer, & M. J. Furlong (Eds.). *The handbook of school violence and school safety: International research and practice* (2nd ed., pp. 191–202). New York: Routledge.

Benbenishty, R., Jedweb, R., Lavi-Sahar, Z., & Lerner-Geva, L. (in press). Predicting the decisions of hospital based child protection teams to report to child protective services, police and community welfare services. Child Abuse and Neglect.

Benbenishty, R., & Oyserman, D. (1991). Clinical information system for the Israeli foster care system. *Chevra U'Revacha, 11*, 148–155. [Hebrew]

Benbenishty, R., & Oyserman, D. (1995). Integrated information systems for human services: A conceptual framework, methodology and technology. *Computers in Human Services, 12*(3–4), 311–325.

Chaffin, M., Bard, D., Bigfoot, D. S., & Maher, E. J. (2012). Is a structured, manualized, evidence-based treatment protocol culturally competent and equivalently effective among American Indian parents in child welfare? *Child Maltreatment, 17*(3), 242–252.

Chalmers, I. (2005). If evidence-informed policy works in practice, does it matter if it doesn't work in theory? *Evidence and Policy: A Journal of Research, Debate and Practice, 1*(2), 227–242. doi:10.1332/1744264053730806

Courtney, M. E., Dworsky, A., Brown, A., Cary, C., Love, K., Vorhies, V., & Hall, C. (2011). *Midwest evaluation of the adult functioning of former foster youth: Outcomes at age 26.* Chicago: Chapin Hall Center for Children at the University of Chicago.

Dettlaff, A. J., Rivaux, S. L., Baumann, D. J., Fluke, J. D., Rycraft, J. R., & James, J. (2011). Disentangling substantiation: The influence of race, income, and risk on the substantiation decision in child welfare. *Children and Youth Services Review, 33*(9), 1630–1637. doi:10.1016/j.childyouth.2011.04.005

Dolev, T., Schmid, H., Sabo-Eliel, R., & Barnir, D. (2008). *The policy of "With the Face to the Community": An evaluation study.* Jerusalem: JDC-Brookdale.

Durlak, J. A., & DuPre, E. P. (2008). Implementation matters: A review of research on the influence of implementation on program outcomes and the factors affecting implementation. *American Journal of Community Psychology, 41*(3–4), 327–350.

Durrant, J. (2012). Physical punishment of children: Lessons from 20 years. *Canadian Medical Association Journal, 184*(12), 12.

Epstein, I. (2010). *Clinical data-mining: Integrating practice and research.* New York: Oxford University Press.

Bloom, M., Fischer, J., & Orme, J. G. (2009). *Evaluating practice: Guidelines for the accountable professional* (6th Edition). Boston: Allyn and Bacon.

Fixsen, D. L., Naoom, S. F., Blasé, K. A., Friedman, R. M., & Wallace, F. (2005). *Implementation research: A synthesis of the literature.* FMHI Publication No. 231. Tampa: University of South Florida, Louis de la Parte Florida Mental Health Institute, National Implementation Research Network.

Friend, C., Shlonsky, A., & Lambert, L. (2008). From evolving discourses to new practice approaches in domestic violence and child protective services. *Children and Youth Services Review, 30*(6), 689–698.

Gambrill, E. (1999). Evidence-based practice: An alternative to authority-based practice. *Families in Society, 80,* 341–350.

Gambrill, E. (2001). Social work: An authority-based profession. *Research on Social Work Practice, 11*(2), 166–175.

Gambrill, E. (2006). Evidence-based practice and policy: Choices ahead. *Research on Social Work Practice, 16*(3), 338–357. doi:10.1177/1049731505284205

Gambrill, E. (2010). Evidence-informed practice: Antidote to propaganda in the helping professions? *Research on Social Work Practice, 20*(3), 302–320. doi:10.1177/1049731509347879

Gershoff, E. T., Grogan-Kaylor, A., Lansford, J. E., Chang, L., Zelli, A., Deater-Deckard, K., & Dodge, K. A. (2010). Parent discipline practices in an international sample: Associations with child behaviors and moderation by perceived normativeness. *Child Development, 81*(2), 487–502.

Gibbs, L. E. (2003). *Evidence-based practice for the helping professions: A practical guide with integrated multimedia.* Pacific Grove, CA: Brooks/Cole-Thomson Learning.

Gilbert, N., Parton, N., & Skivenes, M. (2011). *Child protection systems: International trends and orientations.* New York: Oxford University Press.

Gilbert, R., Fluke, J., O'Donnell, M., Gonzalez-Izquierdo, A., Brownell, M., Gulliver, P., ... Sidebotham, P. (2012). Child maltreatment: Variation in trends and policies in six developed countries. *Lancet, 379*(9817), 758–772.

Goerge, R. M., Wulczyn, F. H., & Harden, A. W. (1995). *An update from the multistate foster care data archive.* Chicago: Chapin Hall Center for Children at the University of Chicago.

Gray, J. A. M. (1997). *Evidence-based healthcare: How to make health policy and management decisions.* New York: Churchill Livingstone.

Gray, J. A. M. (2004). Evidence based policy making: Is about taking decisions based on evidence and the needs and values of the population. *BMJ: British Medical Journal, 329*(7473), 988.

Guyatt, G. H. (1991). Evidence-based medicine. *ACP Journal Club, 114*(supp 2), A–16.

Haynes, R. B., Devereaux, P. J., & Guyatt, G. H. (2002). Clinical expertise in the era of evidence-based medicine and patient choice. *Evidence Based Medicine*, *7*(2), 36–38. doi:10.1136/ebm.7.2.36

Kalibala, S., Schenk, K. D., Weiss, D. C., & Elson, L. (2012). Examining dimensions of vulnerability among children in Uganda. *Psychology, Health and Medicine*, *17*(3), 295–310.

Kamerman, S. B., Phipps, S. A., & Ben-Aryeh, A. (2010). *From child welfare to child well-being: An international perspective on knowledge in the service of policy making.* Dordrecht; New York: Springer.

Littell, J. H., Popa, M., & Forsythe, B. (2005). Multisystemic therapy for social, emotional, and behavioral problems in youth aged 10–17. *Cochrane Database of Systematic Reviews* (3), CD004797. doi:10.1002/14651858.CD004797.pub3

Lorenzo-Blanco, E. I., Unger, J. B., Baezconde-Garbanati, L., Ritt-Olson, A., & Soto, D. (2012). Acculturation, enculturation, and symptoms of depression in Hispanic youth: The roles of gender, Hispanic cultural values, and family functioning. *Journal of Youth and Adolescence*, *41*(10), 1350–1365.

Marmot, M. G., Syme, S. L., Kagan, A., Kato, H., Cohen, J. B., & Belsky, J. (1975). Epidemiologic studies of coronary heart disease and stroke in Japanese men living in Japan, Hawaii and California: Prevalence of coronary and hypertensive heart disease and associated risk factors. *American Journal of Epidemiology*, *102*(6), 514–525.

McCracken, S. G., & Marsh, J. C. (2008). Practitioner expertise in evidence-based practice decision making. *Research on Social Work Practice*, *18*(4), 301–310.

Mullen, E. J., Bledsoe, S. E., & Bellamy, J. L. (2008). Implementing evidence-based social work practice. *Research on Social Work Practice*, *18*(4), 325–338.

Munro, E. (2011). *The Munro Review of Child Protection: Final report—A child-centred system.* CM 8062-8062.pdf. Retrieved April 15, 2013, from http://www.official-documents.gov.uk/document/cm80/8062/8062.pdf

Nutley, S., Walter, I., & Davies, H. T. (2009). Promoting evidence-based practice models and mechanisms from cross-sector review. *Research on Social Work Practice*, *19*(5), 552–559.

O'Donnell, M., Nassar, N., Jacoby, P., & Stanley, F. (2012). Western Australian Emergency Department presentations related to child maltreatment and intentional injury: Population level study utilising linked Health and Child Protection data. *Journal of Paediatrics and Child Health*, *48*(1), 57–65.

Ontario Commission to Promote Sustainable Child Welfare. (2012). *A new approach to accountability & system management—report and recommendations.* Ontario, Canada. Retrieved from http://www.children.gov.on.ca/htdocs/English/documents/topics/childrensaid/commission/2012sept-Accountability_system_management.pdf

Orme, J. G., & Cox, M. E. (2001). Analyzing single-subject design data using statistical process control charts. *Social Work Research-New York*, *25*(2), 115–127.

Pierce, L., & Bozalek, V. (2004). Child abuse in South Africa: An examination of how child abuse and neglect are defined. *Child Abuse and Neglect*, *28*(8), 817–832.

Regehr, C., Stern, S., & Shlonsky, A. (2007). Operationalizing evidence-based practice the development of an institute for evidence-based social work. *Research on Social Work Practice*, *17*(3), 408–416. doi:10.1177/1049731506293561

Sackett, D. L., Richardson, W. S., Rosenberg, W., & Haynes, R. B. (1997). *Evidence-based medicine: How to practice and teach EBM.* New York: Churchill Livingstone.

Schneiderman, J. U., Smith, C., & Palinkas, L. A. (2012). The caregiver as gatekeeper for accessing health care for children in foster care: A qualitative study of kinship and unrelated caregivers. *Children and Youth Services Review, 34,* 2123–2130.

Segal, U. A. (1992). Child abuse in India: An empirical report on perceptions. *Child Abuse & Neglect, 16,* 887–908.

Shlonsky, A., Friend, C., & Lambert, L. (2007). From culture clash to new possibilities: A harm reduction approach to family violence and child protection services. *Brief Treatment and Crisis Intervention, 7*(4), 345.

Shlonsky, A., & Gibbs, L. (2004). Will the real evidence-based practice please stand up?: Teaching the process of evidence-based practice to the helping professions. *Brief Treatment and Crisis Intervention, 4*(2), 137. doi:10.1093/brief-treatment/mhh011

Shlonsky, A., Noonan, E., Littell, J. H., & Montgomery, P. (2011). The role of systematic reviews and the Campbell Collaboration in the realization of evidence-informed practice. *Clinical Social Work Journal, 39*(4), 362–368. doi:10.1007/s10615-010-0307-0

Shlonsky, A., & Wagner, D. (2005). The next step: Integrating actuarial risk assessment and clinical judgment into an evidence-based practice framework in CPS case management. *Children and Youth Services Review, 27*(4), 409–427.

Sundell, K., Ferrer-Wreder, L., & Fraser, M. W. (2013). Going global: A model for evaluating empirically supported family-based interventions in new contexts. *Evaluation and the Health Professions.* Published online prior to print edition 4 January 2013. doi: 10.1177/0163278712469813

The Center for Effective Discipline. (2013). *U.S.: Corporal punishment and paddling statistics by state and race.* Retrieved April 14, 2013, from http://www.stophitting.com/index.php?page=statesbanning

Unicef. (2004). Child care system reform in Romania 2004. Retrieved from https://www.google.com.au/search?q=child%20welfare%20system%20reform%20in%20romania%20unicef&ie=utf-8&oe=utf-8&aq=t&rls=org.mozilla:en-US:official&client=firefox-a

US Department of Health and Human Services, Administration for Children and Families. (2012). *Information memorandum.* ACYF-CB-IM-12-04. Retrieved from http://www.acf.hhs.gov/sites/default/files/cb/im1204.pdf

Walter, I., Nutley, S., & Davies, H. (2005). What works to promote evidence-based practice? A cross-sector review. *Evidence and Policy: A Journal of Research, Debate and Practice, 1*(3), 335–364.

Webster, D., Needell, B., & Wildfire, J. (2002). Data are your friends: Child welfare agency self-evaluation in Los Angeles County with the family to family initiative. *Children and Youth Services Review, 24*(6–7), 471–484. doi:10.1016/S0190-7409(02)00197-4

Wengler, A. (2011). The health status of first-and second-generation Turkish immigrants in Germany. *International Journal of Public Health, 56*(5), 493–501.

Wulczyn, F. (2009). Epidemiological perspectives on maltreatment prevention. *The Future of Children, 19*(2), 39–66.

Wulczyn, F. H., & Goerge, R. M. (1992). Foster care in New York and Illinois: The challenge of rapid change. *Social Service Review, 66*(2), 278–294.

Wulczyn, F., Daro, D., Fluke, J., Feldman, S., Glodek, C., & Lifanda, K. (2010). *Adapting a systems approach to child protection: Key concepts and considerations.* UNICEF.

CHAPTER 2

Baumann, D. J., Fluke, J. Graham, J. C., Wittenstrom, K., Hedderson, J., Riveau, S., Detlaff, A., Rycraft, J., Ortiz, M.J., James, J., Kromrei, L., Craig, S., Capouch, D., Sheets, J., Ward, D., Breidenbach, R., Hardaway, A., Boudreau, B., & Brown, N.... Brown, N. (2010, March). *Disproportionality in child protective services: The preliminary results of statewide reform efforts.* Austin Texas: Texas Department of Family and Protective Services.

Baumann, D., Kern, H., & Fluke, J. (1997). Foundations of the decision making ecology and overview. In Kern, H., Baumann, D. J., & Fluke, J. (Eds.). *Worker Improvements to the Decision and Outcome Model (WISDOM): The child welfare decision enhancement project* (pp. 1–12). Washington, DC: The Children's Bureau.

Benbenishty, R., Osmo, R., & Gold, N. (2003). Rationales provided for risk assessments and for recommended interventions: A comparison between Canadian and Israeli professionals. *British Journal of Social Work, 33*(2), 137–155.

Bowers, K. S. (1984). On being unconsciously influenced and informed. In K. S. Bowers & D. Meichenbaum (Eds.), *The unconscious reconsidered* (pp. 227–272). New York: Wiley.

Dalgleish, L. I. (1988). Decision-making in child abuse cases: Applications of social judgment theory and signal detection theory. In B. Brehmer & C. R. B. Joyce (Eds.), *Human judgment: The SJT view* (pp. 317–360). North Holland: Elsevier.

Dalgleish, L. I. (2003). Risk, needs and consequences. In M. C. Calder (Ed.), *Assessments in child care: A comprehensive guide to frameworks and their use.* (pp. 86–99). Dorset, UK: Russell House.

Dalgleish, L. I., & Newton, D. (1996, August). *Reunification: Risk assessment and decision-making* (Oral presentation). 11th International Congress on Child Abuse and Neglect, Dublin.

Davidson-Arad, B., & Benbenishty, R. (2010). Contribution of child protection workers' attitudes to their risk assessments and intervention recommendations: A study in Israel. *Health and Social Care in the Community, 18*(1), 1365–2524.

Dettlaff, A., Rivaux, S., Baumann, D.J., Fluke, J. D., Rycraft, J. R. & James, J. (2011). Disentangling substantiation: The influence of race, income, and risk on the substantiation decision in child welfare. *Children and Youth Services Review, 33*(9), 1630–1637.

Edwards, W. (1954). The theory of decision-making. *Psychological Bulletin, 41,* 380–417.

Edwards, W. (1961). Behavioral decision theory. *Annual Review of Psychology, 12,* 473–498.

Fluke, J. D., Chabot, M., Fallon, B., MacLaurin, B., & Blackstock, C. (2010). Placement decisions and disparities among aboriginal groups: An application of the decision-making ecology through multi-level analysis. *Child Abuse and Neglect, 34,* 57–69.

Fluke, J. D., Shusterman, G., Hollinshead, D., & Yuan, Y. T. (2008). Longitudinal analysis of repeated child abuse reporting and victimization: Multistate analysis of associated factors. *Child Maltreatment, 13*(1), 76–88.

Fluke, J. D., Parry, C., Shapiro, P., Hollinshead, D., Bollenbacher, V., Baumann, D., & Davis-Brown, K. (2001). *The dynamics of unsubstantiated reports: A multi-state study—final report.* Denver, CO: American Humane Association.

Gigerenzer, G. (1991). How to make cognitive illusions disappear: "Beyond heuristics and biases." In W. Stroebe & M. Hewstone (Eds.), *European Review of Social Psychology* (Vol. 2, pp. 83–115). Chichester, England: Wiley.

Gigerenzer, G. (1993). The bounded rationality of probabilistic mental models. In K. L. Manktelow & D. E. Over (Eds.), *Rationality* (pp. 284–313). London: Routledge.

Gigerenzer, G. (1994). Why the distinction between single-event probabilities and frequencies is relevant for psychology and vice versa. In G. Wright & P. Avion (Eds.), *Subjective probability* (pp. 129–162). New York: Wiley.

Gigerenzer, G. (1996). On narrow norms and vague heuristics: A reply to Kahneman and Tversky. *Psychological Review, 103*(3), 592–596.

Gigerenzer, G (2005). "I think, therefore I err." *Social Research, 72*, 1–24.

Gold, N., Benbenishty, R., & Osmo, R. (2001). A comparative study of risk assessments and recommended interventions in Canada and Israel. *Child Abuse and Neglect, 25*(5), 607–622.

Graham, J. C., Fluke, J., Baumann D. J., & Dettlaff, A., (2013). *The decision-making ecology of placing children in foster care: A structural equation model.* Manuscript in preparation.

Hammond, K. R. (1955). Probabilistic functioning and the clinical method. *Psychological Review, 62*, 255–262.

Hammond, K. (1996). *Human judgment and social policy.* New York: Oxford University Press.

Homans, G. C. (1958). Social behaviour as exchange. *The American Journal of Sociology, 63*(6), 597–606.

Hunink, M. G., Glasziu, P., Siegel, J., Weeks, J., Pliskin, J., Elstien, A., & Weinstein, M. (2003). *Decision making in health and medicine: Integrating evidence and values.* Cambridge, UK: Cambridge University Press.

Jones, E. E., & Davis, K. E., (1966). From acts to dispositions: The attribution process in person perception. *Advances in Experimental Social Psychology, 2*, 219–266.

Kahneman, D. (2002). *Maps of bounded rationality: A perspective on intuitive judgment and choice.* Nobel Prize Lecture, December 8. http://www.nobelprize.org/nobel_prizes/economic-sciences/laureates/2002/kahneman-lecture.html

Kahneman, D., & Tversky, A. (1996). On the reality of cognitive illusions: A reply to Gigerenzer's critique. *Psychological Review, 103*, 582–591.

Kelly, H. (1973, February). The process of causal attribution. *American Psychologist, 28*(2), 107–128.

Mansell, J., Ota, R, Erasmus, R., & Marks, K. (2011). Reframing child protection: A response to a constant crisis of confidence in child protection. *Children and Youth Services Review, 33*, 2076–2086.

Mansell, J. (2006). The underlying instability in statutory child protection: Understanding the system dynamics driving risk assurance levels. *Social Policy Journal of New Zealand, 28*, 97–132.

McMahon, A. (1998). *Damned if you do, damned if you don't—Working in child welfare.* Aldershot, UK: Ashgate.

Munro, E. (2005) Improving practice: Child protection as a systems problem. *Children and Youth Services Review, 27*, 375–391.

Munro, E. (2008). Lessons from research on decision-making. In D. Lindsey & A. Shlonsky (Eds.), *Child welfare research: Advances for practice and policy* (pp. 194–200). New York; Oxford, UK: Oxford University Press.

Munro, E., & Hubbard, A. (2011). A systems approach to evaluating organisational change in children's social care. *British Journal of Social Work, 41*(4), 726–743.

National Research Council. (1989). *Improving risk communication.* Washington, DC: National Academy Press.

Rivaux, S. L., James, J., Wittenstrom, K., Baumann, D. J., Sheets, J., Henry, J., & Jeffries, V. (2008). The intersection of race, poverty and risk: Understanding the decision to provide services to clients and to remove children. *Child Welfare, 87*, 151–168.

Rossi, P. H., Schuerman, J., & Budde, S. (1999). Understanding decisions about child maltreatment. *Evaluation Review, 23*(6), 579–598.

Shapira, M., & Benbenishty, R. (1993). Modeling judgments and decisions in cases of alleged child abuse and neglect. *Social Work Research and Abstracts, 29*(2), 14–20.

Shlonsky, A., & Wagner, D. (2005). The next step: Integrating actuarial risk assessment and clinical judgment into an evidence-based practice framework in CPS case management. *Children and Youth Services Review, 27*(4), 409–427. doi:10.1016/j.childyouth.2004.11.007.

Simon, H. (1956). Rational choice and the structure of the environment. *Psychological Review, 29*(2), 129–138.

Simon, H. (1959). Theories of decision-making in economics and behavioral sciences. *The American Economic Review, 49*(2), 253–283.

Stein, T., & Rzepnicki, T. L. (1983). *Decision-making in child welfare intake: A handbook for practitioners.* New York: Child Welfare League of America.

Swets, J. A., Tanner, W. P., Jr., & Birdsall, T. G. (1955). Decision processes in perception. *Psychological Review, 68*, 301–340.

Triantaphyllou, E., & Mann S. H. (1995). Using the analytic hierarchy process for decision-making in engineering applications: Some challenges. *International Journal of Industrial Engineering: Applications and Practice, 2*(1), 35–44.

Tversky, A., & Kahneman, D. (1974). Judgment under uncertainty: Heuristics and biases. *Science, 185*, 1124–1131.

Weiss, S. M., Kulikowski, C. A., Amarel, S., & Safir, A. (1978). A model-based method for computer-aided medical decision-making. *Artificial Intelligence, 11*(1–2), 145–172.

Wittenstrom, K., Fluke, J., & Baumann, D. (2013). *Disparities and reunification: An analysis of interactions and child race.* Manuscript in preparation.

CHAPTER 3

Ahluwalia J. S., Harris, K. J., Catley, D., Okuyemi, K. S., & Mayo, M. S. (2002) Sustained-release bupropion for smoking cessation in African Americans: A randomized controlled trial. *Journal of the American Medical Association, 288*, 468–474.

Andrée Löfholm, C., Brännström, L., Olsson, M., & Hansson, K. (2013). Treatment-as-usual in effectiveness studies: What is it and does it matter? *International Journal of Social Welfare, 22*, 25–34.

Andrée Löfholm, C., Olsson, T., Sundell, K., & Hansson, K. (2009). Multisystemic therapy with conduct disordered youth: Stability of treatment outcomes two years after intake. *Evidence and Policy, 5*, 373–397.

Axberg, U., & Broberg, A. G. (2012). Evaluation of "The Incredible Years" in Sweden: The transferability of an American parent-training programme to Sweden. *Scandinavian Journal of Psychology, 53*, 224–232.

Baldwin, S. A., Christian, S., Berkeljon, A., & Shadish, W. R. (2012). The effects of family therapies for adolescent delinquency and substance abuse: A meta-analysis. *Journal of Marital and Family Therapy, 38*, 281–304.

Barkley, R. (1997). *Defiant children: A clinician's manual for assessment and parent training* (2nd ed.). New York: Guilford Press.

Berkel, C., Mauricio, A. M., Schoenfelder, E., & Sandler, I. N. (2011). Putting the pieces together: An integrated model of program implementation. *Prevention Science, 12*, 23–33.

Bernal, G., Jiménez-Chafey, M. I., Rodrı́guez, M. M. D. (2009). Cultural adaptation of treatments: A resource for considering culture in evidence-based practice. *Professional Psychology: Research and Practice, 40*, 361–368.

Bloomquist, M. L., & Schnell, S. V. (2002). *Helping children with aggression and conduct problems.* New York: Guilford Press.

Bodenmann, G., Cina, A., Ledermann, T., & Sanders, M. R. (2008). The efficacy of the Triple P-Positive Parenting Program in improving parenting and child behavior: A comparison with two other treatment conditions. *Behaviour Research and Therapy, 46*, 411–427.

Burns, T., Catty, J., Dash, M., Roberts, C., Lockwood, A., & Marshall, M. (2007). Use of intensive case management to reduce time in hospital in people with severe mental illness: Systematic review and meta-regression. *British Medical Journal, 335*, 336–341.

Butler, S., Baruch, G., Hickey, N., & Fonagy, P. (2011). A randomized controlled trial of multisystemic therapy and a statutory therapeutic intervention for young offenders. *Journal of the American Academy of Child and Adolescent Psychiatry, 50*, 1220–1235.

Byrne, B. M., & van De Vijver, F. J. R. (2010). Testing for measurement and structural equivalence in large-scale cross-cultural studies: Addressing the issue of nonequivalence. *International Journal of Testing, 10*(2), 107–132.

Castro, F. G., Barrera, M., & Holleran Steiker, L. K. (2010). Issues and challenges in the design of culturally adapted evidence-based interventions. *Annual Review of Clinical Psychology, 6*, 213–239.

Curtis, N. M., Ronan, K. R., & Borduin, C. M. (2004). Multisystemic treatment: A meta-analysis of outcome studies. *Journal of Family Psychology, 18*, 411–419.

Deković, M., Asscher, J. J., Manders, W. A., Prins, P. J. M., & van der Laan, P. (2012). Within-intervention change: Mediators of intervention effects during multisystemic therapy. *Journal of Consulting and Clinical Psychology, 80*, 574–587. doi: 10.1037/a0028482

Durlak, J., & DuPre, E. (2008). Implementation matters: A review of research on the influence of implementation on program outcomes and the factors affecting implementation. *American Journal of Community Psychology, 41*, 327–350.

.Eisner, M., Nagin, D., Ribeaud, D.,Malti, T. (2012). Effects of a universal parenting program for highly adherent parents: A propensity score matching approach. *Prevention Science, 13*, 252–266. doi:10.1007/s11121-011-0266-x

Enebrink, P., Högström, J., Forster, M., & Ghaderi, A. (2012). Internet-based parent management training: A randomized controlled study. *Behaviour Research and Therapy,50*, 240–249 doi:10.1016/j.brat.2012.01.006

Fairchild, A. J. & MacKinnon, D. P. (2009). A general model for testing mediation and moderation effects. *Prevention Science, 10*, 87–99.

Ferrer-Wreder, L., Stattin, H., Lorente, C. C., Tubman, J., & Adamson, L. (2004). *Successful prevention and youth development programs: Across borders.* New York: Kluwer Academic/Plenum.

Ferrer-Wreder, L., Sundell, K., & Mansoory, S. (2012). Tinkering with perfection: Theory development in the intervention cultural adaptation field. *Child and Youth Care Forum, 41*, 149–171. doi 10.1007/s10566-011-9162-6

Fixsen, D. L., Naoom, S. F., Blasé, K. A., Friedman, R. M., & Wallace, F. (2005). *Implementation research: A synthesis of the literature.* Tampa, Florida: University of South Florida, Louise de la Parte Florida Mental Health Institute, The National Implementation Research Network.

Fossum, S., Mørch, W.-T., Handegård, B. H., Drugli, M. B., & Larsson, B. (2009). Parent training for young Norwegian children with ODD and CD problems: Predictors and mediators of treatment outcome. *Scandinavian Journal of Psychology, 50,* 173–181.

Gardner, F., Burton, J., & Klimes, I. (2006). Randomised controlled trial of a parenting intervention in the voluntary sector for reducing child conduct problems: Outcomes and mechanisms of change. *Journal of Child Psychology and Psychiatry, 47,* 1123–1132.

Ginner-Hau, H., & Smedler, A. C. (2011). Different problems—same treatment: Swedish juvenile offenders in community-based rehabilitative programmes. *International Journal of Social Welfare, 20,* 87–96.

Grant, K. E., Compas, B. E., Stuhlmacher, A. F., Thurm, A. E., McMahon, S. D., & Halpert, J. A. (2003). Stressors and child and adolescent psychopathology: Moving from markers to mechanisms of risk. *Psychological Bulletin, 129,* 447–466.

Grissom, R. J. (1996). The magical number.7 +.2: Meta-meta-analysis of the probability of superior outcome in comparisons involving therapy, placebo, and control. *Journal of Consulting and Clinical Psychology, 64,* 973–982.

Hahlweg, K., Heinrichs, N., Kuschel, A., & Feldmann, M. (2007). Therapist-assisted, self-administered bibliotherapy to enhance parental competence short- and long-term effects. *Behavior Modification, 32,* 659–681.

Hansson, K., Cederblad, M., & Höök, B. (2000). Funktionell familjeterapi. *Socialvetenskaplig tidskrift, 3,* 231–243.

Hansson, K., & Olsson, M. (2012). Effects of multidimensional treatment foster care (MTFC): Results from a RCT study in Sweden. *Children and Youth Services Review, 34,* 1929–1936. doi:10.1016/j.childyouth.2012.06.008Harris, K. J., Ahluwalia, J. S., Okuyemi, K. S., Turner, J. R., Woods, M. N., Backinger, C. L., & Ken, R. (2001). Addressing cultural sensitivity in a smoking cessation intervention: Development of the Kick It at Swope Project. *Journal of Community Psychology, 29,* 447–458.

Hrobjartsson, A., & Gøtzsche, P. C. (2001). Is the placebo powerless? An analysis of clinical trials comparing placebo with no treatment. *New England Journal of Medicine, 344,* 1594–1603.

Jaffe, S. R., Caspi, A., Moffitt, T. E., Polo-Tomás, M., & Taylor, A. (2007). Individual, family, and neighborhood factors distinguish resilient from non-resilient maltreated children: A cumulative stressor model. *Child Abuse and Neglect, 31,* 231–253.

Jungmann, T., Kurtz, V., Brand, T., Sierau, S., & von Klitzing, K. (2010). Präventionsziel Kindergesundheit im Rahmen des Modellprojektes „Pro Kind" Vorläufige Befunde einer längsschnittlichen, randomisierten Kontrollgruppenstudie Leitthema: Frühe Hilfen zum gesunden Aufwachsen von Kindern Hintergrund und Fragestellungen. *Bundesgesundheitsbl, 53,* 1180–1187.

Jungmann, T., Ziert, Y., Kurtz, V., & Brand, T (2009). Preventing adverse developmental outcomes and early onset conduct problems through prenatal and infancy home visitation: The German pilot project "Pro Kind." *European Journal of Developmental Science, 3,* 292–298.

Kling, Å., Forster, M., Sundell, K., & Melin, L. (2010). A randomized controlled effectiveness trial of parent management training with varying degrees of therapist support. *Behavior Therapy, 41,* 530–542.

Koning, I. M., Vollebergh, W. A. M., Smit, F., Verdurmen, J. E. E., van den Eijnden, R. J. J. M., ter Bogt, T. F. M., …Engels, R. C. M. E. (2009). Preventing heavy alcohol use in adolescents (PAS): Cluster randomized trial of a parent and student intervention offered separately and simultaneously. *Addiction, 104,* 1669–1678.

Koutakis, N., Stattin, H., & Kerr, M. (2008). Reducing youth alcohol drinking through a parent-targeted intervention: The Örebro Prevention Program. *Addiction, 103,* 1629–1637.

Kumpfer, K. L., Pinyuchon, M., Teixeira de Melo, A., & Whiteside, H. O. (2008). Cultural adaptation process for international dissemination of the Strengthening Families Program. *Evaluation and the Health Professions, 31,* 226–239.

Kurtz, V., Brand, T., & Jungmann, T. (2010). Förderung der kindlichen Entwicklung durch Frühe Hilfen? Vorlaufige Ergebnisse einer langsschnittlichen, randomisierten Kontrollgruppenstudie zum Modellprojekt "Pro Kind." *Präv Gesundheitsf, 5,* 347–352.

Kyhle Westermark, P., Hansson, K., & Olsson, M. (2011). Multidimensional treatment foster care (MTFC): Results from an independent replication. *Journal of Family Therapy, 33,* 20–41.

Leschied, A. W., & Cunningham, A. (2002). *Seeking effective interventions for serious young offenders—Interim results of a four year randomized study of multisystemic therapy in Ontario, Canada. Centre for Children & Families in the Justice System.* Retrieved February 15, 2010, from www.lfcc.on.ca/mst_final_results.html

Leung, C., Sanders, M. R., Leung, S., Mak, R., & Lau, J. (2003). An outcome evaluation of the implementation of the Triple P-Positive Parenting Program in Hong Kong. *Family Process, 42,* 531–544.

Lipsey, M. W. (1999). Can intervention rehabilitate serious delinquents? *The Annals of the American Academy of Political and Social Science, 564,* 142–166.

Littell, J. H., Popa, M., &Forsythe, B. (2005). *Multisystemic therapy for social, emotional, and behavioural problems in youth aged 10–17,* Cochrane library, issue 4, Chichester, UK: John Wiley and Sons.

Lösel, F., & Beelmann, A. (2003). Effects of child skill training in preventing antisocial behaviour: A systematic review of randomized evaluations. *Annals of the American Academy, 587,* 84–109.

Magill, M., & Ray, L. A. (2009). Cognitive-behavioral treatment with adult alcohol and illicit drug users: A meta-analysis of randomized controlled trials. *Journal of Studies on Alcohol and Drugs, 80,* 516–527.

Malti, T., Ribeaud, D., & Eisner, M. (2011). The effectiveness of two universal preventive interventions in reducing children's externalizing behavior: A cluster-randomized controlled trial. *Journal of Clinical Child and Adolescent Psychology, 40,* 677–692.

Magnusson, M. (1999). *Barnhälsovård: Studier av effektivitet och föräldratillfredsställelse* (Comprehensive summaries of Uppsala dissertations from the Faculty of Medicine, 882). Uppsala: Acta Universitatis Upsaliensis.

McConnell, D., Breitkreuz, R., & Savage, A. (2011). Independent evaluation of the Triple P Positive Parenting Program in family support service settings. *Child and Family Social Work.* Advance online publication. doi: 10.1111/j.1365-2206.2011.00771.x

Matsumoto, Y., Sofronoff, K., & Sanders, M. R. (2010). Investigation of the effectiveness and social validity of the Triple P Positive Parenting Program in Japanese society. *Journal of Family Psychology, 24,* 87–91.

Ogden, T., & Hagen, K. A. (2006). Multisystemic therapy of serious behavior problems in youth: Sustainability of therapy effectiveness two years after intake. *Child and Adolescent Mental Health, 11*, 142–149.

Olds, D. L., (2002). Prenatal and infancy home visiting by nurses: From randomized trials to community replication. *Prevention Science, 3*(3), 153–172.

Petrosino, A., & Soydan, H. (2005). The impact of program developers as evaluators on criminal recidivism: Results from a meta-analysis of experimental and quasi-experimental research. *Journal of Experimental Criminology, 1*, 435–450.

Prinz, R. J., Sanders, M. R., Shapiro, C. J., Whitaker, D. J., & Lutzke, J. R. (2009). Population-based prevention of child maltreatment: The U.S. Triple P system population trial. *Prevention Science, 10*, 1–12.

Resnicow, K., Soler, R., Braithwaite, R. L., Ahluwalia, J. S., & Butler, J. (2000). Cultural sensitivity in substance use prevention. *Journal of Community Psychology, 28*(3), 271–290.

Rutter, M. (1979). Protective factors in children's responses to stress and disadvantage. In M. W. Kent & J. E. Rolf (Eds.), *Primary prevention of psychopathology: Social competence in children* (pp. 49–74). Hanover, NH: University Press of New England.

Schoenwald, S. K., Chapman, J. E., Sheidow, A. J., & Carter, R. E. (2009). Long-term youth criminal outcomes in MST transport: The impact of therapist adherence and organizational climate and structure. *Journal of Clinical Child and Adolescent Psychology, 38*, 91–105.

Schoenwald, S. K., Heiblum, N., Saldana, L., & Henggeler, S. W. (2008). The international implementation of multisystemic therapy. *Evaluation and the Health Professions, 31*, 211–224.

Schoenwald, S. K., Sheidow, A. J., & Chapman, J. E. (2009). Clinical supervision in treatment transport: Effects on adherence and outcomes. *Journal of Consulting and Clinical Psychology, 77*, 410–421.

Shadish, W. R. (2011). Randomized controlled studies and alternative designs in outcome studies: Challenges and opportunities. *Research on Social Work Practice, 21*, 636–643.

Skärstrand, E., Larsson, J., & Andreasson, S. (2008). Cultural adaptation of the Strengthening Families Programme to a Swedish setting. *Health Education, 108*, 287–300.

Skärstrand, E. (2010). Prevention of alcohol and drug preblems among adolescents: Evaluating Swedish version of the strengthening families programme (Doctoral dissertation, Karolinska institutet, Stockholm, Sweden). Retrieved from http://publications.ki.se/jspui/handle/10616/40344

Socialstyrelsen. (2011). *Svensk och internationell forskning om sociala interventioners effekter* [Swedish and international research on the effects of social interventions]. Stockholm: Socialstyrelsen.

Spoth, R., Greenberg, M., Redmond, C., & Shin, C. (2007). Toward dissemination of evidence-based family interventions: Maintenance of community-based partnership recruitment results and associated factors. *Journal of Family Psychology, 21*, 137–146.

Spoth, R., Redmond, C., Trudeau, L., & Shin, C. (2002), Longitudinal substance initiation outcomes for a universal preventive intervention combining family and school program, *Psychology of Addictive Behaviors, 16*, 129–134.

Sundell, K., Hansson, K., Andrée Löfholm, C., Olsson, T., Gustle, L.-H., & Kadesjö, C. (2008). Multisystemic therapy and traditional services for antisocial adolescents in Sweden: Results from a randomized controlled trial after six months. *Journal of Family Psychology, 22*, 550–560.

Sundell, K., Vinnerljung, B., Andrée Löfholm, C., & Humlesjö, E. (2007). Child protection in Stockholm: A local cohort study of childhood prevalence. *Children and Youth Services Review*, *29*, 180–192.

Super, C. M., & Harkness, S. (1999). The environment as culture in developmental research. In S. L. Friedman & T. D. Wachs (Eds.), *Measuring environment across the life span* (pp. 279–323). Washington, DC: American Psychological Association.

Taylor, T. K., Schmidt, F., Pepler, D., & Hodgins, C. (1998). A comparison of eclectic treatment with Webster-Stratton's parents and children series in a children's mental health center: A randomized controlled trial. *Behavior Therapy*, *29*, 221–240.

ter Bogt, T., Schmid, H., Nic Gabhainn, S., Fotiou, A., & Vollebergh, W. (2006). Economic and cultural correlates of cannabis use among mid-adolescents in 31 countries. *Addiction*, *101*, 241–251.

UNICEF. (July 2001). *A league table of teenage births in rich nations*. Innocenti Report Card No. 3. UNICEF Innocenti Research Centre, Florence. Retrieved July 8, 2011, from http://www.unicef-irc.org/publications/pdf/repcard3e.pdf

Webster-Stratton, C. (1996). Early intervention with videotape modeling: Programs for families of children with oppositional defiant disorder or conduct disorder. In E. S. Hibbs & P. S. Jensen (Eds.), *Psychosocial treatments for child and adolescent disorders: Empirically-based strategies for clinical practice* (pp. 435–474). Washington, DC: American Psychological Association.

Wright C. C., & Sim, J. (2003). Intention to treat approach to data from randomized controlled trials: A sensitivity analysis. *Journal of Clinical Epidemiology*, *56*, 533–842.

CHAPTER 4

Ahn, H., & Wampold, B. (2001). Where oh where are the specific ingredients? A meta-analysis of component studies in counseling and psychotherapy. *Journal of Counseling Psychology*, *38*, 251–257.

American Board of Examiners in Clinical Social Work (ABECSW). (2004). *Clinical supervision: A practice specialty of clinical social work*. Retrieved from http://www.abecsw.org/images/ABESUPERV2205ed406.pdf

Anderson, T., Lunnen, K. M., & Ogles, B. M. (2010). Putting models and techniques in context. In B. L. Duncan, S. D. Miller, B. E. Wampold, & M. A Hubble (Eds.), *The heart and soul of change: Delivering what works in therapy* (2nd ed., pp. 143–166). Washington, DC: American Psychological Association.

Anker, M. G., Duncan, B. L., & Sparks, J. A. (2009). Using client feedback to improve couple therapy outcomes: A randomized clinical trial in naturalistic setting. *Journal of Consulting and Clinical Psychology*, *77*, 693–704.

Barth, R. P. (2008). The move to evidence-based practice: How well does it fit child welfare services? *Journal of Public Child Welfare*, *2*, 145–172.

Barth, R. P., Lee, B. R., Lindsey, M., Collins, K. S., Strieder, F., Chorpita, B., ... Sparks, J. (2012). Evidence-based practice at a crossroads: The emergence of common elements and factors. *Research on Social Work Practice*, *22*(1), 108–119. doi: 10.1177/1049731511408440.

Bickman, L. (2008). A measurement feedback system (MFS) is necessary to improve mental health outcomes. *Journal of the American Academy of Child and Adolescent Psychiatry*, *47*(10), 1114–1119.

Bond, G. R., Drake, R. E., & Becker, D. R. (2010). Beyond evidence-based practice: Nine ideal features of a mental health intervention. *Research on Social Work Practice, 20*(5), 493–501. doi: 10.1177/1049731509358085

Burns, B. J., Mastillo, S. A., Farmer, E. M. Z., MacCrae, J., Kolko, D. J., & Libby, A. M. (2010). Caregivers' depression, mental health service use, and children's outcome. In K. D. M. B. Webb, J. Harden, J. Landsverk, & M. F. Testa (Eds.), *Child welfare and child well-being: New perspectives from the National Survey of Child and Adolescent Well-Being.* (pp. 351–379). New York: Oxford University Press.

Cameron, M., & Keenan, E. K. (2010). The common factors model: Implications for transtheoretical clinical social work practice. *Social Work, 55*(1), 63–73.

Chaffin, M., Funderburk, B., Bard, D., Valle, L. A., & Gurwitch, R. (2011). A combined motivation and parent-child interaction therapy package reduces child welfare recidivism in a randomized dismantling field trial. *Journal of Consulting and Clinical Psychology, 79*(1), 84–95. doi: 10.1037/a0021227

Chaffin, M., Hecht, D., Bard, D., Silovsky, J., & Beasley, W. H. (2012). A statewide trial of the SafeCare home-based services model with parents in Child Protective Services. *Pediatrics,* 129, 509–515. doi: 10.1542/peds.2011-1840

Chamberlain, P., Price, J., Leve, L. D., Laurent, H., Landsverk, J. A., & Reid, J. B. (2008). Prevention of behavior problems for children in foster care: Outcomes and mediation effects. *Prevention Science, 9*(1), 17–27. doi: 10.1007/s11121-007-0080-7

Chamberlain, P., Price, J., Reid, J. B., & Landsverk, J. (2008). Cascading implementation of a foster and kinship parent intervention. *Child Welfare, 87*(5), 27–48.

Chapman, J. E., & Schoenwald, S. K. (2011). Ethnic similarity, therapist adherence, and long-term multisystemic therapy outcomes. *Journal of Emotional and Behavioral Disorders, 19*(1), 3–16. doi: 10.1177/1063426610376773

Chorpita, B. F., Becker, K. D., & Daleiden, E. I. (2007). Understanding the common elements of evidence-based practice: Misconceptions and clinical examples. *Journal of the American Academy of Child and Adolescent Psychiatry, 46*(5), 647–652.

Chorpita, B. F., Bernstein, A., & Daleiden, E. L. (2011). Empirically guided coordination of multiple evidence-based treatments: An illustration of relevance mapping in children's mental health Services. *Journal of Consulting and Clinical Psychology, 79*(4), 470–480. doi: 10.1037/a0023982

Chorpita, B. F., Bernstein, A. D., Daleiden, E. L., & the Research Network on Youth Mental Health. (2008). Driving with roadmaps and dashboards: Using information resources to structure the decision models in service organizations. *Administration and Policy in Mental Health and Mental Health Services Research, 35,* 114–123.

Chorpita, B. F., & Daleiden, E. L. (2009). Mapping evidence-based treatments for children and adolescents: Application of the distillation and matching model to 615 treatments from 322 randomized trials. *Journal of Consulting and Clinical Psychology, 77*(3), 566–579.

Chorpita, B. F., Daleiden, E., & Weisz, J. R. (2005). Identifying and selecting the common elements of evidence based interventions: A distillation and matching model. *Mental Health Services Research, 7,* 5–20.

Chorpita, B. F., Rotheram-Borus, M. J., Daleiden, E. L., Bernstein, A., Cromley, T., Swendeman, D., & Regan, J. (2011). The old solutions are the new problem: How do we better use what we already know about reducing the burden of mental illness? *Perspectives on Psychological Science, 6*(5), 493–497. doi: 10.1177/1745691611418240

DePanfilis, D., Filene, J., & Smith, E. (2010, September). *Multi-site findings from the replication of a family strengthening program with diverse populations to prevent child maltreatment.* Symposium conducted at the IVIII ISPCAN International Congress: Strengthening Children and Families Affected by Personal, Intrapersonal, and Global Conflict, Honolulu, Hawaii.

Drisko, J. W. (2004). Common factors in psychotherapy outcome: Meta-analytic findings and their implications for practice and research. *Families in Society: The Journal of Contemporary Human Services, 85*(1), 81–90.

Duncan, B. (2010a). *On becoming a better therapist.* Washington, DC: IVIII ISPCAN International Congress: Strengthening Children and Families Affected by Personal, Intrapersonal, and Global Conflict, Honolulu, Hawaii. American Psychological Association.

Duncan, B. (2010b). *Poor children and psychiatric drugs.* Retrieved November 14, 2010, from http://heartandsoulofchange.com/2010/11/

Duncan, B.L. (n.d.). *What is CDOI?* Retrieved from http://heartandsoulofchange.com/what-is-cdoi/

Duncan, B., & Miller, S. (2006). Treatment manuals do not improve outcomes. In J. Norcross, R. Levant, & L. Beutler (Eds.), *Evidence-based practices in mental health* (pp. 140–148). Washington, DC: American Psychological Association Press.

Duncan, B. L., Miller, S. D., Wampold, B. E., and Hubble, M. A. (2010) *Heart and soul of change: Delivering what works in therapy* (2nd ed.). Washington, DC: American Psychological Association.

Duncan, B. L., Sparks, J. A., Miller, S. D., Bohanske, R. T. & Claud, D. A. (2006). Giving youth a voice: A preliminary study of the reliability and validity of a brief outcome measure for children, adolescents, and caretakers. *Journal of Brief Therapy, 5* (2), 71–88.

Embry, D. D., & Biglan, A. (2008). Evidence-based kernels: Fundamental units of behavioral influence. *Clinical Child and Family Psychology Review, 11*, 75–113. doi: 10.1007/s10567-008-0036-x

Fisher, P., Kim, H., & Pears, K. (2009) Effects of multidimensional treatment foster care for preschoolers (MTFC-P) on reducing permanent placement failures among children with placement instability. *Children and Youth Services Review, 31*, 541–546.

Fraser, M. W., Richman, J. M., Galinsky, M. J., & Day, S. H. (2009). *Intervention research: Developing social programs.* New York: Oxford University Press.

Garland, A. F., Hawley, K. M., Brookman-Frazee, L., & Hurlburt, M. S. (2008). Identifying common elements of evidence-based psychosocial treatments for children's disruptive behavior problems. *Journal of the American Academy of Child and Adolescent Psychiatry, 47*(5), 505–514. doi: 10.1097/CHI.0b013e31816765c2

Hennessy, K. D. & Green-Hennessy, S. (2011). A review of mental health interventions in SAMHSA's National Registry of Evidence-Based Programs and Practices. *Psychiatric Services, 62*, 303–305.

Kazdin, A. E., & Blase, S. L. (2011). Rebooting psychotherapy research and practice to reduce the burden of mental illness. *Perspectives on Psychological Science, 6*, 21–37.

Kendall, P. C., Gosch, E., Furr, J., & Sood, E. (2008). Flexibility within fidelity. *Journal of the American Academy of Child and Adolescent Psychiatry, 47*, 987–993.

Lambert, M. J., & Shimokawa, K. (2011). Collecting client feedback. *Psychotherapy, 48*(1), 72–79. doi: 10.1037/a0022238

Lehninger, L. (2000). *Creating a new profession: The beginnings of social work education in the United States.* Washington, DC: Council on Social Work Education.

Linares, L. O., Montalto, D., Li, M. M., & Oza, V. S. (2006). A promising parenting intervention in foster care. *Journal of Consulting and Clinical Psychology, 74*(1), 32–41. doi: 10.1037/0022-006X.74.1.32

Mildon, R., & Shlonsky, A. (2011). Bridge over troubled water: Using implementation science to facilitate effective services in child welfare. *Child Abuse and Neglect, 35*(9), 753–756. doi: 10.1016/j.chiabu.2011.07.001

Morgan, M. M., & Sprenkle, D. H. (2007). Toward a common factors approach to supervision. *Journal of Marital and Family Therapy, 33*, 1–17.

National Association of Social Workers (NASW) (approved 1996, revised 1999). *Code of Ethics of the National Association of Social Workers*. Washington, DC: Author.

Norcross, J. C., & Wampold, B. E. (2011). Evidence-based therapy relationships: Research conclusions and clinical practices. *Psychotherapy, 48*(1), 98–102. doi: 10.1037/a0022161

Powers, J., Bowen, N., & Bowen, G. (2010). Evidence-based programs in school settings: Barriers and recent advances. *Journal of Evidence Based Social Work, 7*, 313–331.

Price, J. M., Chamberlain, P., Landsverk, J., & Reid, J. (2009). KEEP foster-parent training intervention: Model description and effectiveness. *Child and Family Social Work, 14*(2), 233–242. doi:10.1111/j.1365-2206.2009.00627.x

Prinz, R. J., Sanders, M. R., Shapiro, C. J., Whitaker, D. J., & Lutzker, J. R. (2009). Population-based prevention of child maltreatment: The US Triple P system population trial. *Prevention Science, 10*(1), 1–12. doi: 10.1007/s11121-009-0123-3

Raue, P. J., & Goldfried, M. R. (1994). The therapeutic alliance in cognitive-behavior therapy. In A. O. Horvath & L. S. Greenberg (Eds.), *Alliance: Theory, research, and practice* (pp. 131–148). New York: Wiley.

Rosenzweig, S. (1936). Some implicit common factors in diverse methods of psychotherapy. *American Journal of Orthopsychiatry, 6*, 412–415.

Rubin, A. (2011). Teaching EBP in social work: Retrospective and prospective. *Journal of Social Work, 11*(1), 64–79. doi: 10.1177/1468017310381311

Rubin, A., & Parrish, D. (2007). Challenges to the future of evidence-based practice in social work education. *Journal of Social Work Education, 43*, 403–424.

Schiffman, J., Becker, K. D., & Daleiden, E. L. (2006). Evidence-based services in a statewide public mental health system: Do the treatments fit the problems? *Journal of Clinical Child and Adolescent Psychology, 35*, 13–19.

Sexton, T. L., Ridley, C. R., & Kleiner, A. J. (2004). Beyond common factors: Multilevel-process models of therapeutic change. *Journal of Marriage and Family Therapy, 30*(2), 131–149.

Siev, J., Huppert, J., & Chambless, D.L. (2009). The Dodo bird, treatment technique, and disseminating empirically supported treatments. *The Behavior Therapist, 32*(4), 69–76.

Sparks, J. A., & Muro, M. L. (2009). Client-directed wraparound: The client as connector in community collaboration. *Journal of Systemic Therapies, 28*(3), 63–76.

Sprenkle, D. H., Davis, D. D., & Lebow, J. L. (2009). *Common factors in couple and family therapy: The overlooked foundation for effective practice*. New York: Guilford.

Suveg, C., Comer, J., Furr, J., & Kendall, P. C. (2006). Adapting manualized CBT for a cognitively-delayed child with multiple anxiety disorders. *Clinical Case Studies, 5*, 488–510.

Timmer, S. G., Urquiza, A. J., Herschell, A. D., McGrath, J. M., Zebell, N. M., Porter, A. L., & Vargas, E. C. (2006). Parent-child interaction therapy: Application of an empirically supported treatment to maltreated children in foster care. *Child Welfare, 85*(6), 919–939.

Torrey, E. F. (1986). *Witchdoctors and psychiatrists: The common roots of psychotherapy and its future*. Northvale, NJ: Jason Aronson.

US Department of Health and Human Services, Substance Abuse and Mental Health Services Administration. (2011). *National registry of effective programs and practices*. Available at http://nrepp.samhsa.gov/.

Wampold, B. E., Mondin, G. W., Moody M., Stich, F., Benson, K., & Ahn, H. (1997). A meta-analysis of outcome studies comparing bona fide psychotherapies: Empirically, "all must have prizes." *Psychological Bulletin, 122*, 203–215.

Weisz, J. R., & Chorpita, B. F. (2012). Mod squad for child psychotherapy: Restructuring evidence—based treatment for clinical practice. In P. C. Kendall (Ed.), *Child and adolescent therapy: Cognitive-behavioral procedures* (4th ed.) (pp. 379–397). New York: Guilford.

Weisz, J. R., Chorpita, B. F., Frye, A., Ng, M. Y., Lau, N., Bearman, S. K., … Hoagwood, K. E. (2011). Youth top problems: Using idiographic, consumer-guided assessment to identify treatment needs and to track change during psychotherapy. *Journal of Consulting and Clinical Psychology, 79*(3), 369–380. doi: 10.1037/a0023307

Weisz, J. Chorpita, B. F., Palinkas, L., Schoenwald, S., Miranda, J., Bearman, S. K., … Gibbons, R. D. (2012). Testing standard and modular designs for psychotherapy for youth with anxiety, depression, and conduct problems: A randomized effectiveness trial. *Archives of General Psychiatry, 69*, 274–282. doi:10.1001/archgenpsychiatry.2011.147

Westermark, K., Hannson, K., & Vinnerljung, B. (2008) Does MTFC reduce placement breakdown in foster care? *International Journal of Child & Family Welfare, 4*, 155–171.

CHAPTER 5

Abbott, R. D., O'Donnell, J., Hawkins, J. D., Hill, K. G., Kosterman, R., & Catalano, R. F. (1998). Changing teaching practices to promote achievement and bonding to school. *American Journal of Orthopsychiatry, 68*, 542–552.

Aarons, G. A. (2004). Mental health provider attitudes toward adoption of evidence-based practice: The evidence-based practice attitude scale (EBPAS). *Health Services Review, 6*, 61–74.

Aarons, G. A., Green, A. E., Palinkas, L. A., Self-Brown, S., Whitaker, D. J., Lutzker, … Chaffin, M. J. (2012). Dynamic adaptation process to implement an evidence-based child maltreatment intervention. *Implementation Science, 7*(1), 32–41.

Aarons, G. A., Hurlburt, M., & Horwitz, S. M. (2011). Advancing a conceptual model of evidence-based practice implementation in public service sectors. *Administration and Policy in Mental Health and Mental Health Services Research, 38*, 4–23.

Aarons, G. A., Sommerfeld, D. H., & Walrath-Greene, C. M. (2009). Evidence-based practice implementation: The impact of public versus private sector organisation type on organisational support, provider attitudes and adoption of evidence-based practice. *Implementation Science, 4*, 83.

Aarons, G. A., Sommerfeld, D. H., Hecht, D. B., Silovsky, J. F., & Chaffin, M. J. (2009). The impact of evidence-based practice implementation and fidelity monitoring on staff turnover: Evidence for a protective effect. *Journal of Consulting and Clinical Psychology, 77*(2), 270–280.

Aarons, G. A., Wells, R. S., Zagursky, K., Fettes, D. L., & Palinkas, L. A. (2009). Implementing evidence-based practice in community mental health agencies: A multiple stakeholder analysis. *American Journal of Public Health, 99*, 2087–2095.

Antle, B. F., Barbee, A. P., Sullivan, D. J., & Christense, D. N. (2008). The effects of training rein-forcement on training transfer. *Child Welfare, 88*, 5–26.

Antle, B. F., Barbee, A. P., Christensen, D. N., & Sullivan, D. (2010). The prevention of child maltreatment recidivism through the solution-based casework model of child welfare practice. *Children and Youth Services Review, 31*, 1346–1351.

Barbee, A. P., Antle, B., Sullivan, D., Huebner, R., & Fox, S. (2009). Recruiting and retaining child welfare workers: Is preparing social work students enough for sustained commitment to the field? *Child Welfare, 88*, 69–86.

Barbee, A. P., Christensen, D., Antle, B., Wandersman, A., & Cahn, K. (2011). Successful adop-tion and implementation of a comprehensive casework practice model in a public child welfare agency: Application of the getting to outcomes (GTO) model. *Children and Youth Services Review, 33*, 622–633.

Barth, R. P., Landsverk, J., Chamberlain, P., Reid, J. B., Rolls, J. A., Hurlburt, M. S., et al. (2005). Parent-training programs in child welfare services: Planning for a more evidence-based approach to serving biological parents. *Research on Social Work Practice, 15*(5), 353–371.

Bernotavicz, F., & Locke, A. (2000). Hiring child welfare caseworkers: Using a competency-based approach. *Public Personnel Management, 29*(1), 33–45.

Berdie, J., Leake, R., & Parry, C. (2010). A model for skills-based classroom training. *Protecting Children, 19*(2), 53–63.

Berwick, D. M. (2003). Disseminating innovations in health care. *JAMA, 289*(15), 1969–1975.

Blasé, K. A., Fixsen, D. L., Metz, A. J. R., & Van Dyke, M. (2009). *Systems change to support effec-tive service: Why DITWLY just won't get us there.* Presentation at the U.S. Children's Bureau Meeting for Agencies and Courts, New Strategies for Changing Times, August 5, 2009, Arlington, VA.

Cahn, K. (2003). *Getting there from here: Variables associated with the adoption of innova-tion in child welfare.* Unpublished dissertation, Portland State University School of Social Work.

Chaffin, M., Hecht, D., Bard, D., Silovsky, J. F., & Beasley, W. H. (2012). A statewide trial of the SafeCare home-based services model with parents in child protective services. *Pediatrics, 129*(3), 509–515.

Chamberlain, P., Brown H. C., & Saldana, L. (2011). Observational measure of implementa-tion progress in community based settings: The Stages of implementation completion (SIC). *Implementation Science, 6*, 116.

Chinman, M., Imm, P., & Wandersman, A. (2004). *Getting to outcomes 2004: Promoting account-ability through methods and tools for planning, implementation, and evaluation.* Santa Monica, CA: RAND Corporation TRTR101. Available at http:// www.rand.org/ publications/TR/ TR101/.

Chinman, M., Hunter, S. B., Ebener, P., Paddock, S. M., Stillman, L., Imm, P., & Wandersman, A. (2008). The getting to outcomes demonstration and evaluation: An illustration of the preven-tion support system. *American Journal of Community Psychology, 41*, 206–224.

Chorpita, B. F., Daleiden, E., & Weisz, J. R. (2005a). Identifying and selecting the common ele-ments of evidence based interventions: A distillation and matching model. *Mental Health Services Research, 7*, 5–20.

Chorpita, B. F., Daleiden, E., &Weisz, J. R. (2005b). Modularity in the design and application of therapeutic interventions. *Applied and Preventive Psychology, 11*, 141–156.

Damschroder, L. J., Aron, D, C., Keith, R. E., Kirsh, S. R., Alexander, J. A., & Lowery, J. C. (2009). Fostering implementation of health services research findings into practice: A consolidated framework for advancing implementation science. *Implementation Science, 4*, 50–65.

Dickinson, N. S., & Comstock, A. (2009). Getting and keeping the best people. In C. Potter & C. Brittain (Eds.), *Supervision in child welfare* (pp. 220–261). New York: Oxford.

Dickinson, N.S., & Painter, J.S. (2011). An experimental study of child welfare worker turnover. *Proceedings of the 14ᵗʰ Annual National Human Services Training Evaluation Symposium.* Berkeley, CA: California Social Work Education Center. Retrieved from http://calswec. berkeley.edu/files/uploads/nhstes2011_dickenson_painter_turnover_final_0.pdf

Domitrovich, C. E., Gest, S. D., Gill, S., Jones, D., & Sanford DeRousie, R. (2009). Individual factors associated with professional development training outcomes of the Head Start REDI program. *Early Education and Development, 20*(3), 402–430.

DuBois, D. L., Holloway, B. E., Valentine, J. C., & Cooper, H. (2002). Effectiveness of mentoring programs for youth: A meta-analytic review. *American Journal of Community Psychology, 30*, 157–197.

Durlak, J. A., & DuPre, E. P. (2008). Implementation matters: A review of research on the influence of implementation on program outcomes and the factors affecting implementation. *American Journal of Community Psychology, 41*, 327–350.

Ellett, A. J. (2000). *Human caring, self-efficacy beliefs, and professional organizational culture correlates of employee retention in child welfare.* Baton Rouge: Louisiana State University.

Embry, D. D. (2004). Community-based prevention using simple, low-cost, evidence-based kernels and behaviour vaccines. *Journal of Community Psychology, 32*, 575–591.

Embry, D. D., & Biglan, A. (2008). Evidence-based kernels: Fundamental units of behavioural influence. *Clinical Child Family Psychology Review, 11*, 75–113.

Faller, K. C., Masternak, M., Grinnell-Davis, C., Grabarek, M., Sieffert, J., & Bernotavicz, F. (2009). Realistic job previews in child welfare: State of innovation and practice. *Child Welfare, 88*(5), 23–47.

Felner, R. D., Favazza, A., Shim, M., Brand, S., Gu, K., & Noonan, N. (2001). Whole school improvement and restructuring as prevention and promotion: Lessons from STEP and the project on high-performance learning communities. *Journal of School Psychology, 39*, 177–202.

Flaspohler, P., Anderson-Butcher, D., & Wandersman, A. (2008). Supporting implementation of expanded school mental health services: Application of the interactive systems framework in Ohio. *Advances in School Mental Health Promotion, 1*, 38–48.

Fixsen, D. L., Naoom, S. F., Blase, K.A., Friedman, R. M., & Wallace, F. (2005). *Implementation research: A synthesis of the literature.* Tampa: University of South Florida, The Louis de la Parte Florida Mental Health Institute, Department of Child and Family Studies.

Fixsen, D. L., Blasé, K. A., Naoom, S. F., & Wallace, F. (2009). Core implementation components. *Research on Social Work Practice, 19*(5), 531–540.

Forthman, M. T., Wooster, L. D., Hill, W. C., Homa-Lowry, J. M., & DesHarnais, S. I. (2003). Insights into successful change management: Empirically supported techniques for improving medical practice patterns. *American Journal of Medical Quality, 18*, 181–189.

Gambrill, E., & Shlonsky, A. (2001). The need for comprehensive risk management programs in child protective services. *Children and Youth Services Review, 23*, 79–107.

Gambrill, E. (2010). Evidence-informed practice: Antidote to propaganda in the helping professions? *Research on Social Work Practice, 20*(3), 302–320. doi:10.1177/1049731509347879

Garland, A. F., Hurlburt, M. S., & Hawley, K. M. (2006). Examining psychotherapy processes in a services research context. *Clinical Psychology: Science and Practice, 13*, 30–46.

Glisson, C., & Hemmelgarn, A. (1998). The effects of organizational climate and interorganizational coordination on the quality and outcomes of children's service systems. *Child Abuse and Neglect, 22*(5), 401–421.

Godley, S. H., White, W. L., Diamond, G., Passetti, L., & Titus, J. (2001). Therapists' reactions to manual-guided therapies for the treatment of adolescent marijuana users. *Clinical Psychology: Science and Practice, 8*, 405–417.

Greenwood, C. R., Tapia, Y., Abbott, M., & Walton, C. (2003). A building-based case study of evidence-based literacy practices: Implementation, reading behavior, and growth in reading fluency, K-4. *The Journal of Special Education, 37*, 95–110.

Greenhalgh, T., Robert, G., Macfarlane, F., Bate, P., & Kyriakidou, O. (2004). Diffusion of innovations in service organizations: Systematic review and recommendations. *Milbank Quarterly, 82*(4), 581–629.

Grimshaw, J. M., & Russell, I. T. (1993). Effect of clinical guidelines on medical practice: A systematic review of rigorous evaluations. *Lancet, 342*, 1317–1322.

Grimshaw, J., Shirran, L., Thomas, R., Mowatt, G., Fraser, C., Bero, L., et al. (2001). Changing provider behaviour: An overview of systematic reviews of interventions. *Medical Care, 39*(8), II2–II45.

Grol, R. (2001). Successes and failures in the implementation of evidence-based guidelines for clinical practice. *Medical Care, 39*(8 Suppl 2), 46–54.

Hawley, K. M., & Weisz, J. R. (2002). Increasing the relevance of evidence based treatment review to practitioners and consumers. *Clinical Psychology: Science and Practice, 9*, 225–230.

Henggeler, S. W., Melton, G. B., Brondino, M. J., Scherer, D. G., & Hanley, J. H. (1997). Multisystemic therapy with violent and chronic juvenile offenders and their families: The role of treatment fidelity in successful dissemination. *Journal of Consulting and Clinical Psychology, 65*, 821–833.

Henggeler, S. W., Pickrel, S. G., & Brondino, M. J. (1999). Multisystemic treatment of substance abusing and dependent delinquents: Outcomes, treatment fidelity, and transportability. *Mental Health Services Research, 1*, 171–184.

Hoge, M. A., & Morris, J. A. (Eds.). (2004). Implementing best practices in behavioral health workforce education—Building a change agenda [Special issue]. *Administration and Policy in Mental Health, 32*(2).

Joyce, B., & Showers, B. (1980). Improving inservice training: The messages of research. *Educational Leadership, 37*(5), 379–385.

Kazdin, A. E., & Blase, S. L. (2011). Rebooting psychotherapy research and practice to reduce the burden of mental illness. *Perspectives on Psychological Science, 61*, 21–37.

Kirigin, K. A, Braukmann, C. J, Atwater, J. D, & Wolf, M. M. (1982). An evaluation of Teaching-Family (Achievement Place) group homes for juvenile offenders. *Journal of Applied Behavior Analysis, 15*, 1–16

Kutash, K., Duchnowski, A. J., Sumi, W. C., Rudo, Z. & Harris, K. M. (2002) A school, family, and community collaborative program for children who have emotional disturbances. *Journal of Emotional and Behavioral Disorders, 10*, 99–107

Lee, S. J, Altschul, I, & Mowbray, C. T. (2008) Using planned adaptation to implement evidence-based programs with new populations. *American Journal of Community Psychology, 41*, 290–303.

Lipsey, M. W., Howell, J. C., Kelly, M. R., Chapman, G., & Carver, D. (2010). *Improving the effectiveness of juvenile justice programs: A new perspective on evidence-based practice.* Centre for Juvenile Justice Reform, Georgetown University.

Littell, J. H., & Shlonsky, A. (2010). Toward evidence-informed policy and practice in child welfare. *Research on Social Work Practice, 20*(6), 723–725.

Lyon, A. R., Lau, A., McCauley, E., Vander Stoep, A., & Chorpita, B. F. (2013). A case for modular design: Implications for implementing evidence-based interventions with culturally-diverse youth. Manuscript under review.

Lyon, A. R., Stirman, S. W., Kerns, S. E. U., & Bruns, E. J. (2011). Developing the mental health workforce: Review and application of training approaches from multiple disciplines. *American Journal of Public Health, 38*, 238–253.

Maloney, D. M., Warfel, D. J., Blasé, K. A., Timbers, G. D., Fixsen, D. L., & Phillips, E. L. (1983). A method for validating employment interviews for residential child care workers. *Residential Group Care and Treatment, 1*, 37–50.

Meyers, D. C., Durlak, J. A., & Wandersman, A. (2012). The quality implementation framework: A synthesis of critical steps in implementation process frameworks. *American Journal of Community Psychology, 50*, 462–480.

Mildon, R., & Shlonsky, A. (2011). Bridge over troubled water: Using implementation science to facilitate effective services in child welfare. *Child Abuse and Neglect, 35*, 753–756.

Miller, W. R., Yahne, C. E., Moyers, T. B., Martinez, J., & Pirritano, M. (2004). A randomized trial of methods to help clinicians learn motivational interviewing. *Journal of Consulting and Clinical Psychology, 72*(6), 1050–1062.

Mitchell, P. F. (2011). Evidence-based practice in real-world services for young people with complex needs: New opportunities suggested by recent implementation science. *Children and Youth Services Review, 33*, 207–216.

Munro, E. (2011). *The Munro Review of Child Protection: Final Report—A child-centred system.* Retrieved April 15, 2013, from http://www.official-documents.gov.uk/document/cm80/8062/8062.pdf

National Association of Public Child Welfare Administrators [NAPCWA]. (2005). *Guide for child welfare administrators on evidence based practice.* Washington DC: APHSA.

Oxman, A. D., Thomson, M. A., Davis, D. A., & Haynes, R. B. (1995). No magic bullets: A systematic review of 102 trials of interventions to improve professional practice. *Canadian Medical Association Journal, 153*, 1423–1431.

Proctor, E., Landsverk, J., Aarons, G. A., Chambers, D., Glisson, C. A., & Mittman, B. (2009). Implementation research in mental health services: An emerging science with conceptual, methodological, and training challenges. *Administration and Policy in Mental Health and Mental Health Services Research, 46*, 24–34.

Regehr, C., Hemsworth, D., Leslie, B., Howe, P., & Chau, S. (2004). Predictors of post-traumatic distress in child welfare workers: A linear structural equation model. *Children and Youth Services Review, 26*, 331–346.

Rogers, E. M. (2003). *Diffusion of innovations* (5th ed.). New York: Free Press.

Saunders, R. P., Ward, D. S., Felton, G. M., Dowda, M. & Pate, R. R. (2006). Examining the link between program implementation and behavior outcomes in the Lifestyle Education for Activity Program (LEAP). *Program Evaluation and Planning, 29*, 352–364.

Schoenwald, S. K., Garland, A. G., Chapman, J. E., Frazier, S. L., Sheido, A. J., & Southam-Gerow, M. A. (2010). Toward the effective and efficient measurement of implementation fidelity. *Administration and Policy in Mental Health,38*(1), 32–43.

Schoenwald S. K., Henggeler, S. W., Brondino, M. J., & Rowland, M. D. (2000). Multisystemic therapy: Monitoring treatment fidelity. *Family Process, 39*(1), 83–103.

Sholomskas, D. E., Syracuse-Siewert, G., Rounsaville, B. J., Ball, S. A., Nuro, K. F., & Carroll, K. M. (2005). We don't train in vain: A dissemination trial of three strategies of training clinicians in cognitive-behavioral therapy. *Journal of Consulting and Clinical Psychology, 73*(1), 106–115.

Stirman, S. W., Crits-Christoph, P., & DeRubeis, R. (2004). Achieving successful dissemination of empirically supported adult psychotherapies: A synthesis of dissemination theory. *Clinical Psychology: Science and Practice, 11*, 343–359.

Tobler, N. (1986). Meta-analysis of 143 adolescent drug prevention programs: Quantitative outcomes results of program participants compared to a control or comparison group. *Journal of Drug Issues, 16*, 537–567.

Walker, J. S., & Koroloff, N. (2007). Grounded theory and backward mapping: Exploring the implementation context for wraparound. *Journal of Behavioral Health Services and Research, 34*, 443–458.

Wandersman, A. (2009). Four keys to success (theory, implementation, evaluation, and resource/system support): High hopes and challenges in participation. *American Journal of Community Psychology, 43*, 3–21.

Wandersman, A., Chien, V., & Katz. J. (2012). Toward an evidence-based system for innovation support for implementing innovations with quality: Tools, training, technical assistance, and quality assurance/quality improvement. *American Journal of Community Psychology, 50*, 445–459.

Wandersman, A., Duffy, J., Flaspohler, P., Noonan, R., Lubell, K., Stillman, L., ... Saul, J. (2008). Bridging the gap between prevention research and practice: The interactive systems framework for dissemination and implementation. *American Journal of Community Psychology, 41*, 171–181.

Wandersman, A., Imm, P., Chinman, M., & Kaftarian, S. (2000). Getting to outcomes: A results-based approach to accountability. *Evaluation and Program Planning, 23*, 389–395.

Wanous, J. P. (1992). *Organizational entry: Recruitment, selection, orientation and socialization of newcomers* (2nd ed.) Boston: Addison Wesley.

Weisz, J. R., Southam-Gerow, M., Gordis, E. B., & Connor-Smith, J. (2003). Primary and secondary control enhancement training for youth depression: Applying the deployment-focused model of treatment development and testing. In A. E. Kazdin & J. R. Weisz (Eds.), *Evidence-based psychotherapies for children and adolescents* (pp. 165–183). New York: Guilford.

CHAPTER 6

Baicker, K., Skinner, J., & Chandra, A. (2005). Geographic variation in health care and the problem of measuring racial disparities. *Perspectives in Biology and Medicine, 48*(1), S42–S53.

Braveman, P. (2006). Health disparities and health equity: Concepts and measurement. *Annual Review of Public Health, 27*, 167–194.

Drake, B., & Jonson-Reid, M. (2010). NIS interpretations: Race and the National Incidence Studies of Child Abuse and Neglect. *Children and Youth Services Review, 33*(1), 16–20.

Drake, B., Lee, S. M., & Jonson-Reid, M. (2008). Race and child maltreatment reporting: Are Blacks overrepresented? *Children and Youth Services Review,31*(3), 309–316. doi:10.1016/j.childyouth.2008.08.004

Gibbons, R., Hur, K., Bhaumik, D., & Bell, C. (2007). Profiling of county-level foster care placements using random-effects Poisson regression models. *Health Services and Outcomes Research Methodology, 7*(3), 97–108.

Hines, A., Lee, P., Osterling, K., & Drabble, L. (2007). Factors predicting family reunification for African American, Latino, Asian and White families in the child welfare system. *Journal of Child and Family Studies, 16*(2), 275–289.

Lery, B. (2009). Neighborhood structure and foster care entry risk: The role of spatial scale in defining neighborhoods. *Children and Youth Services Review, 31*(3), 331–337.

Marts, E., Lee, E., McRoy, R., & McCroskey, J. (2008). Point of engagement: Reducing disproportionality and improving child and family outcomes. *Child Welfare, 87*(2), 335–358.

Needell, B., Brookhart, M. A., & Lee, S. (2003). Black children and foster care placement in California. *Children and Youth Services Review, 25*(5–6), 393–408.

Osgood, D. (2000). Poisson-based regression analysis of aggregate crime rates. *Journal of Quantitative Criminology, 16*(1), 21–44.

Osterling, K., D'Andrade, A., & Austin, M. (2008). Understanding and addressing racial/ethnic disproportionality in the front end of the child welfare system. *Journal of Evidence-Based Social Work, 5*(1), 9–30.

Ousey, G. (1999). Homicide, structural factors, and the racial invariance assumption. *Criminology, 37*(2), 405–426.

Putnam-Hornstein, E. (2011). Report of maltreatment as a risk factor for injury death: A prospective birth cohort study. *Child Maltreatment, 16*(3), 163–174.

Raudenbush, S. W., & Bryk, A. S. (2002). *Hierarchical linear models: Applications and data analysis methods* (2nd ed.). Newbury Park, CA: Sage.

Rivaux, S., James, J., Wittenstrom, K., Baumann, D., Sheets, J., Henry, J., & Jeffries, V. (2008). The intersection of race, poverty, and risk: Understanding the decision to provide services to clients and to remove children. *Child Welfare, 87*(2), 151–168.

Sampson, R. J., & Wilson, W. J. (1995). Toward a theory of race, crime, and urban inequality. In J. Hagan & R. D. Peterson (Eds.), *Crime and inequality* (pp. 37–56). Stanford, CA: Stanford University Press.

Sedlak, A., McPherson, K., & Das, B. (2010). *Supplementary analyses of race differences in child maltreatment rates in the NIS-4.* Washington, DC: US Department of Health and Human Services, Administration for Children and Families, Office of Planning, Research, & Evaluation and the Children's Bureau. Retrieved from http://www.acf.hhs.gov/sites/default/files/opre/nis4_supp_analysis_race_diff_mar2010.pdf.

Smedley, B., Stith, A., & Nelson, A. (Eds.). (2003). *Unequal treatment: Confronting racial and ethnic disparities in health care.* Washington, DC: National Academies Press

US Government Accountability Office. (2007). *African American children in foster care: Additional HHS assistance needed to help states reduce the proportion in care.* Retrieved April 10, 2010, from http://www.gao.gov/new.items/ d07816.pdf.

Wilson, W. J. (1987). *The truly disadvantaged.* Chicago: University of Chicago Press.

Wulczyn, F., & Lery, B. (2007). *Racial disparity in foster care admissions.* Chicago, IL: Chapin Hall Center for Children.

CHAPTER 7

Bloom, H. S. (2004). *Randomizing groups to evaluate place-based programs.* New York: MDRC.

Bloom, H. S. (2009). *Modern regression discontinuity analysis.* New York: MDRC.

Courtney, M. E. (2009). The difficult transition to adulthood for foster youth in the US: Implications for the state as corporate parent. *Social Policy Report, 23*(1), 3–18.

Courtney, M. E., Dworsky, A., & Pollack, H. (2007). *When should the state cease parenting? Evidence from the Midwest study.* Chicago: Chapin Hall Center for Children at the University of Chicago.

Courtney, M. E., & Terao, S. (2002). *Classification of independent living services.* Chicago: Chapin Hall at the University of Chicago.

Courtney, M., Zinn, A., Johnson, H., & Malm, K. (2011). *Evaluation of the Massachusetts Adolescent Outreach Program for Youths in Intensive Foster Care: Final Report.* OPRE Report #2011-14. Washington, DC: Office of Planning, Research and Evaluation, Administration for Children and Families, US Department of Health and Human Services.

Courtney, M., Zinn, A., Koralek, R., & Bess, R. (2011). *Evaluation of the Independent Living— Employment Services Program, Kern County, California: Final Report.* OPRE Report # 201113. Washington, DC: Office of Planning, Research and Evaluation, Administration for Children and Families, US Department of Health and Human Services.

Courtney, M. E., Zinn, A., Zielewski, E. H., Bess, R. J., Malm, K. E., Stagner, M., & Pergamit, M. (2008a). *Evaluation of the Life Skills Training Program: Los Angeles County.* Washington, DC: US Department of Health and Human Services, Administration for Children and Families.

Courtney, M. E., Zinn, A., Zielewski, E. H., Bess, R. J., Malm, K. E., Stagner, M., & Pergamit, M. (2008b). *Evaluation of the Early Start to Emancipation Preparation Tutoring Program: Los Angeles County.* Washington, DC: US Department of Health and Human Services, Administration for Children and Families.

Guo, S., & Fraser, W.M. (2010). *Propensity score analysis: Statistical methods and applications.* Thousand Oaks, CA: Sage.

Michalopoulos, C., Bloom, H. S., & Hill, C. J. (2004). *Can propensity score methods match the findings from a random assignment evaluation of mandatory welfare-to-work programs?* New York: MDRC.

Moffitt, R. (1991). Program evaluation with nonexperimental data. *Evaluation Review, 15*(3), 291–314.

Montgomery, P., Donkoh, C., & Underhill, K. (2006) Independent living programs for young people leaving the care system: The state of the evidence. *Children and Youth Services Review, 28,* 1435–1448.

Peters, C. M., Dworsky, A., Courtney, M. E., & Pollack, H. (2009). *Extending foster care to age 21: Weighing the costs to government against the benefits to youth.* Chicago: Chapin Hall at the University of Chicago.

Raudenbusch, S. W., Martinez, A.,& Spybrook, J. (2007). Improving precision in group-randomized experiments. *Educational Evaluation and Policy Analysis, 29*(1), 5–29.

Stein, M., & Munro, E. R. (2008) (Eds.). *Young people's transitions from care to adulthood: International research and practice.* London: Jessica Kingsley.

Trevisan, M. S. (2007). Evaluability assessment from 1986 to 2006. *American Journal of Evaluation, 28*(3), 290–303.

US General Accounting Office (November 1999). *Foster Care: Effectiveness of independent living services unknown*. Washington, DC: Author.

CHAPTER 8

American Academy of Child and Adolescent Psychiatry. (1997a). Practice parameters for the psychiatric assessment of children and adolescents. *Journal of the American Academy of Child and Adolescent Psychiatry, 36*(10 Suppl), 4S–20S.

American Academy of Child and Adolescent Psychiatry. (1997b). Practice parameters for the psychiatric assessment of infants and toddlers (0–36 months). *Journal of the American Academy of Child and Adolescent Psychiatry, 36*(10 Suppl), 21S–36S.

American Academy of Child and Adolescent Psychiatry. (2007). Practice parameters for the assessment of the family. *Journal of the American Academy of Child and Adolescent Psychiatry, 46*(7), 922–937.

Bergman, L. R., & Magnusson, D. (1997). A person-oriented approach in research on developmental psychopathology. *Development and Psychopathology, 9*, 291–319.

Bickman, L. (1996). The evaluation of a children's mental health managed care demonstration. *Journal of Mental Health Administration, 23*(1), 7–15.

Bromfield, L., Lamont, A., Parker, R., & Horsfall, B. (2010). *Issues for the safety and wellbeing of children in families with multiple and complex problems: The co-occurrence of domestic violence, parental substance misuse, and mental health problems*. Melbourne, Australia: National Child Protection Clearinghouse.

Burns, B., Mustillo, S., Farmer, E., Kolko, D., McCrae, J., Libby, A., & Webb, M. B. (2009). Caregiver depression, mental health service use, and child outcomes. In M. B. Webb, K. Dowd, B. J. Harden, J. Landsverk, & M. Testa (Eds.), *Child welfare and child well-being: New perspectives from the National Survey of Child and Adolescent Well-Being* (pp. 351–379). New York: Oxford University Press.

Burnside, L. (2012). *Youth in care with complex needs*. Special report for the Office of the Children's Advocate, Manitoba, Canada.

Chaffin, M., Bard, D., Hecht, D., & Silovsky, J. (2011). Change trajectories during home-based services with chronic child welfare cases. *Child Maltreatment, 16*(2) 114–125.

Chernoff, R., Combs-Orme, T., Risley-Curtiss, C., & Heisler, A. (1994). Assessing the health status of children entering foster care. *Pediatrics, 93*(4), 594–601.

Clausen, J. M., Landsverk, J., Ganger, W., Chadwick, D., & Litrownik, A. (1998). Mental health problems of children in foster care. *Journal of Child and Family Studies, 7*, 283–296.

Cleaver, H. Nicholson, D., Tarr, S., & Cleaver, D. (2007). *Child protection, domestic violence and parental substance misuse: Family experiences and effective practice*. London: Jessica Kingsley.

Curry, J., Rohde, P., Simons, A., Silva, S., Vitiello, B., Kratochvil, C., …March, J. (2006). Predictors and moderators of acute outcome in the Treatment for Adolescents with Depression Study (TADS). *Journal of the American Academy of Child and Adolescent Psychiatry, 45*(12), 1427–1439.

Drake, B. (1996). Unraveling unsubstantiated. *Child Maltreatment, 1*(5), 261–271.

Fixsen, D. L., Blase, K. A., Naoom, S. F., & Wallace, F. (2009). Core implementation components. *Research on Social Work Practice, 19*, 531–540.

Fluke, J., Shusterman, G., Hollinshead, D., & Yuan, Y. T. (2008) Longitudinal analysis of repeated child abuse reporting and victimization: Multistate analysis of associated factors. *Child Maltreatment, 13*(1), 76–88.

Gibbs, L. E. (2003). *Evidence-based practice for the helping professions: A practical guide with integrated multimedia.* Pacific Grove, CA: Brooks/Cole–Thomson Learning.

Gibbs, L., & Gambrill, E. (2002). Evidence-based practice: Counterarguments to objections. *Research on Social Work Practice, 12,* 452–476.

Gilbert, N., Parton, N., & Skivenes, M. (Eds.) (2011). *Child protection systems: International trends and orientations.* New York: Oxford University Press.

Hawkins, J. D., Brown, E. C., Oesterle, S., Arthur, M. W., Abbott, R. D., & Catalano, R. F. (2008). Early effects of Communities That Care on targeted risks and initiation of delinquent behavior and substance use. *Journal of Adolescent Health, 43,* 15–22.

Hessle, S., & Vinnerljung, B. (1999). *Child Welfare in Sweden: An Overview.* Stockholm: Stockholm University Department of Social Work.

Hinshaw, S. P. (2007). Moderators and mediators of treatment outcome for youth with ADHD: Understanding for whom and how interventions work. *Ambulatory Pediatrics, 7,* 91–100.

Jensen, P. S., Arnold, L. E., Swanson, J., Vitiello, B., Abikoff, H.B., Greenhill, L.L., ... Hur, K. (2007). Follow-up of the NIMH MTA study at 36 months after randomization. *Journal of the American Academy of Child and Adolescent Psychiatry, 46,* 988–1001.

Johnson, M. A., Stone, S., Lou, C., Vu, C., Ling, J., Mizrahi, P. & Austin, M. J. (2006). *Family assessment in child welfare services: Instrument comparisons.* Bay Area Social Services Consortium, University of California, Berkeley.

Lambert, M. J., Hansen, N. B., & Finch, A. E. (2001). Patient-focused research: Using patient outcome data to enhance treatment effects. *Journal of Consulting and Clinical Psychology, 69*(2), 159–172.

Leslie, L. K., Gordon, J. N., Lambros, K., Premji, K., Peoples, J., & Gist, K. (2005). Addressing the developmental and mental health needs of young children in foster care. *Journal of Developmental and Behavioral Pediatrics, 26*(2), 140–151.

Lou, C., Anthony, E. K., Stone, S., Vu, C., & Austin, M. J. (2006). *Assessing child and youth well-being: Implications for child welfare practice.* Bay Area Social Services Consortium, University of California, Berkeley.

Magnusson, D. (1995). Individual development: A holistic, integrated model. In P. Moen, G. H. Elder, & K. Luscher (Eds.), *Examining lives in context: Perspective on the ecology of human development* (pp. 19–60). Washington, DC: American Psychological Association.

Magnusson, D. (1998). The logic and implications of a person approach. In R. B. Cairns, L. R. Bergman, & J. Kagan (Eds.), *Methods and models for studying the individual* (pp. 33–64). Thousand Oaks, CA: Sage.

Owens, G. P., & Chard, K. M. (2003). Comorbidity and psychiatric diagnoses among women reporting child sexual abuse. *Child Abuse & Neglect, 27*(9), 1075–1082.

Pilowsky, D. (1995). Psychopathology among children placed in foster care. *Psychiatric Services, 46*(9), 906–910.

Rosengard, A., Laing, I., Ridley, J., & Hunter, S. (2007). *A literature review on multiple and complex needs.* Edinburgh: Scottish Executive Social Research.

Samuels, (2012). Trauma and treatment in child welfare policy and practice. Presentation at the Society for Social Work Research, Washington, DC.

Schor, E. L. (1982). The foster care system and the health status of foster children. *Pediatrics, 69*(5), 521–528.

Scottish Executive. (2005). *Getting it right for every child: Proposals for action.* Edinburgh: Crown, St. Andrew's House.

Spivak, H., Sege, R., Flanigan, E., & Licenziato, V. (Eds.); American Academy of Pediatrics. (2006). *Connected kids: Safe, strong, secure clinical guide.* Elk Grove Village, IL: American Academy of Pediatrics.

Simms, M. D. (1989). The foster care clinic: A community program to identify treatment needs of children in foster care. *Journal of Developmental and Behavioral Pediatrics, 10,* 121–128.

Stein, E., Evans, V., Mazumdar, R., & Rae-Grant, N. (1996). The mental health of children in foster care: A comparison with community and clinical samples. *Canadian Journal of Psychiatry, 41,* 385–391.

Szilagyi, M. (1998). The pediatrician and the child in foster care. *Pediatrics in Review, 19*(2), 39–50.

Trocmé, N., Fallon, B., MacLaurin, B., Sinha, V., Black, T., Fast, E., …Holroyd, J. (2010). Characteristics of children and families. In *Canadian incidence of reported child abuse and neglect—2008: Major findings.* Ottawa, Canada: Public Health Agency.

US Department of Health and Human Services (USDHHS). (2006). *Child and family services reviews: Statewide assessment instrument.* Washington, DC: Administration on Children, Youth, and Families.

US Department of Health and Human Services. (2011). *Child and family services reviews: aggregate report: Findings for round 2 fiscal years 2007–2010.* Washington, DC: Administration on Children, Youth, and Families.

US Department of Health and Human Services, Administration for Children and Families (USDHHS-ACF). (2005). *National Survey of Child and Adolescent Well-Being, No. 3: Children's cognitive and socioemotional development and their receipt of special educational and mental health services. Research brief: Findings from the NSCAW Study.* Washington, DC: Author.

US Department of Health and Human Services, Administration for Children and Families. (2007a). *National Survey of Child and Adolescent Well-Being, No. 7: Special health care needs among children in child welfare, Research brief: Findings from the NSCAW study.* Washington, DC: Author.

US Department of Health and Human Services, Administration for Children and Families. (2007b). *National Survey of Child and Adolescent Well-Being, No. 8: Need for early intervention services among infants and toddlers in child welfare. Research brief: Findings from the NSCAW study.* Washington, DC: Author.

US Department of Health and Human Services, Administration for Children and Families. (2007c). *National Survey of Child and Adolescent Well-Being, No. 9: Does substantiation of child maltreatment relate to child well-being and service receipt? Research brief: Findings from the NSCAW study.* Washington, DC: Author.

US Department of Health and Human Services, Administration for Children and Families. (2008a). *National Survey of Child and Adolescent Well-Being, No. 10: From early involvement with child welfare services to school entry: Wave 5 follow-up of infants in the national survey of child and adolescent well-being. Research brief: Findings from the NSCAW study*. Washington, DC: Author.

US Department of Health and Human Services, Administration for Children and Families. (2008b). *National Survey of Child and Adolescent Well-Being, No. 11: Adolescents involved with child welfare: A transition to adulthood. Research brief: Findings from the NSCAW study*. Washington, DC: Author.

US Department of Health and Human Services, Administration for Children and Families. (2009). *National Survey of Child and Adolescent Well-Being, No. 13: Depression among caregivers of young children reported for child maltreatment. Research brief: Findings from the NSCAW study*. Washington, DC: Author.

Wulczyn, F., Barth, R. P., Yuan, Y. T., Harden, B. J., & Landsverk, J. (2005). *Beyond common sense: Child welfare, child well-being, and the evidence for policy reform*. New Brunswick, NJ: Aldine Transaction.

CHAPTER 9

Aarons, G. A., Hurlburt, M., & Horwitz, S. M. (2011). Advancing a conceptual model of evidence-based practice implementation in public service sectors. *Administration in Policy Mental Health, 38*, 4–23.

Aldrich, H., & Reuf, M. (2006). *Organizations evolving*. Thousand Oaks, CA: Sage.

Arndt, M., & Bigelow, B. (1999). In their own words: The presentation of corporate restructuring in hospitals' annual reports. *Journal of Health Care Management, 44*, 117–131.

Arndt, M., & Bigelow, B. (2009). Evidence-based management in health care organizations: A cautionary note. *Health Care Management Review, 34*, 206–213.

Bartunek, J. M., & Moch, M. K. (1987). First-order, second-order and third-order change and organization development interventions: A cognitive approach. *Journal of Applied Behavioral Science, 23*, 483–500.

Bartunek, J. M., & Moch, M. K. (1994). Third-order organizational change and the western mystical tradition. *Journal of Organizational Management, 7*, 24–41.

Blanchard, K., & Johnson, S. (1983). *The one-minute manager*. New York: Harper Collins Business.

Briggs, H. E., & McBeath, B. (2009). Evidence-based management: Origins, characteristics, and implications for social service administration. *Administration in Social Work, 33*, 242–261.

Burns, T., & Stalker, G. M. (1961). *The management of innovation*. Chicago: Quadrangle.

Chagnon, F., Pouliot, L., Malo, C., Gervais, M., & Pigeon, M. (2010). Comparison of determinants of research knowledge utilization by practitioners and administrators in the field of child and family social services. *Implementation Science, 5*, 1–12.

Collins-Camargo, C., McBeath, B., & Ensign, K. (2011). Privatization and performance-based contracting in child welfare: Recent trends and implications for social service administrators. *Administration in Social Work, 35*, 494–516.

Damore, J. F. (2006). Making evidence-based management usable in practice. *Frontiers of Health Services Management, 22*(3), 37–39.

Fine, D. J. (2006). Toward the evolution of a newly skilled managerial class for health care organizations. *Frontiers of Health Services Management, 22*(3), 31–35.

Fixen, D., Naoom, S. F., Blase, D. A., Friedman, R. M., & Wallace, F. (2005). *Implementation research: A synthesis of the literature*. University of South Florida, Louis de la Parte Florida

Mental Health Institute, The National Implementation Research Network (FMHI Publication #231). Retrieved from http://nirn.fmhi.usf.edu/sources/publications/monograph/index.cfm

Gambrill, E. (2003). Evidence-based practice: Sea change or the emperor's new clothes? *Journal of Social Work Education, 29,* 3–23.

Gambrill, E. (2006). Evidence-based practice and policy: Choices ahead. *Research on Social Work Practice, 16,* 338–357.

Hasenfeld, Y. (1988). *Human service organizations.* Englewood Cliffs, NJ: Prentice-Hall.

Hasenfeld, Y. (1992). *Human services as complex organizations.* Newbury Park, CA: Sage.

Hasenfeld, Y. (2010). The attributes of human service organizations. In Y. Hasenfeld (Ed.), *Human services as complex organizations* (2nd ed., pp. 9–32). Newbury Park, CA: Sage.

Hasenfeld, Y., & Schmid, H. (1989). The community center as a human service organization. *Nonprofit and Voluntary Sector Quarterly, 18,* 47–61.

Johnson, M., & Austin, M. J. (2006). Evidence-based practice in the social services: Implications for organizational change. *Administration in Social Work, 30,* 75–104.

Kotter, J. P. (1982). What effective general managers really do. *Harvard Business Review, 60*(6), 156–167.

Kovner, A. R. (2003). Agenda setting for health care management research: Report of a conference. *Health Care Management Review, 28,* 319–322.

Kovner, A. R., Elton, J. J., & Billings, J. (2000). Evidence-based management. *Frontiers of Health Services Management, 16*(4), 3–24.

Kovner, A. R., & Rundall, T. (2006). Evidence-based management reconsidered. *Frontiers of Health Services Management, 22*(3), 3–22.

Learmonth, M., & Harding, N. (2006). Evidence-based management: The very idea. *Public Administration, 84,* 245–266.

McBeath, B., Briggs, H. E., & Aisenberg, G. (2009). The role of child welfare managers in promoting agency performance through experimentation. *Children and Youth Services Review, 31,* 112–118.

McCracken, S. G., & Marsh, J. C. (2007). Practitioner expertise in evidence-based practice decision-making. *Research on Social Work Practice, 18,* 301–310.

Meezan, W., & McBeath, B. (2011). Moving toward performance-based managed care—contracting out of child welfare: Perspectives on staffing, financial management, and information technology. *Administration in Social Work, 35,* 180–206.

Mendelson, D., & Carino, T. V. (2005). Evidence-based medicine in the United States: De-rigueur or dream deferred? *Health Affairs, 24,* 133–136.

Miller, J. A., Bogotova, T., & Carnohan, B. (2012). *Improving performance in service organizations.* Chicago, IL: Lyceum Books.

Mintzberg, H. (1973). *The nature of managerial work.* New York: Harper & Row.

Pfeffer, J., & Sutton, R. I. (2006a). *Hard facts, dangerous half-truths, and total nonsense.* Boston, MA: Harvard Business School Press.

Pfeffer, J., & Sutton, R. I. (2006b). Profiting from evidence-based management. *Strategy and Leadership, 34*(2), 35–42.

Proctor, E. K. (2007). Implementing evidence-based practice in social work education: Principles, strategies and partnerships. *Research on Social Work Practice, 17,* 583–291.

Rousseau, D. M. (2006a). Is there such a thing as evidence-based management? *Academy of Management Review, 31,* 256–269.

Rousseau, D. M. (2006b). Keep an open mind about evidence-based management. *Academy of Management Review, 31,* 1089–1091.

Rousseau, D. M., & McCarthy, S. (2007). Educating managers from an evidence-based perspective. *Academy of Management Learning and Education, 6,* 84–101.

Rynes, S. L., Colbert, A. E., & Brown, K. G. (2002). HR professionals' beliefs about effective human resource practices: Correspondence between research and practice. *Human Resource Management, 41,* 149–174.

Sackett, D. L., Rosenberg, W. M., Gray, J. A., Haynes, R. B., & Richardson, W. S. (1996). Evidence-based medicine: What it is and what it isn't. *British Medical Journal, 312,* 71–72.

Sackett, D. L., Straus, S. E., Richardson, W. S., Rosenberg, W., & Haynes, R. B. (2000). *Evidence-based medicine: How to practice and teach EBM.* New York: Churchill Livingstone.

Schmid, H. (1990). Staff and line relationships revisited: The case of community service organizations. *Public Personnel Management, 19,* 71–83.

Schmid, H. (2009). Agency-environment relations. In R. Patti (Ed.), *The handbook of human services management* (pp. 411–433). Thousand Oaks, CA: Sage.

Schmid, H. (2010). Organizational change in human service organizations: Theories, boundaries, strategies and implementation. In Y. Hasenfeld (Ed.), *Human services as complex organizations* (2nd ed., pp. 455–479). Newbury Park, CA: Sage.

Schmid, H. (2013). Nonprofit human services: Between identity blurring and adaptation to changing environments. *Administration in Social Work. 37,* 242–256.

Schmid, H., Bargal, D., & Hasenfeld, Y. (1991). Executive behavior in community service organizations. *Journal of Social Service Research, 15*(1/2), 23–39.

Schmid, H., & Blit-Cohen, E. (2009). University and social involvement at the neighborhood level: Implications for social work education. *Journal of Teaching in Social Work, 29,* 271–290.

Shoham, A., Ruvio, A., & Vigoda-Gadot, E. (2006). Market orientation in the nonprofit and voluntary sector: A meta-analysis of their relationships with organizational performance. *Nonprofit and Voluntary Sector Quarterly, 35,* 453–476.

Simon, H. A. (1991). *Models of my life.* New York: Basic Books.

Stern, Z., Schmid, H., & Nirel, R. (1994). Administrative behavior of directors in hospitals: The Israeli case. *Hospital and Health Services Administration, 39,* 249–263.

Weick, K. E. (1995). *Sense making in organizations.* Thousand Oaks, CA: Sage.

Walker, J., Briggs, H. E., Koroloff, N. M., & Friesen, B. J. (2007). Implementing and sustaining evidence-based practice in social work. *Journal of Social Work Education, 43,* 1–15.

Walshe, K., & Rundall, T. G. (2001). Evidence-based management: From theory to practice in health care. *Milbank Quarterly, 79,* 429–457.

Williams, L. L. (2006).What goes around comes around: EBM for consideration. *Administration in Social Work, 30,* 5–18.

Woodward, J. (1965). *Industrial organization: Theory and practice.* London: Oxford University Press.

Wuenschel, P. C.(2006).The diminishing role of social work administrators in social service agencies: Issues for consideration. *Administration in Social Work, 30,* 5–18.

CHAPTER 10

Begun, A., Berger, L. K., Otto-Salaj, L., & Rose, S. F. (2010). Developing effective social work university-community research collaborations. *Social Work, 55,* 54–62.

Bellamy, J. L., Bledsoe, S. E., Mullen, E. J., Fang, L., & Manuel, J. I. (2008). Agency- university partnership for evidence-based practice in social work. *Journal of Social Work Education, 44*, 55–75.

Benbenishty, R. (1996). Integrating research and practice: Time for a new agenda. *Research on Social Work Practice, 6*, 77–82.

Bitonti, C. (1993). Cognitive mapping: A qualitative research method for social work. *Social Work Research and Abstracts, 29*, 9–16.

Bogo, M. (2005). Field instruction in social work: A review of the research literature. *The Clinical Supervisor, 24*, 163–193.

Chalmers, I. (2005). If evidence-informed policy works in practice, does it matter if it doesn't work in theory? *Evidence and Policy: A Journal of Research, Debate and Practice, 1*, 227–242.

Cheetham, J. (1997). Evaluating social work: Progress, and prospects. *Research on Social Work Practice, 7*, 291–310.

Cnaan, R., & Dichter, M. E. (2008). Thoughts on the use of knowledge in social work practice. *Research on Social Work Practice, 18*, 278–284.

Corcoran, K., & Fischer, J. (2000). *Measures for clinical practice.* New York: The Free Press.

Dorfman, R. A. (1988). Clinical social work: The development of a discipline. In R. A. Dorfman (Ed.), *Paradigms of clinical social work* (pp. 3–24). New York: Brunner/Mazel Publishers.

Edmond, T., Megivern, D., Williams, C., Rochman, E., & Howard, M. (2006). Integrating evidence-based practice and social work field education. *Journal of Social Work Education, 42*, 377–396.

Epstein, I. (2009). Promoting harmony where there is commonly conflict: Evidence-informed practice as an integrative strategy. *Social Work in Health Care, 48*, 216–231.

Epstein, I. (2010). *Clinical data-mining: Integrating practice and research.* NY: Oxford University Press.

Fernandez, S., & Rainey, H. G. (2006). Managing successful organizational change in the public sector. *Public Administration Review, 66*, 168–176.

Flexner, A. (1915, as cited in 2001). Is social work a profession? *Research on Social Work Practice, 11*, 152–165.

Foster, M., Harris, J. Jackson, K., & Glendinning, C. (2008). Practitioners' documentation of assessment and care planning in social care: The opportunities for organizational learning. *British Journal of Social Work, 38*, 546–560.

Gambrill, E. (2006). Evidence-based practice and policy: Choices ahead. *Research on Social Work Practice, 16*, 338–357.

Gibbs, L. (2003). *Evidence-based practice for the helping professions.* Pacific Grove, CA: Brooks/ Cole.

Gibbs, L., & Gambrill, E. (2002). Evidence-based practice: Counterarguments to objections. *Research on Social Work Practice, 12*, 452–476.

Grady, M. (2010). The missing link: The role of social work schools and evidence-based practice. *Journal of Evidence-Based Practice, 7*, 400–411.

Greenhalgh, T., Robert, G., MacFarlane, F., Bate, P., & Kyriakidou, O. (2004). Diffusion of innovations in service organizations: Systematic review and recommendations. *The Milbank Quarterly, 82*, 581–629.

Grinnell, R. M., & Unrau, Y. A. (2008). *Social work research and evaluation.* New York: Oxford University Press.

Haynes, R. B., Devereaux, P. J., & Guyatt, G. H. (2002). Clinical expertise in the era of evidence-based medicine and patient choice. *ACP Journal Club, 136*(2), A11–14.

Howard, M. O., McMillen, C., J., & Pollio, D. E. (2003). Teaching evidence-based practice: Toward a new paradigm for social work education. *Research on Social Work Practice, 13*, 244–259.

Hudson, W. W. (1982). *The clinical measurement package: A field manual.* Homewood, IL: Dorsey Press.

Ivanoff, A., Blythe, B. J., & Tripodi, T. (1994). *Involuntary clients in social work practice.* New York: Aldine de Gruyter.

Levin-Rozalis, M. (2003). Evaluation and research: differences and similarities. *The Canadian Journal of Program Evaluation, 18*, 1–31.

Long, K., & Wodarski, J. S. (2010). The importance of educating, understanding, and empirical research in social work: The nuts and bolts of the business. *Journal of Evidence-Based Social Work, 7*, 173–199.

Morris, K., & Barnes, M. (2008). Prevention and social exclusion: New understanding for policy and practice. *British Journal of Social Work, 38*, 1194–1211.

Mullen, E. J. (1998). Linking the university and the social agency in collaborative evaluation research: Principles and examples. *Scandinavian Journal of Social Welfare, 7*, 152–158.

Mullen, E. J., & Bacon, W. (2006). Implementation of practice guidelines and evidence-based treatments: A survey of psychiatrics, psychologists, and social workers. In A. R. Roberts & K. R. Yeager (Eds.), *Foundations of evidence-based social work practice* (pp. 81–92). New York: Oxford University Press.

Mullen, E. J., Bledsoe, S. E., & Bellamy, J. L. (2008). Implementing evidence-based social work practice. *Research on Social Work Practice, 18*, 325–338.

Mullen, E. J., Shlonsky, A., Bledsoe, S. E., & Bellamy, J. L. (2005). From concept to implementation: Challenges facing evidence-based social work. *Evidence and Policy, 1*, 61–84.

Nevo, I., & Slonim-Nevo, V. (2011). The myth of evidence-based practice: Towards evidence-informed practice. *British Journal of Social Work, 41*(6), 1176–1197. doi:10.1093/bjsw/bcq149

Odom, S. L., & Strain, P. S. (2002). Evidence-based practice in early intervention/early childhood special education: Single-subject design research. *Journal of Early Intervention, 25*, 151–160.

Parrish, D. E., & Rubin, A. (2011). An effective model for continuing education training in evidence-based practice. *Research on Social Work Practice, 21*, 77–87.

Pawson, R., Boaz, A., Grayson, L., Long, A., & Barnes, C. (2003). *Types and quality of knowledge in social care.* London: Social Care Institute for Excellence.

Petr, C. G., & Walter, U. M. (2009). Evidence-based practice: A critical reflection. *European Journal of Social Work, 12*, 221–232.

Proctor, E. K., & Rosen, A. (2008). From knowledge production to implementation: Research challenges and imperatives. *Research on Social Work Practice, 18*, 285–291.

Proctor, E., Knudsen, K., Fedoravicius, N., Hovmand, P., Rosen, A., & Perron, B. (2007). Implementation of evidence-based practice in community behavioral health: Agency director perspectives. *Administration and Policy in Mental Health, 34*, 479–488.

Reid, W. J. (2002). Knowledge for direct social work practice: An analysis of trends. *Social Service Review, 76*, 6–33.

Reid, W. J., & Smith, A. D. (1989). *Research in Social Work.* NY: Columbia University Press.

Rosen, A. (1993). Systematic planned practice. *Social Service Review, 67*, 84–100.

Rosen, A. (1994). Knowledge use in direct practice. *Social Service Review, 68,* 561–577.

Rosen, A. (2003). Evidence-based practice: Challenges and promises. *Social Service Research, 27,* 197–208.

Rosen, A., & Proctor, E. K. (1978). Specifying the treatment process: The basis for effectiveness research. *Journal of Social Service Research, 2,* 25–41.

Rosen, A., Proctor, E. K., & Livne, S. (1985). Planning and direct practice. *Social Service Review, 59,* 161–167.

Rosen, A., & Proctor, E. K. (2003). *Developing practice guidelines for social work intervention: Issues, methods and research agenda.* NY: Columbia University Press.

Rosen, A., Proctor, E. K., Morrow-Howell, N., & Staudt, M. (1995). Rationales for practice decisions: Variations in knowledge use by decision task and social work service. *Research on Social Work Practice, 5,* 501–5023.

Royse, D., Thyer, B. A., & Padgett, D. K. (2006). *Program evaluation.* Belmont, CA: Wadsworth.

Rubin, A., & Parrish, D. (2010). Development and validation of the EBP Process Assessment Scale: Preliminary findings. *Research on Social Work Practice, 20,* 629–640.

Sackett, D. L., Straus, S. E., Richardson, W. S., Rosenberg, W., & Haynes, R. B. (2000). *Evidence-based medicine: How to practice and teach EBM* (2nd ed.). Edinburgh: Churchill Livingstone.

Shaw, I. (2005). Practitioner research: Evidence or critique. *British Journal of Social Work, 35,* 1231–1248.

Shaw, I., & Shaw, A. (1997). Keeping social work honest: Evaluating as profession and practice. *British Journal of Social Work, 27,* 847–869.

Shlonsky, A., & Gibbs, L. (2004). Will the real evidence-based practice please stand up? Teaching the process of evidence-based practice to the helping professions. *Brief Treatment and Crisis Intervention, 4,* 137–153.

Soydan, H. (2007). Improving the teaching of evidence-based practice: Challenges and priorities. *Research on Social Work Practice, 17,* 612–618.

Thyer, B. A. (2004). What is evidence-based practice? *Brief Treatment and Crisis Intervention, 4,* 167–176.

Thyer, B. A. (2008). The quest for evidence-based practice? We are all positivists! *Research on Social Work Practice, 18,* 339–345.

Vaughn, M. G., Howard, M. O., & Thyer, B. A. (2009). *Readings in evidence-based social work: Syntheses of the intervention knowledge base.* New York: Sage.

Weiss, H. (1997). Results-based accountability for child and family services. In E.J. Mullen & J. L. Magnabosco (Eds.), *Outcomes measurement in the human services* (pp. 173–180). Washington, DC: NASW Press.

Yunog, H., & Fengzhi, M. (2009). A reflection on reasons, preconditions, and effects of implementing evidence-based practice in social work. *Social Work, 54,* 177–181.

Zeira, A. (2002). Promoting self-evaluation of programs for children at risk and their families. In T. Vecchiato, A. Maluccio, & C. Canali (Eds.), *Clients and program perspectives on outcome evaluation in child and family services* (pp. 183–194). New York: Aldine de Gruyter.

Zeira, A. (2010). Testing practice wisdom in child welfare. In S. Kamerman, S. Phipps, and A. Ben Arieh (Eds.), *From child welfare to child well-being: An international perspective on knowledge in the service of making policy* (pp. 49–63). New York: Springer.

Zeira, A., & Rosen, A. (2000). Unraveling "tacit knowledge": What social workers do and why they do it. *Social Service Review, 74*, 103–123.

Zeira, A., Canali, C., Vecchiato, T., Jergeby, U., Thoburn, J., & Neve, E. (2008). Evidence- based social work practice with children and families: A cross national perspective. *European Journal of Social Work, 11*, 1–18.

Zeira, A., & Wolfsfeld, L. (2003). *Developing a model for training manpower to evaluate intervention programs for children at-risk and their families: The second year* (in Hebrew). Jerusalem: The Hebrew University of Jerusalem, Paul Baerwald School of Social Work.

CHAPTER 11

Aarons, G. A., & Palinkas, L. A. (2007). Implementation of evidence-based practice in child welfare: Service provider perspectives. *Administration and Policy in Mental Health and Mental Health Services Research, 34*, 411–419.

Amara, N., Ouimet, M., & Landry, R. (2004). New evidence on instrumental, conceptual, and symbolic utilization of university research in government agencies. *Science Communication, 26*, 75–106.

Barwick, M. A., Boydell, K. M., Stasiulis, E., Ferguson, H. B., Blase, K., & Fixsen, D. (2008). Research utilization among children's mental health providers. *Implementation Science, 3*(19). Retrieved October 1, 2010, from www.implementationscience.com/content/3/1/19/about

Bate, S., & Robert, G. (2002). Knowledge management and communities of practice in the private sector: Lessons for modernizing the National Health Service in England and Wales. *Public Administration, 80*, 643–663.

Baumbusch, J., Kirkham, S., Khan, K., McDonald, H., Semeniuk, P.,…Anderson, J. M. (2008). Pursuing common agendas: A collaborative model for knowledge translation between research and practice in clinical settings. *Research in Nursing and Health, 31*, 130–140.

Bowlus, A., McKenna, K., Day, T., & Wright, D. (2003). *The economic costs and consequences of child abuse in Canada: Report to the Law Commission of Canada*. London, ON: University of Western Ontario.

Briggs, H. E., & McBeath, B. (2009). Evidence-based management: Origins, challenges and implications for social service administration. *Administration in Social Work, 33*, 242–261.

Canadian Health Services Research Foundation (CHSRF). (2003). *The theory and practice of knowledge brokering in Canada's health system: A report based on a CHSRF national consultation and a literature review*. Ottawa, ON: Author.

Chagnon, F., Pouliot, L., Malo, C., Gervais, M., & Pigeon, M. (2010). Comparison of determinants of research knowledge utilization by practitioners and administrators in the field of child and family social services. *Implementation Science, 5*, 1–12. Retrieved on February 27, 2012, from http://www.implementationscience.com/content/5/1/41/prepub

Clark, G., & Kelly, L. (2005). *New directions for knowledge transfer and knowledge brokerage in Scotland*. Edinburgh: Scottish Executive Social Research.

Cousins, J. B., & Simon, M. (1996). The nature and impact of policy-induced partnerships between research and practice communities. *Educational Evaluation and Policy Analysis, 18*(3), 199–218.

Dash, P., Gowman, N., & Traynor, M. (2003). Increasing the impact of health services research. *British Medical Journal, 327*, 1339–1341.

Davis, P., & Howden-Chapman, P. (1996). Translating research findings into health policy. *Social Science & Medicine, 43*(5), 865–872.

Denis, J. L., & Lomas, J. (2003). Convergent evolution: The academic and policy roots of collaborative research. *Journal of Health Services Research Policy, 8,* 1–6.

Dobrow, M. J., Goel, V., & Upshur, R. E. G. (2004). Evidence-based health policy: Context and utilisation. *Social Science and Medicine, 58,* 207–217.

Eccles, M., & Foy, R. (2009). Linkage and exchange interventions. In S. Strauss, J. M. Tetroe, & I. D. Graham (Eds), *Knowledge translation in health care: Moving from evidence to practice* (pp. 176–182). London: Wiley-Blackwell.

Fixsen, D., Naoom, S. F., Blase, D. A., Friedman, R. M., & Wallace, F. (2005). *Implementation research: A synthesis of the literature.* University of South Florida, Louis de la Parte Florida Mental Health Institute, The National Implementation Research Network (FMHI Publication #231). http://nirn.fmhi.usf.edu/resources/publications/Monograph/index.cfm

Flynn, R. J., & Bouchard, D. (2005). Randomized and quasi-experimental evaluations of program impact in child welfare in Canada: A review. *Canadian Journal of Program Evaluation, 20,* 65–100.

Funk, S., Champagne, M., Wiese, R., & Tornquist, E. (1991). BARRIERS: The barriers to Research Utilization Scale. *Applied Nursing Research, 4,* 39–45.

Gollop, R., Ketley, D., Buchanan, D., Whitby, E., Lamont, S., Jones, J., Neath, A.,…Fitzgerald, L. (2006). Research into practice: A model for healthcare management research. *Evidence and Policy, 2,* 257–267.

Goyette, C., & Charest, P. (2007). *Rapport du comité de travail sur la santé mentale des jeunes suivis par les Centres Jeunesses.* Québec: Sante et Services Sociaux.

Greenhalgh, J., Knight, C., Hind, D., Beverley, C., & Walters, S. (2005). Clinical and cost-effectiveness of electroconvulsive therapy for depressive illness, schizophrenia, catatonia and mania: systematic reviews and economic modelling studies. *Health Technology Assessment, 9,* 1–156, iii–iv.

Grol, R. (2002). Changing physicians' competence and performance: Finding the balance between the individual and the organization. *Journal of Continuing Education in the Health Professions, 22,* 244–251.

Heller, C., & Arozullah, A. (2001). Implementing change—It's as hard as it looks. *Disease Management and Health Outcomes, 9,* 551–563.

Hemmelgarn, A. L., Glisson, C., & James, L. R. (2006). Organizational culture and climate: Implications for services and interventions research. *Clinical Psychology: Science and Practice, 13,* 73–89.

Hemsley-Brown, J. (2004). Facilitating research utilisation: A cross-sector review of research evidence. *International Journal of Public Sector Management, 17,* 534–552.

Hemsley-Brown, J., & Sharp, C. (2003). The use of research to improve professional practice: A systematic review of the literature. *Oxford Review of Education, 29,* 449–471.

Hoagwood, K., & Johnson, J. (2003). School psychology: a public health framework: I. From evidence-based practices to evidence-based policies. *Journal of School Psychology, 41,* 3–21.

Huberman, M. (1993). Linking the practitioner and researcher communities for school improvement. *School Effectiveness and School Improvement: An International Journal of Research, Policy and Practice, 4,* 1–16.

Johnson, M. A., & Austin, M. J. (2006). Evidence-based practice in the social services: Implications for organizational change. *Administration in Social Work, 30*, 75–104.

Kothari, A., Birch, S., & Charles, C. (2005). "Interaction" and research utilisation in health policies and programs: Does it work? *Health Policy, 71*, 117–125.

Kramer, D., & Cole, D. (2003). Sustained, intensive engagement to promote health and safety knowledge transfer to and utilization by workplaces. *Science Communication, 25*, 56–82.

Kramer, D., & Wells, R. (2005). Achieving buy-in: building networks to facilitate knowledge transfer. *Science Communication, 26*, 428–444.

Landry, R., Amara, N., & Lamari, M. (2001). Utilization of social science research knowledge in Canada. *Research Policy, 30*, 333–349.

Locock, L., Dopson, S., Chambers, D., & Gabbay, J. (2001). Understanding the role of opinion leaders in improving clinical effectiveness. *Social Science and Medicine, 53*, 745–757.

Lomas, J. (2000). Using "linkage and exchange" to move research into policy at a Canadian foundation. *Health Affairs, 19*, 236–240.

Lomas, J. (2003). Health services research. *British Medical Journal, 327*, 1301–1302.

Nutley, S., & Davies, H. (2001). Developing organizational learning in the NHS. *Medical Education, 35*, 35–42.

Nutley, S., Walter, I., & Davies, H. (2009). Promoting evidence-based practice: models and mechanisms from cross-sector review. *Research on Social Work Practice, 19*, 552–559.

Orlandi, M. A. (1996). Health promotion technology transfer: Organizational perspectives. *Canadian Journal of Public Health, 87*, 28–33.

Pfeffer, J., & Sutton, R. I. (2006). Evidence-based management. *Harvard Business Review, 84*, 62–74.

Proctor, E., Landsverk, J., Aarons, G., Chambers, D., Glisson, C., & Mittman, B. (2009). Implementation research in mental health services: an emerging science with conceptual, methodological, and training challenges. *Administration and Policy in Mental Health and Mental Health Services Research, 36*, 24–34.

Proctor, E. K., Knudsen, K. J., Fedoravicius, N., Hovmand, P., Rosen, A., & Perron, B. (2007). Implementation of evidence-based practice in community behavioral health: Agency director perspectives. *Administration and Policy in Mental Health and Mental Health Services Research, 34*, 479–488.

Rogers, E. M. (2003). *Diffusion of innovations* (5th ed.). New York: Free Press.

Rycroft-Malone, J. (2008). Evidence-informed practice: from individual to context. *Journal of Nursing Management, 16*, 404–408.

Scott, S., & Bruce, R. (1995). Decision-making style: The development and assessment of a new measure. *Educational & Psychological Measurement, 55*, 818–831.

Sharp, C. (2005). *The improvement of public sector delivery: Supporting evidence based practice through action research*. Edinburgh: Scottish Executive Social Research.

Titler, M. G., Steelman, V. J., Budreau, G., Buckwalter, K. C. & Goode, C. J. (2001). The Iowa model of evidence-based practice to promote quality care. *Critical Care Nursing Clinics of North America, 13*, 497–509.

Tribble, D. S.-C., Lane, J., Boyer, G., Aubé, D., Blackburn, F., . . . LeGall, J. (2008). *Le cadre de référence "Trans-Action" en transfert des connaissances*. Sherbrooke, Quebec: Centre de santé et de services sociaux—Institut universitaire de gériatrie de Sherbrooke.

Trocmé, N., Esposito, T., Laurendeau, C., Thomson, W., & Milne, L. (2009). La mobilisation des connaissances en protection de l'enfance. *Criminologie, 42*, 33–59.

Trocmé, N., Fallon, B., MacLaurin, B., Sinha, V., Black, T., Fast, E.,...Holroyd, J. (2010). *Canadian Incidence Study of Reported Child Abuse and Neglect—2008: Major Findings.* Public Health Agency of Canada: Ottawa, 122 pp.

Turcotte, D., Lamonde, G., & Beaudoin, A. (2009). Evaluation of an in-service training program for child welfare practitioners. *Research on Social Work Practice, 19*, 31–41.

VanDeusen Lukas, C., Holmes, S., Restuccia, J., Cramer, I., Shwartz, M., & Charns, M. (2007). Transformational change in health care systems: An organizational model. *Health Care Management Review, 32*, 309–320.

Waddell, C., Lavis, J., Abelson, J., Lomas, J., Shepherd, C.,...Offord, D. (2005). Research use in children's mental health policy in Canada: Maintaining vigilance amid ambiguity. *Social Science & Medicine, 61*, 1649–1657.

Walter, I., Nutley, S., & Davies, H. (2003). *Research impact: A cross sector review.* St. Andrews: Research Unit for Research Utilisation. University of St. Andrews.

Walter, I., Nutley, S., Percy-Smith, J., McNeish, D., & Frost, S. (2004). Improving the use of research in social care practice. *Social Care Institute for Excellence Knowledge Review 07.* Retrieved February 27, 2012, from http://www.scie.org.uk/publications/knowledgereviews/kr07.asp

Webb, S. (2002). Evidence-based practice and decision analysis in social work: An implementation model. *Journal of Social Work, 2*, 45–63.

Werr, A., & Stjernberg, T. (2003). Exploring management consulting firms as knowledge systems. *Organization Studies, 24*, 881–908.

EPILOGUE

Sackett, D. L., Richardson, W. S., Rosenberg, W., & Haynes, R. B. (1997). *Evidence-based medicine: How to practice and teach EBM.* New York: Churchill Livingstone.

Index